SCHOLAR Study Guide
Advanced Higher Busine

Authored by:

Alan Hamilton (Stirling High School)

Reviewed by:

Frances McCrudden (The Mary Erskine School)

Julie Nicoll (West Calder High School)

Previously authored by:

Jane McFarlane

Linda Alison

Heriot-Watt University

Edinburgh EH14 4AS, United Kingdom.

First published 2019 by Heriot-Watt University.

This edition published in 2019 by Heriot-Watt University SCHOLAR.

Copyright © 2019 SCHOLAR Forum.

Members of the SCHOLAR Forum may reproduce this publication in whole or in part for educational purposes within their establishment providing that no profit accrues at any stage, Any other use of the materials is governed by the general copyright statement that follows.

All rights reserved. No part of this publication may be reproduced, stored in a retrieval system or transmitted in any form or by any means, without written permission from the publisher.

Heriot-Watt University accepts no responsibility or liability whatsoever with regard to the information contained in this study guide.

Distributed by the SCHOLAR Forum.

SCHOLAR Study Guide Advanced Higher Business Management

Advanced Higher Business Management Course Code: C810 77

ISBN 978-1-911057-67-3

Print Production and Fulfilment in UK by Print Trail www.printtrail.com

Acknowledgements

Thanks are due to the members of Heriot-Watt University's SCHOLAR team who planned and created these materials, and to the many colleagues who reviewed the content.

We would like to acknowledge the assistance of the education authorities, colleges, teachers and students who contributed to the SCHOLAR programme and who evaluated these materials.

Grateful acknowledgement is made for permission to use the following material in the SCHOLAR programme:

The Scottish Qualifications Authority for permission to use Past Papers assessments.

The Scottish Government for financial support.

The content of this Study Guide is aligned to the Scottish Qualifications Authority (SQA) curriculum.

All brand names, product names, logos and related devices are used for identification purposes only and are trademarks, registered trademarks or service marks of their respective holders.

Contents

1 The external business environment — 1

1. Globalisation and its effects on business 3
2. Multinationals 13
3. Effects on host country and home countries 35
4. Current developments in the EU and their effect on UK organisations 45
5. Asian nations and their effect on UK businesses 55
6. Business ethics and corporate social responsibility 61
7. Government influence / technological developments 71
8. The external business environment test 93

2 The internal business environment — 103

1. Management theory 105
2. Leadership 137
3. Teams 155
4. Time and task management 167
5. Managing change 179
6. Equality and diversity 205
7. The internal business environment test 215

3 Researching a business — 221

1. Research 223
2. Analytical research 235
3. Evaluating financial information 249

Glossary — 259

Answers to questions and activities — 265

The external business environment

1 **Globalisation and its effects on business** 3
   1.1 Globalisation issues 4
   1.2 Effects of globalisation on UK businesses 6
   1.3 Globalisation strategies 9
   1.4 Summary 10
   1.5 End of topic test 11

2 **Multinationals** 13
   2.1 Introduction to multinational companies (MNCs) 14
   2.2 Reasons for growth of MNCs 16
   2.3 Methods of growth 19
   2.4 Transfer pricing 27
   2.5 Summary 32
   2.6 End of topic test 33

3 **Effects on host country and home countries** 35
   3.1 Introduction 36
   3.2 Effects on host country 36
   3.3 Effects on home country 39
   3.4 Summary 41
   3.5 End of topic test 42

4 **Current developments in the EU and their effect on UK organisations** 45
   4.1 The European Union (EU) 46
   4.2 Single market 49
   4.3 Social Chapter 51
   4.4 Summary 52
   4.5 End of topic test 53

5 **Asian nations and their effect on UK businesses** 55
   5.1 Association of Southeast Asian Nations (ASEAN) 56
   5.2 China 56
   5.3 Summary 58
   5.4 End of topic test 59

6	Business ethics and corporate social responsibility	61
6.1	Business ethics	62
6.2	Corporate social responsibility	64
6.3	Summary	68
6.4	End of topic test	69
7	**Government influence / technological developments**	**71**
7.1	Environmental factors	72
7.2	Government influence	76
7.3	Other external influences	79
7.4	Technological factors	82
7.5	E-commerce	86
7.6	Summary	88
7.7	End of topic test	89
8	**The external business environment test**	**93**

Unit 1 Topic 1

Globalisation and its effects on business

Contents

1.1 Globalisation issues	4
1.2 Effects of globalisation on UK businesses	6
1.3 Globalisation strategies	9
1.4 Summary	10
1.5 End of topic test	11

Learning objective

After studying this topic, you should be able to:

- describe the reasons for an increase in globalisation;
- discuss the effects this increase has had on business.

1.1 Globalisation issues

The increase in multinationals has led to an increase in **globalisation**.

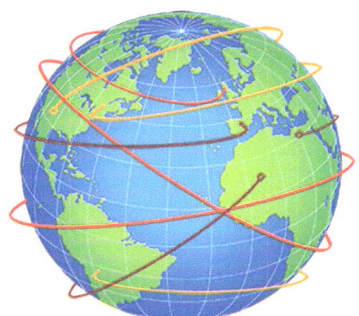

Globalisation

The main reasons for the increasing pace of global business operations are:

- **Removal of global trade barriers** which means removing the political barriers of trading between two countries, such as tariffs stipulating the amount of value of goods that can be traded or the type of goods that can be traded. The EU trading blocs and the changes as a result of negotiations with China and other Asian countries have given way to the removal of many barriers. As a result, organisations from both countries have seen trade increase, which results in an increased profit for the companies involved, as well as increase tax revenue for the Governments of these countries;

- **Advances in communications and technology** - the biggest of which is the explosion in e-commerce. These advances have also increased in communications between organisations and foreign suppliers using email, video and audio conference and mobile technologies;

- **Growth in global trade** as a result of low cost air travel making it easier for people (and cargo) to move between countries;

- **New opportunities in emerging markets**, such as China and Japan, and their capital investment in infrastructure and manufacturing capabilities;

- **Increasing opportunities for global travel**, such as low cost jet travel, making it easier for people, including company executives, to move between countries. This may reinforce some of the above factors through changed demand patterns and co-ordination of companies;

- **Technological developments in transport**, such as the use of large containers in shipping and bulk air freight, which has enabled goods to be transported across the world much more readily. Scotland has recently taken advantage of this growth by focussing on freight transportation in its Prestwick Airport operations;

TOPIC 1. GLOBALISATION AND ITS EFFECTS ON BUSINESS

- ***The development of global media*** has also changed demand patterns and made them less variable between countries, e.g. satellite television regularly broadcasts state television from multiple countries across the world.

Globalisation issues　　　　　　　　　　　　　　　　　　　　　　　Go online

Q1: Low cost transportation allows organisations to ship products all over world more easily than ever before.

a) True
b) False

....

Q2: Global trade barriers are increasing.

a) True
b) False

....

Q3: New management techniques can be discovered and filtered down the organisation.

a) True
b) False

....

Q4: Organisations which are decentralised may find it difficult to react to changes in the local market.

a) True
b) False

....

Q5: Preferences are not universal so standardised products may not be feasible, e.g. Tesco sells live turtles in China.

a) True
b) False

....

Q6: Transfer pricing can reduce tax bills.

a) True
b) False

1.2 Effects of globalisation on UK businesses

For UK businesses the effects of globalisation have led to the following:

- *cost savings* through purchasing, production and marketing economies of scale;
- *choice of cheaper locations* as businesses no longer stick to the one country;
- *higher consumer expectations* as customers can now browse the internet and compare products very easily;
- *increased competition* as a result of the increase of global companies setting up in the UK and online;
- *challenge of multi-cultural societies* as businesses move into new areas of Asia and the Americas;
- *increased lobbying from anti-globalisation groups* who would rather see an end to the exploitation of foreign workers and who oppose the increased pollution caused by increased air and sea transportation;
- *access to cheaper raw materials* as the cost of buying materials in developing countries is often less;
- *transfer pricing* can reduce tax bills and therefore increase profits;
- *new management techniques* can be discovered and brought back to the home country and businesses can benefit from experiencing different cultures, although this may lead to misunderstanding;
- *new production techniques* can be learned and used in other countries;
- *legislation* may have limited growth in the home country;
- *allows organisation to control production* from start to finish, e.g. car manufacturing;
- *low cost transportation* allows organisations to transport goods all over globe;
- *large organisations* may be able to influence government policy in their favour;
- *opportunity to take advantage of lower wages and less restrictive (expensive) working conditions* in host countries, therefore increasing profitability;
- *organisations may find it difficult to react to changes in the local market* if they have no local knowledge;
- *different parts of the world have different tastes and preferences*, for example horse meat is considered a delicacy in Japan;
- *increased travel for senior managers* of organisations means time away from office and can expensive; technology can help but it is often necessary for senior managers to spend time in the new country;
- *may have employees working in politically unstable countries*, which may put them at risk;
- *customers are more aware of tax avoidance schemes and can build pressure*, for example with businesses such as Amazon;

- *language barriers* can cause issues with communication with local workforce and communities.

Effects of globalisation on UK businesses　　　　　　　　　　Go online

Identify which of the following effects are positive or negative for the UK.

Q7: Access to cheaper raw materials.

a) Positive effect
b) Negative effect

....

Q8: Allows organisation to control production from start to finish, e.g. oil industry.

a) Positive effect
b) Negative effect

....

Q9: Can allow expansion where monopoly legislation in home country prevents it.

a) Positive effect
b) Negative effect

....

Q10: Can learn new techniques from other countries.

a) Positive effect
b) Negative effect

....

Q11: Can serve a gap in the market.

a) Positive effect
b) Negative effect

....

Q12: Closer to source of raw materials, cutting down transport costs.

a) Positive effect
b) Negative effect

....

Q13: Consumers more aware of tax avoidance methods and can assert pressure, e.g. Starbucks.

a) Positive effect
b) Negative effect

....

Q14: Cultural difficulties may lead to conflicts and misunderstandings.

a) Positive effect
b) Negative effect

....

Q15: Exploitation of local resources, e.g. lower labour costs.

a) Positive effect
b) Negative effect

....

Q16: Increased competition when new multinationals enter countries can damage the long serving, smaller businesses.

a) Positive effect
b) Negative effect

....

Q17: Increased consumer awareness of costs and product availability.

a) Positive effect
b) Negative effect

....

Q18: Increased demand for Western products in newly industrialised countries.

a) Positive effect
b) Negative effect

....

Q19: Increased travel and (expensive) time away from office for senior managers of organisations.

a) Positive effect
b) Negative effect

....

Q20: Large organisations may be able to influence government policy in their favour.

a) Positive effect
b) Negative effect

....

Q21: Larger market that allows for increased sales and economies of scale.

a) Positive effect
b) Negative effect

1.3 Globalisation strategies

Many businesses have prepared strategies to reduce the competition and challenges of globalisation.

The anti-globalisation lobby argues that globalisation has led to a convergence of consumer demand throughout the world. Global brands such as Sony, McDonalds and Nike promote and sell their brands in similar ways in every country in which they operate. But does one size really fit all? Are markets really the same in every country?

For this reason many global companies are developing a more local approach to try and gain a competitive edge. This approach can be referred to as **glocalisation** - an approach in which they operate globally but act locally in a way that shows sensitivity to and awareness of local markets and issues. This can be done through changing a recipe, altering packaging or in its approach to CSR and environmental issues.

For example, McDonalds used to use a standard menu across their franchise but have moved to adopting local menus to appeal to local tastes. Whilst every McDonalds will serve up the Big Mac, you can also chose a spicy paneer wrap in Indian restaurants, chicken with spaghetti in Indonesia, a pineapple pie in Thailand or a Pizzarotto in Italy!

HSBC

Read the article and answer the questions which follow.

> Headquartered in London, HSBC is one of the largest banking and financial services organisations in the world. It has over 10,000 offices in 83 countries and territories in Europe, the Asia-Pacific region, the Americas, the Middle East and Africa. Through an international network linked by advanced technology, including a rapidly growing e-commerce capability, HSBC provides a comprehensive range of financial services to its global customers. In 2002, HSBC launched a campaign to differentiate its brand from those of its competitors by describing the unique characteristics which distinguish HSBC, summarised by the words 'The world's local bank'.
>
> As part of its core principles and values it states "a commitment to comply with the spirit and letter of all laws and regulations wherever we conduct our business and to exercise our corporate social responsibility through detailed assessments of lending proposals and investments along with the promotion of good environmental practice and sustainable development and commitment to the welfare of each local community based on consultation".

Source: http://www.hsbc.com/.

Q22: What has helped HSBC increase its global capacity and efficiency?

....

Q23: How can having so many offices in so many countries benefit HSBC?

....

Q24: What was the purpose of HSBC's re-branding in 2002?

....

Q25: Referring to the core principle stated in the case study, assess how acting locally as a global company may affect HSBC. *(5 marks)*

1.4 Summary

Summary

You should now be able to:

- describe the reasons for an increase in globalisation;
- discuss the effects this increase has had on business.

1.5 End of topic test

End of Topic 1 test   Go online

Q26: What is meant by globalisation?

a) The increasing universal nature of the business environment.
b) The increasing universal use of ICT in business.
c) The increasing impact of transfer pricing in business.
d) The increasing benefits of economies of scale to the business environment.

....

Q27: Referring to the rise of globalisation in recent years, which statement below is false?

a) Increasing levels of world trade because of reduced trade barriers.
b) Transportation improvements creating global travellers and consumers.
c) Freezing up of financial markets.
d) Technology advances improving communication networks.

....

Q28: Which of the following statements, referring to the reasons for the increase in the pace of globalisation, is false?

a) New opportunities in communications and technological advances.
b) New opportunities in emerging markets.
c) New opportunities in home markets.
d) New opportunities in global trade.

....

Q29: Glocalisation means using cost savings of globalisation to:

a) improve customer services.
b) find cheaper locations.
c) enhance its reputation in the local community.
d) support local cultures and issues.

....

Q30: Which of the following is *not* a benefit of globalisation to businesses?

a) Learning new techniques from others.
b) Increasing awareness from consumers.
c) Access to cheaper raw materials.
d) Reduced tax bills due to transfer pricing.

....

Q31: Globalisation has promoted the removal of trade barriers.

a) True
b) False

Q32: Cultural and time differences may lead to confusion and misunderstandings.

a) True
b) False

Q33: Currency rates will negatively harm UK businesses.

a) True
b) False

Q34: Discuss the effects of globalisation on UK organisations. *(10 marks)*

Unit 1 Topic 2

Multinationals

Contents

2.1 Introduction to multinational companies (MNCs) 14
2.2 Reasons for growth of MNCs 16
    2.2.1 MNC case studies 18
2.3 Methods of growth 19
    2.3.1 Foreign direct investment (FDI) 19
    2.3.2 Joint ventures 21
    2.3.3 Mergers and acquisitions revision 23
    2.3.4 Franchise 25
2.4 Transfer pricing 27
    2.4.1 Transfer pricing - case studies 30
2.5 Summary 32
2.6 End of topic test 33

Learning objective

After studying this topic, you should be able to:

- assess the operations of multinational companies;
- describe, using examples, the reasons and methods of business growth.

2.1 Introduction to multinational companies (MNCs)

A **multinational** company (MNC) is one that manages productive operations or delivers services in at least two countries. It has a **centralised** head office in its **home country** where it coordinates its global management. Multinational companies tend to be very large organisations employing thousands of workers. Examples of UK multinationals are BP, Royal Bank of Scotland and Vodafone.

Some large multinationals have budgets that exceed that of some of the countries they operate in and therefore MNCs can have a very powerful influence in the economy of these countries. They can, for example, put pressure on these governments to lower taxes or offer incentives such as tax breaks. They have the threat of moving activities to another county to use as leverage.

A **transnational** company also operates on a global basis but has no clear head office in any of the countries in which it operates. However the term multinational is often used to describe both types of company.

Supporters of multinationals argue that they increase efficiency as they rationalise resources while critics say they are too powerful and can gain an unfair advantage, particularly in developing economies. In reality, the arguments both for and against will apply in certain circumstances with certain MNCs at certain times, mostly dependent on the global business environment and the economic cycles of the countries they operate in.

A new breed of MNCs is growing in numbers enabled by Internet communications. These are small to medium sized businesses known as **micro-multinationals** who face the limitations and challenges of small businesses. They use various internet tools to overcome the challenges of remote collaboration and customer service. Internet giants such as Apple, Google, eBay and Amazon facilitate these organisations in reaching potential customers in other countries.

Head office locations   Go online

Q1: The top 500 companies, measured by revenue, are described annually by Forbes magazine. Of the top 500 global companies how many have head offices in the following countries? (Source The Global 500 (http://fortune.com/global500/)). Attempt to complete the table on your own before using the internet to source the answer.

- 128;
- 95;
- 57;
- 31;
- 28;
- 17;
- 13;
- 10;
- 8;
- 3.

TOPIC 2. MULTINATIONALS

Country	Number of head offices
Canada	
China	
France	
India	
Japan	
Netherlands	
South Korea	
Sweden	
UK	
USA	

Q2: Look back at previous Global 500 years. Discuss the reasons why some countries have increased the number of MNCs whilst some have lowered.

Multinational companies (MNCs)   Go online

Q3: Multinational companies are businesses that have outlets or production facilities in several countries.

a) True
b) False

....

Q4: Governments in other countries rarely offer incentives to multinationals to entice them to set up in that country.

a) True
b) False

....

Q5: Multinationals never set up in countries where high skilled workers are available at higher costs.

a) True
b) False

....

Q6: Multinationals may be deterred from setting up abroad if the county's infrastructure is poor.

a) True
b) False

© HERIOT-WATT UNIVERSITY

2.2 Reasons for growth of MNCs

Companies become multinational in many different ways and for many different reasons but why have multinationals become so prominent in recent years? Some of the reasons are listed in the bullet points below.

- **Increased market share and dominance** - Existing on a larger scale allows for market dominance - you quickly become associated with a particular product or service and become the go to business for that product, as happened with Apple dominating the tablet market in the early days.

- **Closeness to local markets - tailor products to customer preferences** - Setting up as a multinational, opposed to a business that sets up in only one country but exports products to other countries, allows the multinational to engage with the local community and consumers. Cadbury is a good example of this. The UK company has an established production plant in Australia and New Zealand, amongst other countries. The product range in these countries differs from that of the UK, as local tastes dictate.

- **Can avoid import tariffs or taxes eg Japanese car production in UK and US** - Any product that is imported into or exported out of the UK is subject to import taxes being applied. One way around this additional charge is to manufacture the product within the country of sale. The UK car manufacturing sector used to be highly competitive with many Japanese, American and European businesses setting up production plants in the UK to avoid import charges. Sadly, these plants have closed over recent years as costs of production mitigate the savings made on any import taxes.

- **Often leads to lower labour costs particularly when setting up in less developed countries** - A disparity remains between those workers in the European Union and those from developing countries. The European Commission works towards establishing a universal minimum wage for countries within the Euro Zone, but has no influence on the wage given to the working poor in developing countries. Public awareness of this disparity is increasing, which may affect a MNC's decision to establish itself in such a country. MNCs need to be aware of the public backlash against such a move, or must be prepared to pay over the average wage for the region. In doing so, the MNC can avoid negative publicity whilst still reducing its wage bill.

- **Can benefit from government incentives** - An Australian energy firm, Clough, opened up a new office at Bellshill, North Lanarkshire, is 2014 as part of the company's expansion plan to target work in Europe, the Middle East and Africa. One of the main reasons the firm chose Scotland was to take advantage of a £1.5 million grant given to the business by the Scottish Government.

- **Falling cost of transportation of people and goods** - The cost of freight and passenger travel continues to come down, as competition increases and cost of oil drops. This means that it is more economical for producers to export across the globe. This will result is transportation being less of a reason against setting up in a foreign country.

- **Reduction in barriers to trade** - In the past, certain tariffs had to be paid when exporting goods from one country to another. These tariffs were greatly reduced in 1947 with the formation of the General Agreement of Tariffs and Trade, which saw 23 countries work together to remove costly barriers. This was superseded by the creation of the World Trade Organisation in 1994. There are currently 120 member countries, and the work that they

TOPIC 2. MULTINATIONALS

do has greatly reduced the cost and paper work involved in importing and exporting goods globally.

- **Low cost communications enabled by ICT** - Video conferencing, audio conferencing, VLEs and cloud computing have all resulted in the increase in global growth. It is now just as easy for employees from different countries to meet as it is for employees in the same office.
- **To gain economies of scale** - Economies of scale suggest that the more you produce of something, the cheaper it becomes to produce one item. This is because businesses become more efficient the more thy make, waste is reduced with practice and discounts become available when large quantities of raw materials are ordered. Many MNCs will manufacture their raw materials in house (backward vertical integration) which reduces costs further.
- **To avoid monopoly legislation in its home country** - Monopoly legislation exists to ensure that consumers are protected against price rises. If no competition exists, a business would be free to increase their prices, knowing that customers cannot go elsewhere for that product or service. In the UK, the Competition Commission exists to ensure this does not happen. This may result in certain organisations being unable to grow within their home country, prompting them to set up in an additional country.
- **Markets are saturated in the home country and new markets need to be found elsewhere** - There comes a point when an organisation outgrows its market, due to prolonged dominance or a platitude of competitors entering the market. One way to combat this saturation is to set up in a foreign country. This practice, known as foreign direct investment, is further detailed later in this subject.

Reasons for growth of MNCs Go online

Q7: Match the following examples with the reasons for growth in the table below:

- Apple dominated the computer tablet market for years;
- Cadbury established production plants in Australia and New Zealand where the cocoa is harvested;
- Japanese car producers setting up in the UK;
- Scottish Government offered Clough a £1.5m grant.

Reason for growth of MNCs	Example
Increased market share	
Closeness to local market	
Can avoid import tariffs	
Can benefit from government incentives	

© HERIOT-WATT UNIVERSITY

2.2.1 MNC case studies

Vodafone

Vodafone is a UK-based company that is a world leader in providing voice and data communications services to consumers in Europe, the Middle East, Africa, Asia and the United States. It employs approximately 90,000 people in 30 different countries. It is very proud of its success in emerging markets.

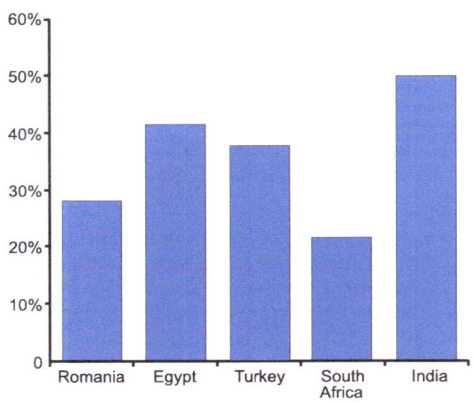

Vodafone revenue growth - emerging markets

Q8: Explain why Vodafone may be described as a multinational company. *(2 marks)*

....

Q9: Explain why the company may have become a multinational. *(4 marks)*

Santander UK call centre Go online

As of July 1 2011, all calls handled by the Indian centres were transferred to Santander UK staff based in Glasgow, Leicester and Liverpool. Abbey, as it was then called, outsourced its call centre operations in 2003 to two centres in India - one in Bangalore and one in Pune. The UK's third-biggest bank, owned by Spanish parent Banco Santander, said the move has created 500 UK-based jobs. The decision was taken after feedback from customers who said dealing with an offshore call centre was "a frustration that can lead to dissatisfaction".

Above text adapted from an article in The Independent (http://ind.pn/1JMIB3v)

Q10: Why did Santander decide to move its call centre operation back to the UK?

a) Increase in market share
b) Lower labour costs
c) Government incentive
d) Responding to customer need

2.3 Methods of growth

Many foreign multinational companies decide to choose the UK as a base for their operations. Government statistics for 2012 showed that over 22,000 foreign owned companies established operations in the UK. This was a small decrease from 2011 figures despite an increase in overall turnover of these firms.

What attracts foreign companies to invest in the UK?

While the UK cannot necessarily compete with emerging economies on cost, foreign investors are attracted by the UK's general business environment and the fact that English is the international language of business. The country is economically stable, has a skilled and adaptable workforce and is renowned for its unrivalled research and development (R&D) capabilities. Investing companies recognise the importance of operating in a market in which it is easy to set-up and which provides a platform for reaching markets in Europe.

The growth methods take the form of:

- **Foreign direct investment**;
- **Joint ventures**;
- **Mergers** and **acquisitions**;
- **Franchise**.

2.3.1 Foreign direct investment (FDI)

Foreign direct investment (FDI) occurs when overseas companies set-up or purchase operations in another country. FDI encompasses new projects, expansions of existing projects, or mergers and acquisitions activity.

The main reasons often quoted for FDI include the following:

- to access new overseas markets or better serve existing markets (e.g. investing in the UK in order to reach customers in Europe);
- to take advantage of lower manufacturing and wage costs (e.g. **outsourcing**);
- to access new technology and skills - particularly in R&D;
- to locate a business function near clusters of similar or related companies.

UNIT 1. THE EXTERNAL BUSINESS ENVIRONMENT

The two methods of FDI are:

- **Creating new facilities in the host country** - this method takes time, effort and finance, e.g. building, hiring, training. An advantage is that it can effectively replicate **corporate culture**.
- **Building over an existing company in the host country** - this is a quick way to expand into new markets. The advantages are that an overseas company can gain knowledge and experience of local markets and can often buy loss making companies and "turn them around".

Advantages of each method of FDI   Go online

Q11: Choose the advantage from the following list and put into the appropriate column:

- Able to reduce competition;
- Allows a large market presence to be built up quickly;
- Can gain competitive advantage in emerging markets;
- Custom built to suit the organisations requirements;
- Enables moves into markets where you can attract a different segment;
- Enables the company to establish its own business philosophy and corporate culture;
- Ensures uniform global facilities;
- Gain access to management and their experience of local conditions reducing risk of failure;
- May be able to acquire a loss making business cheaply;
- Only option as no suitable facilities are available;
- Problems of integration into the existing business structure are minimised;
- Start earning revenue and profits straight away.

Creating new facilities in host country	Buying over an existing company in host country

Disadvantages of FDI

There are also many disadvantages of using FDI.

A business using this method could be disadvantaged if the firms bought were previously struggling to maintain custom and reputation. It may take a long time to build up confidence again, especially if the business is seen as operating the same organisation but under a different name. It is costly to rebrand and update signage and equipment.

TOPIC 2. MULTINATIONALS

Investing directly in a country to set up a new operation will take a lot of time. New staff need to be hired and trained and new sites need to be sourced and premises built/modified. This is also expensive and time consuming to organise.

Many multinationals choose set up in countries with less stringent safety laws. Whilst this cuts the costs of production the business could be damaged by negative press.

What benefits does FDI bring to the UK?

Foreign investment is essential for the long-term health of the UK economy because of its contribution to creating and underpinning British jobs, as well as boosting local and regional economies. International investors are some of our biggest and most innovative manufacturers, and service providers, bringing enormous benefits to the UK. These include not only job and wealth creation but also an injection of innovation to process and produce which add to UK capacity in output, R&D and exports.

International investment allows companies to achieve growth and economies of scale that domestic markets alone would not allow. This makes them more productive and profitable with greater capacity for job and wealth creation. The expansion of high productivity businesses helps strengthen competition within the economy as companies are exposed to new ideas and practices.

Q12: From the above text, highlight seven benefits brought to the UK by FDI.

Stagecoach Go online

Q13: Stagecoach chose to expand its operations abroad by purchasing existing companies. Assess the benefits and costs to Stagecoach of this method of foreign direct investment. *(8 marks)*

2.3.2 Joint ventures

A joint venture is formed when two or more businesses undertake a project together. They each agree to contribute capital for the project and then share in revenues, expenses and control of the enterprise. The venture can be for one specific project after which the arrangement is dissolved or it can be a continuing business relationship.

1. A company or individual has an idea for a one-off project.
2. Two or more companies work together to take on the project.
3. Once the project has been completed, the joint venture dissolves.

Joint ventures are common in the oil and gas industries and are often co-operations between a local and a foreign company as they can complement their skills sets and offers the foreign company a geographical presence.

© HERIOT-WATT UNIVERSITY

Reasons for forming joint ventures

Q14: Write down what you think are the main reasons for forming joint ventures in terms of *internal reasons* and *competitive goals*.

Advantages and disadvantages of joint ventures

Businesses who chose to set up a joint venture together are able to learn from one another. The cost of the short term venture can also be shared, meaning a greater return on the investment for the two businesses involved in the venture. Once the venture is complete, the businesses can take what they have learned and continue to apply this knowledge to their existing business.

During the time of the venture the businesses can benefit from the usual advantages of a growing business, namely:

- economies of scale;
- stronger, more competitive operations;
- access to more customers and increased profits.

There are, of course, disadvantages. Specialist knowledge is lost to a future competitor (remember joint ventures do not last). The venture may not succeed as both parties need to be willing to compromise. This may not be possible if the separate businesses want to push the venture in different directions. Risks are shared, but so are profits meaning each business will not receive the maximum return.

Edrington

> The maker of whiskies including Famous Grouse, Highland Park and The Macallan yesterday unveiled a new joint venture to sell its Scotch in the Americas alongside brands including Disaronno, Tennent's lager and Tia Maria.
>
> Edrington has teamed up with World Equity Brand Builders (Webb) to launch Edrington Webb Travel Retail Americas.
>
> The new entity will market drinks in the duty-free sections of airports, cruise liners and other travel retail locations in the Americas, including Canada and the Caribbean. This new partnership will allow both businesses to spread their costs and risks.
>
> More than five million cases of spirits are sold through travel retail in the Americas each year, accounting for nearly one quarter of global duty free volumes and worth a total of more than £660 million. Glasgow-based Edrington - which also makes Brugal rum, Cutty Sark blended whisky and Snow Leopard vodka - announced in August that it was in exclusive talks with Webb, which has been marketing and distributing the Scottish group's brands in the Caribbean for the past four years.
>
> The switch is in-keeping with Edrington's recent strategy of taking closer control of its brands in key markets, using joint ventures or setting up dedicated companies rather than employing third party distributors, as a longer term relationship can be developed under this model.

Other brands marketed by Webb in the Americas include Armand de Brignac Champagne, Cape Classics wines, Magners cider and Tito's Handmade Vodka.

Juan Gentile, Edrington's area director for the Americas, said: "The creation of Edrington Webb expands our reach and bring us closer to customers and consumers in this valuable and dynamic market.

"Edrington and Webb have worked together in the Caribbean since 2010 and I am delighted at this opportunity to extend such a successful relationship."

Case study adapted from The Press and Journal (http://bit.ly/1GKr6CL) .

Q15: From the Edrington case study above, highlight five reasons for the joint venture, including advantages to be gained.

2.3.3 Mergers and acquisitions revision

A **takeover** is the term used to describe when one company literally "takes over" another company. This usually results in the company being taken over being rebranded - for example, Safeway was taken over by Morrisons. A takeover can be voluntary (where a company puts itself up for sale as Safeway did) or hostile (where a large company buys enough shares in another company to force through a takeover - this happened when Kraft took over Cadbury's).

A merger is where two companies integrate on equal terms - a "friendly" combining of companies, where elements of both brands/names will be retained. For example Halifax and Bank of Scotland became HBoS.

Organic growth is where a company grows naturally, without becoming involved in merging with or taking over another company. This can be achieved through increasing sales and opening new branches, or launching a new product range.

Horizontal and vertical integration

Integration of companies occurs when organisations combine to become larger and more powerful. Four types of integration are:

- *Horizontal integration* - occurs when two companies which operate at the same stage of production merge to become one entity. The reasons for doing this include market domination, avoidance of future takeovers and increased efficiency.

- *Vertical integration* occurs when two companies which operate at different stages of production in the same industry decide to join. Advantages here include increased efficiency and less need to contract out work to other companies as more expertise at all stages of production is now available.

- *Forward vertical integration* occurs when an organisation takes over a customer. Control can be exercised over the chain of distribution and supply.

- *Backward vertical integration* occurs when an organisation takes over a supplier giving a guaranteed source of stock.

Diversification

Diversification is the result of the takeover or merger of different firms operating in different markets, for example when Mackies began to sell crisps along side their ice cream range.

Reasons for diversification include:

- growth and development;
- spread of risk in case one area of the business fails;
- acquisition of assets;
- collection of new knowledge and experience.

Diversification is often a business's response to a change in its market or may be used as an opportunity to enter new markets. For example, many tobacco companies based in the UK have moved to diversify into leisure and food industries to offset the falling demand for their core products of cigarettes and tobacco. Organisations can also choose to reverse the process of growth to focus on key areas.

Deintegration/demerger and divestment

A deintegration, or demerger, is where an organisation splits into two separate businesses. This allows each business to focus on their core activity and therefore improve efficiency and performance.

Divestment is where a business chooses to sell off (usually less profitable or loss making) elements of operations or some assets. This raises finance which can be invested into improving remaining areas of the business.

Mergers and acquisitions   Go online

Q16: Greggs making their own sausage rolls is an example of forward vertical integration.

a) True
b) False

....

Q17: A merger takes place on friendly terms.

a) True
b) False

....

Q18: Taylor Wimpey building more houses due to a boom in the economy is an example of organic growth.

a) True
b) False

....

Q19: Barrs coming together with Britvic would have been an example of horizontal integration.

a) True
b) False

....

Q20: Mackie's selling chocolate is an example of diversification.

a) True
b) False

2.3.4 Franchise

This is a contractual agreement under which the owner of a business idea or name (franchisor) gives another person or company (franchisee) the right to sell a good or service or use a company name under the specifications of the franchisor. The franchisor may provide marketing and other support such as training and advice.

Examples of organisations operating under franchise in more than one country are:

- Burger King;
- Century 21 estate agents;
- Harry Ramsden's.

Franchising is advantageous to the franchisor as it enables them to increase their market share and gives them a steady stream of income. For the franchisee the risk of failure is reduced as they are selling a branded product or service.

Franchisor and franchisee - advantages and disadvantages

Q21: Put the following advantages and disadvantages for the franchisor and franchisee into the correct column in the table below:

- Additional brands can be added to existing portfolio very cheaply;
- Can be costly to buy a successful franchise;
- Franchise contract may not be renewed;
- Has less control over products, selling prices and store layout;
- Market share increased with little investment;
- Only receives a small share of profits;
- Receives a percentage or turnover or set royalty payments;
- Recognised brand therefore minimal advertising needs;
- Reputation can be tarnished by franchisee;
- Risk of failure is reduced;
- Royalty payments of a percentage of profits are paid to franchisor;
- Training and support offered by franchisor.

Advantages for franchisor	Advantages for franchisee	Disadvantages for franchisor	Disadvantages for franchisee

AG Barr

AG Barr has grown by investing in infrastructure and distribution, marketing and advertising and expanding its range of products through inhouse new product development, acquisition and partnerships. Its organic growth brands include IRN-BRU, IRN-BRU 32, Barr flavours (returnable glass bottles) and Simply Citrus.

Over the years, Barr has acquired a number of other companies, e.g. Tizer (1972), Mandora St Clements (1988), Findlays Mineral Water (2002) and more recently Strathmore Spring Water (2006), TAUT sports drink (2008) and Vitsmart functional water (2008). Focussing on brands is at the heart of AG Barr's marketing strategy. Barr's has further developed its interests by securing some franchising agreements.

IRN-BRU is produced and sold under franchise, by Pepsi Bottling Group, in Russia. Other franchise agreements for IRN-BRU with local distributors have been agreed in USA, Australia and Spain. Barr's has also secured an agreement with Schweppes International Limited (SIL) for the franchise of the Orangina brand in the UK (a franchise that Barrs secured in 1995 when the brand was owned by Pernod Ricard before it was acquired by SIL). Barrs also has the franchise from SIL for the Snapple brand in the UK.

Q22: Write a short paragraph analysing advantages and disadvantages of AG Barr's franchise agreements. *(10 marks)*

Hints: Focus on the advantages this will bring to Barrs both as a franchisor and a franchisee. Think about the diverse products now in its portfolio and how this fits in to its marketing strategy (your knowledge of marketing from Higher Business Management should help with this). Develop you answer - do not use bullet points.

2.4 Transfer pricing

As multinational companies operate in many different countries the goods and services produced by them are regularly transferred between the parent company and its foreign operations. Once transferred, these goods may undergo further processes before they can be sold to the consumer as a final good or service. e.g. BP extract crude oil from its Gulf of Mexico subsidiary and transfer it to its US Whiting refinery in Indiana where the crude oil is processed into transport fuels.

Additionally, it is common for international subsidiaries of multinational companies to specialise in different stages of production to benefit from **economies of scale**. Therefore goods or partly finished goods from a branch in one country are transferred to a branch in another country for assembly of the final good. eg car manufacturing.

Transfer pricing refers to the price charged between one international subsidiary of a multinational company and another for the goods supplied between them. This is an internal transfer of goods or services and therefore the price charged between the subsidiaries is set by the company and is not influenced by market forces.

Transfer pricing aims to achieve the company's strategies and goals and is mainly used to minimise the company's overall tax liability.

In terms of bookkeeping most of the company's profit is declared in the country with low taxes, thus shifting the profits to reduce the overall taxes paid by the multinational group. The multinational will set a high transfer price when transferring goods to subsidiaries based in high tax countries and a low transfer price when transferring goods to subsidiaries in low tax countries.

This has the effect of lowering profit margins in the high tax country so less tax is paid in that country but it increases profit margins in the low tax country. However, as the amount of tax paid in the low tax country is relatively small compared to the high tax country, the overall tax payable has been minimised.

How transfer pricing works

Go online

A multinational company transfers goods from the low tax country in Asia where its subsidiary company is based to the high tax country where the company has its head office.

	Low tax country	High tax country
Tax Rate	20%	50%
Costs of Production	£100	
Final Selling Price		£300

Example 1: Transfer price £200

	Low tax country	High tax country
Selling price	**£200**	£300
Costs of production	£100	£200
Profit before tax	£100	£100
Tax paid	£20	£50
Profit after tax	£80	£50

Total tax paid = £70

Example 2: Transfer price £250

	Low tax country	High tax country
Selling price	**£250**	£300
Costs of production	£100	£250
Profit before tax	£150	£50
Tax paid	£30	£25
Profit after tax	£120	£25

Total tax paid = £55

Example 3: Transfer price £300

	Low tax country	High tax country
Selling price	**£300**	£300
Costs of production	£100	£300
Profit before tax	£200	£0
Tax paid	£40	£0
Profit after tax	£160	£0

© HERIOT-WATT UNIVERSITY

Total tax paid = £40

In reality, the total profit before tax is always the same (£200) but by arbitrarily increasing the transfer price between the subsidiaries, after-tax profits are increased. This may enable the company to increase investment, spend more on R&D or pay bigger dividends to shareholders.

Transfer pricing   Go online

Q23: What is transfer pricing?

....

Q24: A transfer price is determined by market forces.

a) True
b) False

....

Q25: Transfer price relates to an internal transfer of goods and services between subsidiaries.

a) True
b) False

....

Q26: A policy of transfer pricing can give MNC's adverse publicity if they are exposed to be evading taxes.

a) True
b) False

....

Q27: From a MNC point of view it is better to structure its business so that fewer profits are earned in a country which taxes at 10% than at 35%.

a) True
b) False

....

Q28: To reduce its overall tax paid on profits a MNC will fix a high transfer price on goods and services coming from a high tax country.

a) True
b) False

....

Q29: Tax authorities in subsidiary countries are increasingly setting limits on transfer pricing manipulation to safeguard that country's legitimate income.

a) True
b) False

....

Q30: A manager in a subsidiary country encouraged to purchase at a high transfer price from a low tax country will be happy to do so.

a) True
b) False

Impact of using transfer pricing

Q31: Assess the impact on a multinational company of using transfer pricing between its subsidiaries. *(6 marks)*
Hints: start with a definition of transfer pricing; highlight the advantages this will bring to the MNC giving an example; think about possible drawbacks for the MNC; develop you answer - do not use bullet points.

2.4.1 Transfer pricing - case studies

Starbucks

Over the past three years, Starbucks has reported no profit, and paid no income tax, on sales of 1.2 billion pounds in the UK. McDonald's, by comparison, had a tax bill of over 80 million pounds on 3.6 billion pounds of UK sales. Kentucky Fried Chicken, part of Yum Brands Inc., the no. 3 global restaurant or cafe chain by market capitalization, incurred taxes of 36 million pounds on 1.1 billion pounds in UK sales, according to the accounts of their UK units.

Starbucks, for example, sources its UK coffee from a wholesale trading subsidiary in Switzerland.

In 2014, as a result of consumer pressure, Starbucks UK agreed to end this practice of transfer pricing and paid UK Corporation tax voluntarily. It promises to end its tax avoidance schemes in the future.

Adapted from a Reuters article on Starbucks (http://reut.rs/1CPf3gN)

Q32: What benefit can multinationals gain from using transfer pricing?

....

Q33: Why do you think Starbucks decided to end their practice of transfer pricing?

TOPIC 2. MULTINATIONALS   31

Is Britain up for sale?

Read the article 'Britain for sale?' (http://bbc.in/1czcA3X) and answer the questions below.

Q34: Using the article, identify the multinationals for which the UK is a home country or a host country:

- 29% of grocery brands operating in the UK;
- Aston Martin;
- BP;
- Branston pickle;
- Cadbury;
- Diageo;
- HP sauce;
- HSBC;
- Jaguar;
- Land Rover;
- Rolls Royce and Bentley;
- Santander;
- Standard Chartered;
- Tesco;
- Unilever;
- Vodafone.

UK is home country	UK is host country

Q35: Select the percentage figure from the options below to complete the following sentence: "Since 2000, inflows of investment income have averaged ..... of GDP compared to outflows which have averaged 12.4% of GDP. This means each year Britain has received a net flow of investment income equal to 1.1% of GDP from the rest of the world."

a) 13.5%
b) 23.5%
c) 33.5%

© HERIOT-WATT UNIVERSITY

2.5 Summary

Summary

You should now be able to:

- assess the operations of multinational companies;
- describe, using examples, the reasons and methods of business growth.

2.6 End of topic test

End of topic 2 test Go online

Q36: An advantage of multinational companies to society is:

a) their power to manipulate governments due to their size and financial power.
b) they can create wealth in an area by providing local jobs.
c) they often exploit natural resources in less developed countries.
d) they often switch production between countries to further their own needs.

....

Q37: Which of the following statements, referring to the growth of multinational operations worldwide, is false?

a) Low cost communications enabled by ICT.
b) Markets are saturated at home and new markets need to be found.
c) New management skills can be learned from the host country.
d) Government incentives are offered by the host country.

....

Q38: Creating new facilities in a host country is beneficial to the company as:

a) it enables the company to establish its own culture and philosophy.
b) it can start earning revenue and profits straight away.
c) it allows a large market presence to be built up very quickly.
d) local knowledge of market conditions can be utilised.

....

Q39: Buying over other businesses in a host country is beneficial to the multinational as it:

a) eliminates problems of integrating the new business into the existing one.
b) eliminates takeover risks by another company.
c) enables you to move into markets where you have limited expertise.
d) ensures uniform global facilities.

....

Q40: Which of the following statements, referring to reasons for forming joint ventures, is false?

a) You can gain access to new technologies.
b) It spreads business costs and risks.
c) Both companies have head offices in the same country.
d) Specialist knowledge is shared between them.

....

Q41: A disadvantage of a franchise for the franchisee is:

a) risk of failure is reduced.
b) franchise contract may not be renewed.
c) substantial advertising is needed to support the brand.
d) training and support is not offered by the franchisor.

....

Q42: Which of the following statements, referring to transfer pricing, is true?

a) Multinationals use transfer pricing to reduce its overall profit margin.
b) It is more advantageous for the MNC to use a high transfer price when transferring goods from a high tax country.
c) The transfer price charged to subsidiaries is set by market forces.
d) It is more advantageous for the MNC to use a low transfer price when transferring goods from a high tax country.

....

Q43: Transfer pricing can adversely impact on a MNC by:

a) reducing the amount of funds available to distribute to shareholders.
b) decreasing its overall profit margins.
c) aggravating relationships with governments.
d) reducing the amount of funds available for research and development.

....

Q44: Which of the following statements, in relation to arguments stating that MNC's can exploit foreign economies, is false?

a) Environmental concerns are often overlooked in the production process.
b) Working conditions of employees in subsidiary countries compare favourably to those in the home country.
c) Governments in subsidiary countries are too over-reliant on them in providing jobs.
d) Working conditions of employees in subsidiary countries are less favourable than those in the home country.

....

Q45: Explain the importance of transfer pricing on UK business. *(4 marks)*

....

Q46: Describe four possible methods of growth for a multinational company. *(4 marks)*

....

Q47: Firms may expand their operations into other countries through setting up their own facilities abroad and buying existing overseas firms.
Examine the advantages and disadvantages of these options. *(8 marks)*

Unit 1 Topic 3

Effects on host country and home countries

Contents

- 3.1 Introduction 36
- 3.2 Effects on host country 36
  - 3.2.1 Effects on a host country - case study 39
- 3.3 Effects on home country 39
- 3.4 Summary 41
- 3.5 End of topic test 42

> **Learning objective**
>
> After studying this topic, you should be able to:
>
> - discuss the effects multinational companies have on their host country;
> - discuss the effects multinational companies have on their home country.

3.1 Introduction

Are multinational companies (MNCs) good for the global economy? If not, why do countries compete so fiercely to attract them?

By studying this topic you will reach your own conclusions. However, recent research suggests that the overall benefits of multinational activity outweigh the costs for both the home and host countries. Although FDI originates predominantly from economically advanced countries it also predominantly goes to economically advanced countries, though the share of FDI going to developing countries has increased in recent years. Those arguing in favour of FDI state that any jobs lost by domestic firms locating abroad can be offset by foreign firms locating there.

The line graph below shows the number of FDI projects ongoing within economically established European countries.

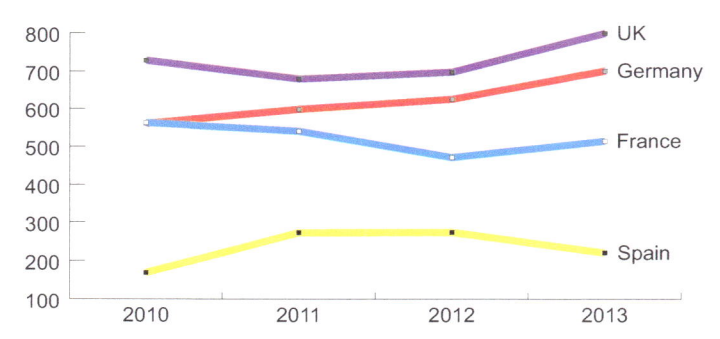

Source: EY Attractiveness Survey, June 2014 (http://bit.ly/1Ea1kAS) - based on announced FDI projects and capturing only certain types of investment

3.2 Effects on host country

In the European manufacturing industry alone foreign owned multinationals employ one worker in every five and sell one euro worth in every four of goods manufactured there. Over the last 20 years worldwide inflows of FDI from multinationals creating, acquiring or expanding in a host country has far outpaced growth in trade. This one-off initial capital inflow of the investment brings in money to the host country which benefits its **balance of payments**.

How else does the presence of foreign owned companies affect the host country?

Advantages to host country

- **Gross National Product (GNP)** will increase. This is the measure of a countries economic performance - the amount of goods that were produced and sold within a country. A higher GNP shows strong economic activity which results in further investment in that country and a good independent rating.
- More direct employment opportunities are created by the multinational and many indirect jobs are created as a consequence. Often employees learn new skills which can be transferred to

TOPIC 3. EFFECTS ON HOST COUNTRY AND HOME COUNTRIES

other employment opportunities.
- Standard of living improves due to wealth creation from better employment as in general foreign owned firms pay higher wages than domestically owned firms.
- Balance of payments show how much is being spent by consumers and businesses in the UK on imported goods and services against how successful UK businesses have been in exporting to other countries. The UK's balance of payments benefits from:
    - Initial injection of capital to the country;
    - Increase in exports if goods/services are sold to other countries;
    - Reduction of imports if the investment eliminates the need to buy from abroad.
- Tax raised from multinationals profits is a source of revenue for the government.
- Local companies can benefit from **technology transfer** improving their skills and making them more efficient as MNCs will bring the technology knowledge from the home country to the host country.
- Competition within the host country can be stimulated leading to improved efficiency and increased productivity - both directly improving GNP further.
- Greater choice of goods and services are now available within the host country, leading to higher sales and increased taxation collected by government.

Disadvantages to host country

- Multinational profits are repatriated to the home country - this means some of the profits can be returned to the home country and not reinvested in the home country.
- Multinationals usually employ staff from the home country in managerial positions and use the local labour for the lower skilled jobs.
- Multinationals may be socially irresponsible by exploiting local resources for a number of years and then relocating back to the home country.
- Multinationals have no loyalty to the host country and can easily switch production to another location to suit their needs resulting in job losses and lowering economic growth.
- Multinationals can manipulate transfer pricing between subsidiaries to reduce their tax liability. MNCs can move stock from one country to another at an inflated or deflated price to impact the amount of profit made - they may wish to record a stronger profit in a country with lower tax rates and a lower profit in a country with a higher tax rate.
- Local companies may be forced to close because they cannot compete with larger companies.
- Local governments can feel pressure from large MNCs to offer incentives to keep them operating within the country.

Investing in a host country

Go online

When a multinational company invests in a host country, decide whether the following statements are true or false.

Q1: The balance of payments of that country deteriorates.

a) True
b) False

....

Q2: Taxes paid on the multinationals profits improves the country's standard of living.

a) True
b) False

....

Q3: Many direct and indirect jobs are created.

a) True
b) False

....

Q4: Benefits of technology transfer can be gained.

a) True
b) False

....

Q5: Highly skilled managerial jobs are usually offered to local employees.

a) True
b) False

....

Q6: Exports and economic growth are boosted.

a) True
b) False

....

Q7: GNP of the host country will decrease.

a) True
b) False

....

Q8: Local companies could be driven out of business.

a) True
b) False

....

Q9: They usually pay lower wages than domestic companies.

a) True
b) False

....

Q10: The government is pleased if the multinational switches production to another country.

a) True
b) False

3.2.1 Effects on a host country - case study

GlaxoSmithKline   Go online

Read the article which follows and answer the question.

> GlaxoSmithKline is a UK research-based pharmaceutical company whose mission is to improve the quality of human life by enabling people to do more, feel better and live longer. Their business employs over 100,000 people in 117 countries. As a company with a firm foundation in science, they have a flair for research and a track record of turning that research into powerful, marketable drugs. They produce medicines that treat six major disease areas - asthma, virus control, infections, mental health, diabetes and digestive conditions. In addition, they are developing new treatments for cancer and every hour spend more than £300,000 (US $562,000) developing and finding new medicines. As an impact of their mission they declare that they are committed to providing discounted medicines where they are most needed.
>
> *Source: http://www.gsk.com*

Q11: Assess the effects on the host countries as a result of GlaxoSmithKline (GSK) expanding overseas. *(10 marks)*

Note the word "assess" in the question. You must always give some positive and negative effects.

3.3 Effects on home country

Critics of globalisation view the foreign ventures of multinational companies as damaging exports, jobs and wages of their home country whilst those in favour argue that the critics fail to see the broader picture.

In the UK many service sector firms, particularly call centre operations, have now shifted production abroad increasing our unemployment but this is often offset by foreign-owned companies moving to the UK. Additionally, there is evidence to suggest that many companies who do operate abroad strengthen and expand the strategic activities in their home country facilitated by technological upgrading leading to more skill intensive and productivity growth.

What are the advantages and disadvantages for the home country when a multinational company shifts its production abroad?

Advantages for home country

- Creation of additional high quality technical and managerial jobs at the MNC's HQ - enhance spending power in the UK as the nationals employed to these new positions are financially rewarded according to the amount of responsibility they are given.
- People seeking further and higher education due to less demand for unskilled labour - as unskilled work moves abroad UK citizens will retrain, benefitting themselves as well as the taxation received by government.
- Company profits are returned to home country which boosts balance of payments - a UK business may own a business overseas and send back some of the operating profits to the UK. This would count as a credit item for the UK current account as it is a stream of profits flowing back into the UK.
- Demand for home country exports can increase if foreign subsidiary creates a demand for them.
- Other firms in the home country may gain opportunities from any expertise gained which will in turn create wealth for the country in the form of increased taxation collected.

Disadvantages for home country

- Employment opportunities may be reduced as MNCs wind down operations leading to less tax revenue for government and increased spending on unemployment benefits.
- Increased burden on government to provide college and university places.
- Balance of payments suffer in the short run from the outflow of money to the foreign country as profits are reinvested in the host country to provide additional capital investment on buildings, machinery, etc.
- Increased burden on government to provide training and skills development to help workers find suitable jobs.
- Competition from foreign-based subsidiaries may lead to greater need for home-based companies to become more efficient or result in losing customers and profit.

Expanding abroad   Go online

There are implications for the home country when a multinational company expands abroad. Decide which of the following are true and which are false.

TOPIC 3. EFFECTS ON HOST COUNTRY AND HOME COUNTRIES

Q12: The government must provide more support and training to alleviate unemployment.

a) True
b) False

....

Q13: In the short term the balance of payments will improve.

a) True
b) False

....

Q14: There is more demand for less skilled workers in the home country.

a) True
b) False

....

Q15: The government must provide more opportunities at colleges and universities.

a) True
b) False

....

Q16: Multinational's profits are returned to the home country.

a) True
b) False

3.4 Summary

Summary

You should now be able to:

- discuss the effects multinational companies have on their host country;
- discuss the effects multinational companies have on their home country.

3.5 End of topic test

End of Topic 3 test   Go online

Decide which of the following are an advantage or disadvantage of multinational companies in society.

Q17: Providing direct jobs for the local economy.

a) Advantage
b) Disadvantage

....

Q18: Furthering their own interests as powerful institutions.

a) Advantage
b) Disadvantage

....

Q19: Providing local workers with new skills via training.

a) Advantage
b) Disadvantage

....

Q20: Bringing expertise in the use of new technology for local enterprises.

a) Advantage
b) Disadvantage

....

Q21: Helping improve the infrastructure of the country.

a) Advantage
b) Disadvantage

....

Q22: Switching production between different countries to suit the multinational's needs.

a) Advantage
b) Disadvantage

....

Q23: Introducing management expertise and techniques.

a) Advantage
b) Disadvantage

....

TOPIC 3. EFFECTS ON HOST COUNTRY AND HOME COUNTRIES

Q24: Exploiting resources in less developed countries for economic gain.

a) Advantage
b) Disadvantage

Q25: Referring to reasons why governments wish to attract inward investment to their countries, which one of the following statements is false?

a) Multinationals create and sustain jobs in the host country.
b) Companies in host countries can benefit from new business ideas and practices.
c) Host governments find multinationals easy to control.
d) It boosts the GNP of the host country.

....

Q26: Which of the following statements is an advantage to the host country of multinational investment in their country?

a) Multinationals usually bring in their own managers to oversee operations.
b) Balance of payments is improved due to the capital injection from multinational.
c) Governments can lose out on taxation due to transfer pricing practices of multinationals.
d) Multinationals' profits are repatriated to their own country.

....

Q27: Which of the following statements is an advantage to the home country of multinational investment in other countries?

a) Tax revenue increases for governments in home country.
b) Other businesses in the home country may become more efficient because of technology transfer.
c) Governments need to provide more training and skills development for workers.
d) The outward investment improves the balance of payments.

....

Q28: What is meant by technology transfer?

a) The introduction of highly skilled workers.
b) The introduction of technology to improve efficiency.
c) The introduction of performance related pay.
d) The introduction of scientific and technological developments to businesses who can develop them into new processes and products.

....

Q29: Explore the possible effects on the UK of a British-based multinational expanding its operations overseas. *(8 marks)*

Unit 1 Topic 4

Current developments in the EU and their effect on UK organisations

Contents

4.1 The European Union (EU) 46
    4.1.1 EU institutions 47
4.2 Single market 49
4.3 Social Chapter 51
4.4 Summary 52
4.5 End of topic test 53

Learning objective

After studying this topic, you should be able to:

- discuss the single European market and its effects on businesses;
- discuss the social chapter and its effects on businesses;

4.1 The European Union (EU)

The origins of the European Union (EU) grew of the desolation left behind after Europe had experienced two devastating world wars and a serious economic depression. Some countries in Western Europe looked for ways to make sure that they never went to war against each other again. As coal and steel production was of great importance to these countries, it was agreed they should be jointly controlled and in 1952 the European coal and steel community (ECSC) was founded.

A brief history of the EU   Go online

Date	Event
1952	Treaty of Paris signed by Belgium, France, Italy, Luxemburg, the Netherlands and West Germany, creating the European Coal and Steel Community (ECSC).
1957	Treaty of Rome signed to establish European Economic Community (EEC) and the European Atomic Energy Community (Euratom).
1967	Merger Treaty signed amalgamating ESCS and EEC, now known as the European Community (EC).
1973	Denmark, Ireland and the UK join the EC bringing membership to nine.
1986	Greece joins the EC.
1990	Portugal and Spain join the EC taking its membership to 12.
1992	The Treaty of Maastricht is signed, effective from 1 January 1993, marking the change of the EC to the European Union (EU).
1996	Austria, Finland and Sweden join the EU taking its membership to 15.
1999	Single currency adopted by 11 member countries - Austria, Belgium, Finland, France, Germany, Ireland, Italy, Luxemburg, the Netherlands, Portugal and Spain. Denmark and the UK chose to 'opt-out' whilst Greece and Sweden did not fulfill the convergence criteria.
2001	Greece deemed to fulfill the convergence criteria and joined the single currency on 1 January 2001.
2002	Coins and bank notes are entered into circulation in the 12 member countries and is traded in the financial markets; the name 'euro' is adopted for the single currency.
2004	Cyprus, the Czech Republic, Estonia, Hungary, Latvia, Lithuania, Malta, Poland, Slovakia and Slovenia join the EU, increasing the number of members to 25.
2007	Bulgaria and Romania join the EU, membership now stands at 27. Slovenia becomes the thirteenth member state to adopt the euro.
2008	Cyprus and Malta adopt the euro, taking the number of countries to 15.
2009	Slovakia becomes the 16th country to adopt the euro.
2011	Estonia becomes the 17th country to adopt the euro.
2013	Croatia joins the EU, membership now stands at 28.
2014	Latvia adopts the euro, taking the number of countries to 18.
2015	Lithuania becomes the 19th country to adopt the euro.

A brief history of the EU

TOPIC 4.   CURRENT DEVELOPMENTS IN THE EU AND THEIR EFFECT ON UK ORGANISATIONS

As of 2015, the EU consists of 28 European countries. The countries that make up the EU remain independent sovereign nations but they pool their decision making powers to shared institutions that have been created in order to gain strength and world influence none of them could have achieved on their own.

The creation of the EU established a free trade area where tariffs and quotas were removed between member states thereby allowing the free movement of goods, services, capital and people. This means that any business within an EU country (or outwith as long as a subsidiary operates within an EU country) can import and export between EU counties without the need for additional payments, levies or taxes. The same applies to employees and capital purchases. The benefits to businesses are that they can move goods, workers and equipment within the EU countries freely. For consumers this means more choice and reduced selling prices (as the business has reduced costs).

A customs union was also established by member countries to create a common external tariff for trade with non-members, i.e. all members charge the same tariffs on goods imported from countries outside the EU. Many American and Japanese firms have created subsidiaries in Europe to avoid this external common tariff.

4.1.1   EU institutions

The four key institutions in the EU and their functions are listed in the table below.

The European Commission	The Council of the European Union	The European Parliament	The European Court of Justice
Represents and upholds the interests of the EU as a whole.	Agrees or adopts legislation based on Commission's proposals.	Elections held every five years.	Staffed by one judge from each member state.
Proposes EU policy and legislation.	Each member state acts as president for six months.	751 MEPs (Members of the European Parliament) from 28 countries.	Deals with disputes between member states.
Carries out decisions taken by Council of Ministers.	Meetings attended by one minister from each national government.	Provides opinion on proposals before Commission can implement them.	Ensures established laws are observed the same way in all member states.
Manages day-to-day business of the European Union.	Decides which minister attends what topic on agenda.	MEPs sit in seven Europe-wide political groups.	Rules on interpretation and application of EU laws and hears appeals.

Four key EU institutions and their functions

EU institutions

In each of the following questions, choose the EU institution to which the statement applies.

Q1: Each country sends one government minister to its meetings.

a) The Council of EU
b) The European Commission
c) The Court of Justice
d) The European Parliament

....

Q2: Manages the day-to-day business of the EU.

a) The Council of EU
b) The European Commission
c) The Court of Justice
d) The European Parliament

....

Q3: Deals with disputes between member states.

a) The Council of EU
b) The European Commission
c) The Court of Justice
d) The European Parliament

....

Q4: Proposes EU policy and legislation.

a) The Council of EU
b) The European Commission
c) The Court of Justice
d) The European Parliament

....

Q5: Elections are held every five years.

a) The Council of EU
b) The European Commission
c) The Court of Justice
d) The European Parliament

....

Q6: Main decision-making body.

a) The Council of EU
b) The European Commission
c) The Court of Justice
d) The European Parliament

....

Q7: Ensures laws are observed in all member countries.

a) The Council of EU
b) The European Commission
c) The Court of Justice
d) The European Parliament

....

Q8: Main task is to debate and ratify proposals made by the Commission.

a) The Council of EU
b) The European Commission
c) The Court of Justice
d) The European Parliament

4.2 Single market

The single market is one of the EU's greatest achievements. It extends the EU's basic principle of free trade to cover free movement of factors of production within the EU. Its success hinges on the fact that in terms of trade all the member countries operate co-operatively as if they were one large country. Restrictions between member countries on trade and competition have gradually been eliminated ultimately resulting in increased standards of living for member countries. However, the single market has not yet become a single economic area as some sectors of the economy (public services) are still subject to national laws.

Although individual EU member countries still largely have responsibility for their own taxation and social welfare systems, the single market is supported by a number of related policies put in place by the EU over the years, e.g. removal of barriers to competition in banking and insurance, mutual recognition of product standards. These policies help ensure that market liberalisation benefits as many businesses and consumers as possible.

The European Commission says that the single market has helped create 2.5 million new jobs and generated 800 billion euros in additional wealth since 1993. Since 2004 businesses selling in the single market now have access to more than 450 million consumers. This enlarged market eases mergers and joint ventures between national companies, e.g. the purchase of Powergen (UK company) by E-On (German Company) and the proposed takeover of Edinburgh based Scottish and Newcastle by Danish and Dutch brewing giants Carlsberg and Heineken.

The EU's economy, measured in terms of the goods and services it produces (GDP), is now bigger than that of the USA. EU GDP in 2012 was €12,945,402 million.

Costs and benefits of a single market   Go online

Identify each of the following statements as a cost or a benefit.

Q9: Can have a short term negative impact on some sectors of the economy due to increased international competition.

a) Cost
b) Benefit

....

Q10: Business that previously had market protection and national subsidies may find it difficult to compete in such an open market leading to failure and unemployment in the country.

a) Cost
b) Benefit

....

Q11: Reduced production costs because of free movement of goods and common standards.

a) Cost
b) Benefit

....

Q12: Opens up new markets to businesses leading to new opportunities.

a) Cost
b) Benefit

....

Q13: Efficient companies producing for a larger market can benefit from economies of scale.

a) Cost
b) Benefit

....

Q14: Differences in cultures and tastes may prove to be a barrier in entering some markets.

a) Cost
b) Benefit

....

Q15: Consumers can benefit from increased choice and cheaper products.

a) Cost
b) Benefit

....

Q16: Innovation in the creation of new products improves as businesses compete for customers.

a) Cost
b) Benefit

....

Q17: Innovation in processes and procedures improves as businesses strive to cut costs whilst simultaneously maintaining quality.

a) Cost
b) Benefit

Q18: Explain three ways in which the single European market may pose a threat to a medium sized UK based manufacturer

4.3 Social Chapter

The Maastricht Treaty of 1992 sought to bring members of the EU closer together by creating the Social Chapter. Its aim was to create a "level playing field" for all EU members as regards conditions at work. Many of the initiatives contained within the Social Chapter had already been taken up by many of the member countries.

The Social Chapter included directives which guaranteed workers the right to:

- join a trade union;
- take industrial action;
- have a minimum wage;
- take parental leave (either gender);
- have a maximum 48 hour working week;
- have at least four weeks paid annual leave;
- be treated equally whether they are part time or full time;
- improve health and safety protection;
- have access to vocational training;
- participate in decision making.

Effects on businesses include:

- workers become more motivated as working conditions are improved;
- as a consequence productivity usually increases;
- better industrial relations and worker participation due to improved consultation;
- raises labour costs to business (eg minimum wage);
- more difficult to compete on price basis with non EU firms e.g. China and India;
- increased regulations make labour market less flexible.

Social Chapter impact

Q19: Discuss how the Social Chapter may impact on UK businesses. *(6 marks)*
Hint: Start with a definition of the Social Chapter then give both positive and negative effects.

4.4 Summary

Summary

You should now be able to:

- discuss the single European market and its effects on businesses;
- discuss the social chapter and its effects on businesses.

4.5 End of topic test

End of Topic 4 test Go online

Q20: The Single European Market refers to free movement of:

a) goods and services between EU members.
b) goods and services between all trading partners.
c) goods, services, capital and people between EU members.
d) government officials between member states.

....

Q21: Which of the following is a disadvantage of the Single European Market?

a) Innovation in the creation of new products is stifled.
b) National differences in cultures and tastes can be a barrier to market entry.
c) Increases business costs of production.
d) Opens up new markets with 450 million potential customers.

....

Q22: The Social Chapter refers to measures designed to harmonise:

a) going to the theatre.
b) social awareness within the EU.
c) competition laws within EU.
d) social legislation within the EU.

....

Q23: Which of the following is an advantage of the Social Chapter for business?

a) It lower costs because of minimum wage laws.
b) It can increase workers' productivity due to the motivational effect.
c) It makes it easier to compete with non EU businesses.
d) It offers a more flexible labour market.

Unit 1 Topic 5

Asian nations and their effect on UK businesses

Contents

5.1 Association of Southeast Asian Nations (ASEAN)	56
5.2 China	56
5.2.1 Case study - Marks and Spencer	57
5.3 Summary	58
5.4 End of topic test	59

Learning objective

After studying this topic, you should be able to:

- describe the impact of Asian nations on UK businesses.

5.1 Association of Southeast Asian Nations (ASEAN)

The Association of Southeast Asian Nations (ASEAN) was established on 8 August 1967. The members are Indonesia, Malaysia, Philippines, Singapore and Thailand (founding members in 1967), Brunei Darussalam (Brunei) (joined 1984), Vietnam (1995), Laos and Myanmar (Burma) (1997) and Cambodia (1999).

The ten Asian countries in ASEAN are shown in the map below.

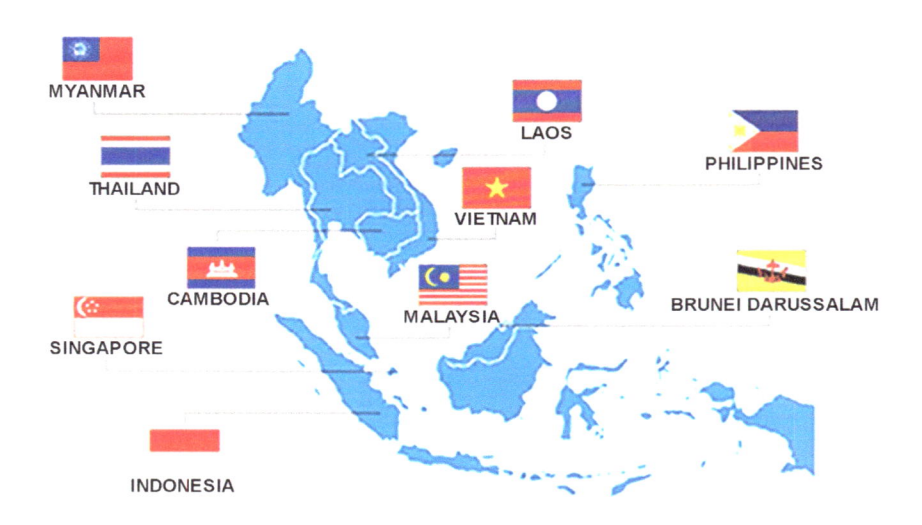

ASEAN member countries

The ASEAN charter was proposed in 2005 and agreed in 2007 (becoming active in 2008) and sets clear targets for the association, as well as setting out its rules and values. The Chair of the association changes annually with each member country taking it in turn.

Currently, each member of ASEAN has its own currency. 80% of the exports from the member countries go to countries outside of ASEAN, which makes a formal currency less necessary.

ASEAN, China, Korea, Japan, Australia, New Zealand and India concluded a free trade agreement in 2015. They are currently negotiating a free trade agreement with the European Union.

5.2 China

China is the world's second biggest economy (behind the United States of America) but is growing at the fastest rate. It uses its wealth to invest in other businesses from around the globe. For example, in recent years China has invested $3bn in Barclays bank, $2bn in BP and $1.9bn in Weetabix. The growing dominance of China, as well as the increasing force of ASEAN will have both positive and negative effects on UK and UK business.

Positive effects for UK businesses include:

- **Inward investment** - the investment China provides to UK businesses is expected to pass £105 billion ($170 billion) in the emerging energy, property and transport sectors by 2025. In 2012, China Investment Corp, the country's sovereign wealth fund, bought an 8.68 per cent stake in Thames Water Utilities Ltd and a 10 per cent stake in Heathrow Airport Holdings. Another example is Cheung Kong Infrastructure Holdings purchasing the UK utility company Northumbrian Water for £2.4 billion in 2011;
- **Cheaper materials** - raw materials from ASEAN/China may be cheaper due to lower wage rates/lower production costs in these countries. China does not have a national minimum wage, but sets a minimum per region. The average minimum wage across China is £0.79, compared to £6.50 in the UK (as of Feb 2015);
- **Newer technologies** - owing to its vast size, population and GDP per capita, ASEAN/China have access to newer technologies, allowing for better quality products to be manufactured and used in UK production processes. This allows them to be at the cutting edge of product innovation;
- **Production processes** - UK businesses can learn from the production processes of ASEAN/Chinese businesses. China manufactures 90% of the world's computers, 80% of all air conditioners and 70% of all mobile phones. This means they also have the largest knowledge of how best to manufacture these products. Chinese companies investing in the UK will bring the lessons they have learned with them, resulting in a technology transfer to UK businesses;
- **Large market** - China has a population of 1.4 billion people, with ASEAN adding another 380 million, meaning UK businesses have a larger market in which to export their luxury goods.

Negative effects for UK businesses include:

- **Price wars** - as previously discussed, the wage and manufacturing costs of products coming out of Asia are much below that of the UK. As a result, UK businesses may have to lower their prices to compete with Chinese/ASEAN businesses;
- **Buying power** - the buying power of Chinese businesses may leave UK businesses vulnerable to a takeover. A Chinese firm bought out pizza Express in July 2014 and there have been rumours that Tate and Lyle may be vulnerable;
- **Corporate culture** - cultural differences could make trading with China/ASEAN nations problematic as UK businesses may be unfamiliar with local customs and cultures. The Chinese are very respectful people, and do not appreciate tardy appearances or time keeping. Language and currency differences may also reduce the success of international trade;
- **Transport costs** - with a distance of almost 5000 miles between China and the UK, transportation costs will be high. Importers must also take account of the time taken to transport. As environmental awareness increases, less consumers want UK businesses to trade with Asia, given the increased carbon footprint of doing so.

5.2.1 Case study - Marks and Spencer

UK clothing and retail giant Marks and Spencer entered China in 2008 with a single store in Shanghai. It grew to open a further 14 stores in the Shanghai areas, but failed to make any impact in the country. The company had a disastrous launch initially as the company failed to properly research local knowledge and thought they could simply mirror their experience in Hong Kong. They failed to stock enough small sizes and suffered badly when an accident caused the death of a customer in store - this led to locals talking of a Marks and Spencer "curse".

Despite the appeal of a large market in China, many UK businesses, such as Tesco and B&Q, have also struggled to impregnate the Chinese market. Reasons include rising costs in the home market, a lack of understanding of the culture of the Chinese and the challenge of competing with existing Chinese businesses. To make any impact in China, UK business require to spend billions of pounds. They are reluctant to do that, as the recent recession has left them cutting costs at home.

Q1: Why are UK businesses so keen to expand into China?

....

Q2: List the reasons Marks and Spencer's failed to make an impact on China, using the case study stimulus.

....

Q3: Why are UK businesses reluctant to spend vast sums of money investing in China, despite the possible gains to be made?

5.3 Summary

Summary

You should now be able to:

- describe the impact of Asian nations on UK businesses.

5.4 End of topic test

End of Topic 5 test   Go online

Q4: China has the largest population of any country in the world.

a) True
b) False

....

Q5: China has the largest share of world output.

a) True
b) False

....

Q6: The countries that make up ASEAN share a common currency.

a) True
b) False

....

Q7: The Chinese people have respectful cultures that permeate their business world.

a) True
b) False

....

Q8: UK businesses are vulnerable to a takeover from Chinese organisations.

a) True
b) False

....

Q9: Discuss the impact of ASEAN and China on UK business.

(6 marks)

Unit 1 Topic 6

Business ethics and corporate social responsibility

Contents

6.1	Business ethics	62
	6.1.1 Case study - Waitrose and Fairtrade Foundation	63
6.2	Corporate social responsibility	64
	6.2.1 Case study - Diageo	67
6.3	Summary	68
6.4	End of topic test	69

Learning objective

After studying this topic, you should be able to:

- explain what it meant by business ethics, social responsibility and corporate social responsibility;
- analyse how they impact on all aspects of businesses such as profitability, stakeholder satisfaction, operations, marketing and planning future strategies.

6.1 Business ethics

Business ethics are the moral principles underpinning decision making. Ethical decisions involve more than just financial factors or the interests of shareholders.

We often hear in the news about companies investing in countries that have oppressive regimes or of following business activities that are highlighted as "unethical", e.g. child labour. Popular opinion would seem to shun such a company's products and services in favour of a more "ethical" alternative.

Ethical issues include:

- Should firms use child labour?
- What wages should be paid to Third World countries?
- What extent should firms seek to be environmentally friendly?
- Should firms get involved in certain activities, e.g. manufacturing weapons, animal research, manufacturing cigarettes and alcohol?

However, do moral and social factors really affect buying and investment decisions or do price, brand loyalty, customer service and high dividends sway these decisions regardless of ethics?

Since many businesses are now choosing to set out formal published codes of ethics it would appear they believe this has a huge influence both on customers' buying decisions and on investors' choice of which company to invest in.

A recent survey concluded that the main reasons for having a code of ethics were to:

- define what is acceptable behaviour;
- promote the highest standards of behaviour;
- have a benchmark against which employees/owners can compare themselves;
- provide a means of establishing an individual identity.

The same survey also concluded that:

- ethics programmes appear to work;
- practicing ethics is correlated to positive business outcomes;
- positive leader role-models result in positive business outcomes.

Business ethics Go online

Q1: Why might a business introduce an ethical code of practice? *(2 marks)*

Decide whether each of the following actions was motivated by ethical considerations and explain your decision. *(2 marks each)*

TOPIC 6. BUSINESS ETHICS AND CORPORATE SOCIAL RESPONSIBILITY   63

Q2: An advertising agency refusing to accept business from a company known to use child labour.

....

Q3: In an emergency situation, a private hospital refusing to treat a person whose only income is the state pension.

....

Q4: Celebrity chefs, like Jamie Oliver, encouraging consumers to boycott intensively farmed chickens in favour of purchasing more expensive organically reared chickens.

....

Q5: A baker refusing to accept supplies of genetically modified (GM) flour.

....

Q6: Animal rights activists using "bullying" tactics such as letter bombs and damage to property to "encourage" commercial banks to withdraw their support to a medical research company that use animals as an integral part of its research.

6.1.1 Case study - Waitrose and Fairtrade Foundation

Waitrose and Fairtrade Foundation

Read the article below and answer the questions that follow.

Waitrose has signed a deal with the Fairtrade Foundation to allow the latter to advise and endorse the supermarket's own ethical food sourcing programme. The partnership sees the Foundation take a new direction as it is the first time that it has allowed its label to be used on products that it has not been responsible for producing.

For Waitrose, the benefits are obvious - by being the only UK supermarket to work in partnership with the well-respected Fairtrade Foundation they are able to move away from the price wars that have dominated the UK supermarket market. They can promote the fact that they are now working in partnership with producers in Africa, Ghana and Kenya. The Waitrose Foundation, a charitable arm of the supermarket, already puts a share of profits towards educational, social and healthcare projects called for by communities in those countries where it sources fruit and flowers. Unlike Fairtrade, however, it does not guarantee a minimum price.

Both organisations are due to gain from the new partnership.

Adapted from an article in The Guardian (http://bit.ly/1HgDoOe)

Q7: What is meant by ethics? *(2 marks)*

....

Q8: How has Waitrose benefited from its partnership with Fairtrade Foundation? *(1 mark)*

© HERIOT-WATT UNIVERSITY

6.2 Corporate social responsibility

Social responsibility is a business obligation to a wider society, particularly to external holders.

Corporate social responsibility (CSR) refers to a more holistic approach that an organisation takes to meet or exceed both internal and external stakeholders' expectations beyond those of simply making profits and meeting legal obligations.

Key areas covered by CSR are shown in the following table.

Community involvement	CSR requires organisations to treat their local community with respect and to engage in some kind of community investment. This can be through: • giving cash donations; • by offering your staffs' time and skills in developing and maintaining local projects; • loaning equipment for a particular project.
Employee relations	CSR employers treat their staff fairly, equally and value diversity. This is done through: • respecting the talents and human rights of all individuals; • being fair in the recruitment and promotion processes; • supporting a good work/life balance; • acting ethically and with integrity at all times.
Environmental practices	CSR means doing more than complying with the law in treating the environment with respect by: • reducing energy consumption and minimising waste; • preventing or minimising pollution; • recycling and using recycled materials.
Stakeholder responsibilities	CSR means you have an obligation to best serve the interests of stakeholders, e.g. customers, shareholders, government, wider society, by: • meeting conflicting stakeholder demands, e.g. maximising ROI for investors while providing high quality and low cost for customers; • building sustainable relationships with your stakeholders to earn long-term profitability and respect.

Key areas covered by CSR (all images designed by Freepik.com)

Some organisations such as the Body Shop and the Co-operative Bank have built their entire brand around social responsibility, thereby differentiating themselves from competitors. In direct response to social responsibility issues, Vodafone developed a speaking phone for the blind. Boots have partnered with MacMillan Cancer Support, encouraging its staff to take part in community events. Prudential have set up a scheme called 'Community Investment' where staff are given time out of their working week to work with local schools and charities. Many hotels now give guests the option of not having their towels and linen changed every day. This gives guests the feel good factor and the hotel benefits by saving energy and time spent doing laundry.

As issues such as climate change become more pressing, emissions targets and environmental guidelines are likely to be replaced by legislation. Organisations engaging in CSR programmes will have a better opportunity to minimise financial risk by anticipating change and planning and budgeting for the future accordingly.

Costs and benefits of pursuing a policy of CSR   Go online

State whether the following are costs or benefits to an organisation when actively engaging in a corporate social responsibility programme.

Q9: It will improve the business's public image and strengthen the brand.

a) Cost
b) Benefit

....

Q10: It can attract good quality staff and improve employee retention and productivity.

a) Cost
b) Benefit

....

Q11: Increased business costs lead to reduction in dividends for shareholders.

a) Cost
b) Benefit

....

Q12: Due to the increase of ethical investors there is the ability to access new sources of capital for expansion.

a) Cost
b) Benefit

....

Q13: Turning down a lucrative contract because you disagree with the prospective client's business philosophy.

a) Cost
b) Benefit

TOPIC 6. BUSINESS ETHICS AND CORPORATE SOCIAL RESPONSIBILITY

....

Q14: Raw ingredients in food production are more expensive when using for example organic ingredients.

a) Cost
b) Benefit

....

Q15: You may be less likely to face litigation and fines.

a) Cost
b) Benefit

Effects of a CSR policy   Go online

Q16: Assess the effects of a CSR policy on an organisation's profits. *(10 marks)*

Hints: Start with a definition of corporate social responsibility, highlight how CSR impacts on profits in positive and negative ways, highlight how CSR may help maintain current levels of profitability and develop your answer - do not use bullet points.

6.2.1 Case study - Diageo

Diageo

Read the passage and answer the questions which follow it.

Diageo is one of the world's 300 biggest companies. It owns major brands such as Guinness, Haagen-Dazs and Smirnoff. It has a CSR policy and for some year now Diageo has committed 1% of its worldwide pre-tax profits (some £18m) to community involvement and it encourages other organisations to contribute to the local and international community through its own foundations and charities.

The Diageo Foundation, which receives £3.5m of the £18m made available, divides its work into five main areas: 'Skills for Life', 'Water of Life', 'Global Brands', 'Local Citizens' and 'Our People'.

The 'Water of Life' initiative provides clean drinking water to communities in Africa and in the 'Our People' initiative Diageo promises to match employees' charitable contributions up to a limit of £1,200 per year and employees' fundraising efforts up to £1,500 per year. Any employee can apply for funding for a community project however strict criteria apply so only projects that are likely to succeed are selected. Most importantly each project must have an exit strategy in place to ensure that the benefits derived are sustainable. Diageo's aim 'is to be measured above all by what they achieve rather than what they give'.

Q17: Explain the difference between social responsibility and corporate social responsibility. *(2 marks)*

Q18: What are the main benefits to Diageo of its community involvement? *(4 marks)*

Q19: Discuss to what extent Diageo is a truly corporate socially responsible company in view of the major brands it owns. *(6 marks)*

6.3 Summary

> **Summary**
>
> You should now be able to:
>
> - explain what it meant by business ethics, social responsibility and corporate social responsibility;
> - analyse how they impact on all aspects of businesses such as profitability, stakeholder satisfaction, operations, marketing and planning future strategies.

6.4 End of topic test

End of Topic 6 test Go online

Q20: Which of the following statements, referring to a business having a code of ethics, is false?

a) It promotes the highest standards of behaviour in the business.
b) The public image of the company is improved.
c) Positive business outcomes are achieved.
d) Businesses are unwilling to give up profits to increase shareholders' returns.

....

Q21: Businesses are increasingly introducing a code of ethics because:

a) it always gives them a competitive advantage.
b) consumers and investors are now expecting it.
c) consumers and investors want to feel good.
d) it encourages business practices to change for the better.

....

Q22: CSR-related community involvement projects include:

a) encouraging customers to spend time working in the community.
b) offering your staff's time and skills in developing and maintaining local projects.
c) respecting the talents of all individuals in helping the community.
d) offering your staff's time and skills in developing and maintaining business projects.

....

Q23: Which of the following statements, referring to employee relations and CSR, is false?

a) Businesses support and promote work practices that encourage positive work/life balance.
b) Staff motivation and turnover rates increase.
c) Staff motivation and turnover rates decrease.
d) Staff and the business act ethically and with integrity at all times.

....

Q24: Which of the following is a cost of pursuing a CSR policy?

a) Decreased employee motivation.
b) New sources of capital for expansion are harder to obtain.
c) Having to turn down a lucrative contract.
d) You are more likely to face litigation and fines.

....

Q25: A CSR policy can help increase profits as:

a) it usually comes in tandem with decreased costs of production.
b) the good publicity gained generates more customers for the business.
c) it reduces competition for the business.
d) staff turnover and retention increases.

....

Q26: Explain how a policy of corporate social responsibility can affect an organisation's functional areas. *(13 marks)*

Unit 1 Topic 7

Government influence / technological developments

Contents

- 7.1 Environmental factors 72
  - 7.1.1 United Nations Framework Convention on Climate Change (UNFCCC) 72
  - 7.1.2 UK and EU governments' response to UNFCCC 73
- 7.2 Government influence 76
  - 7.2.1 Government influence on business activity 77
- 7.3 Other external influences 79
  - 7.3.1 Case study - Starbucks 80
  - 7.3.2 Case study - AG Barr 81
- 7.4 Technological factors 82
  - 7.4.1 Costs and benefits to businesses of technological change 83
  - 7.4.2 Legislation 84
- 7.5 E-commerce 86
  - 7.5.1 Internet shopping 88
- 7.6 Summary 88
- 7.7 End of topic test 89

Learning objective

After studying this topic, you should be able to:

- explain opportunities and threats to an organisation arising from changes in government influence or technological developments;
- build on your understanding and knowledge of external factors affecting business;
- explain opportunities and threats to an organisation arising from changes in environmental factors, government influence or technological developments.

7.1 Environmental factors

During the production process businesses create external costs which are borne by society such as pollution, the greenhouse effect and global warming. The more that is produced the greater the cost to the environment. Who pays for these costs?

The prices paid by consumers for the goods and services produced only take into account the businesses internal running costs with a mark up for profit. Governments therefore intervene to limit the effect of the external costs to society by using the following approaches:

- imposing a tax on businesses to take account of these external costs to society;
- offering a subsidy to businesses if they produce in a more environmentally friendly way;
- introducing laws which force businesses to operate in a more environmentally friendly way.

Countries all over the world, including the UK, have legislated to tackle climate change. There is a growing awareness that greenhouse gas emissions have global consequences, no matter where they come from.

Tackling climate change therefore requires a coordinated effort by all nations around the globe. The UK and the EU are party to international legislation that aims to achieve this by signing up to the United Nations Framework Convention on Climate Change (UNFCCC).

7.1.1 United Nations Framework Convention on Climate Change (UNFCCC)

The UNFCCC was created in 1992 with the intention of speaking with one voice internationally and securing an agreement on tackling climate change. One hundred and ninety-six countries have since joined the international treaty. Negotiations focused on four key areas:

- strategies to adopt to climate change;
- finance to enable action on mitigation and adaptation;
- a reduction of greenhouse gas emissions;
- technology development and transfer to allow green development.

Industrialised countries continue to be encouraged to reduce their emissions under the UNFCCC. Thirty-seven industrialised countries set emissions targets under the Kyoto Protocol in 1997. The Kyoto Protocol set a 5% reduction below 1990 levels for the first commitment period (2008-2012). They achieved this but recognised that it was not been enough to offset the quickly increasing emissions from the other countries of the world who did not self-administer the same commitments.

The UK's commitment under the Protocol was a 12.5% reduction and has been achieved, with emissions being reduced by 27% by 2011.

It has been agreed that a second Kyoto commitment period should run from 2013 to 2020. Although there has been a reduction in the countries remaining as signatories, the UK and the EU continue to participate. Many other UNFCCC countries have made voluntary pledges to cut their emissions by 2020. The UK's 2050 target is consistent with a global effort to achieve this.

The UNFCCC say that they "support countries to meet their targets and provides a variety of support". In 2010 the Cancun Adaptation Framework was adopted. During this summit it was agreed that adaptation must be given the same priority as mitigation.

TOPIC 7. GOVERNMENT INFLUENCE / TECHNOLOGICAL DEVELOPMENTS

Prior to this, a meeting of the Intergovernmental Panel on Climate Change (IPCC) in Bali reported that urgent action was needed from all politicians to combat climate change and therefore work on a replacement for the Kyoto Protocol was needed to set out how to further reduce emissions beyond Kyoto.

7.1.2 UK and EU governments' response to UNFCCC

Some of the UK and EU governments' responses have been to:

- deliver on the new targets via the Climate Change Act, introduced in 2008, to reduce carbon emissions by 30% by 2020 and 60% by 2050;
- create a new independent body to monitor progress of carbon reduction targets;
- create a new commission to spearhead company investment in green technology;
- introduce a Climate Change Levy (2001) which taxes businesses on every unit of energy used in an effort to encourage greater efficiency of use;
- increase landfill taxes;
- implement recycling legislation which places more responsibility on manufacturers for the collection, dismantling and disposal of electrical goods they sell to consumers, such as washing machines, televisions and computers, when they reach the end of their useful life;
- increase the number of lofts and walls being insulated and boilers upgraded, including moves to low-carbon heat such as ultra-efficient heat pumps;
- progress government policies such as the Green Deal and those involving Electricity Market Reform (EMR).

The UK Government last reported to Parliament in 2012 when they were on track to meet their 2020 and 2050 commitments.

In order to minimise any loss of competitiveness for UK firms, the UK government needs to ensure through organisations like the EU and the World Trade Organisation that all governments take similar measures.

For UK businesses, this means:

- new production methods will have to be investigated that uses less fuel and produces less emissions this may also increase cost;
- manufacturers may need to re-consider the design of their products to take into account the make-up of the component parts and how they can be recycled or disassembled for safe disposal at the end of their useful life - increases costs;
- further spending on research and development may be needed to create more environmentally friendly components and packaging;
- packaging may have to be altered to be more biodegradable;
- ways of reducing and recycling waste may have to be found in order to comply with legislation, e.g. carbon footprint reduction by using less paper. Firms will have to train employees and customers to have a more environmentally friendly attitude;

- possible cost reductions in the long-term;
- possible increased demand for their goods and services from consumers attracted to "greener" companies.

Marks & Spencer

Read the article and answer the questions which follow it.

Marks & Spencer embarked on a five-year "ecoplan" called Plan A which aimed for the organisation to be **carbon neutral** by 2012. They updated this plan in 2010 realising that their original plan was over-ambitious but still worth pursuing. Focusing on five key areas for improvement, the plan sets out 100 practical measurable targets that M&S intends to reach. This original plan cost the company £200m and was not passed on to customers. M&S was willing to risk lower margins in the short term in the belief that its greener credentials will pay off in the longer term. Some of its areas for improvement are:

- *Tackle climate change* - using green energy by running its stores on renewable power and by developing low carbon products and services;
- *Reduce waste* - reducing packaging and using more recyclable materials, reducing the number of carrier bags it uses, helping suppliers and customers reduce waste by labelling products with recycling guidance;
- *Safeguard raw materials* - develop a long-term strategy to source all its cotton from sustainable sources, trial and introduce new sustainable fibres, ensure that all its fresh meats are free range;
- *Be a fair partner* - supporting suppliers, helping the communities it does business with, giving farmers at home and overseas a fair deal;
- *Promote health and well-being* - selling more healthy food, improving labelling, offering advice to customers and employees.

Some of these plans have already been put into action. It has launched new care labels for its clothing encouraging customers to wash at 30°C, it has opened several "eco-stores" which use 25% less energy and 50% less carbon dioxide than traditional M&S stores, it is switching to renewable energy to power its stores, it is trialling fleeces for staff that are made from recycled plastic bottles and it has introduced 1500 Healthy Eating Advisors into its food halls.

The first phase of Plan A in 2007 saw them make 100 commitments to reduce the social and environmental footprint of the business including in their hundreds of stores and thousands of supply chain locations. In 2010 they entered a second phase with 80 new commitments and a goal to become the world's most sustainable major retailer.

They are currently entering the third phase, Plan A 2020. They still have 100 commitments but there is a change of emphasis.

TOPIC 7. GOVERNMENT INFLUENCE / TECHNOLOGICAL DEVELOPMENTS

For employees, Plan A 2020 is about four key areas:

1. Inspiration - aiming to excite and inspire our customers at every turn;
2. In touch - listen actively and act thoughtfully;
3. Integrity - always strive to do the right thing;
4. Innovation - being restless in their aim to improve things for the better.

They say they have been working hard with their international business to roll out Plan A in the more than 50 countries where they have retail businesses. They have built the local capacity in their teams to work with their customers, employees and stakeholders on what matters to them locally. Plan A as a global framework but with local application.

According to the company, Plan A 2020 retains the best bits of what they have done before. They believe that by aligning social and environmental outcomes with their business goals they can deliver greater value for all and achieve our goal of becoming the world's most sustainable major retailer.

Source: http://corporate.marksandspencer.com/plan-a

Q1: What do you think has prompted M&S's decision to embark on Plan A? *(3 marks)*

....

Q2: Give three examples of actions that M&S has taken to reduce its carbon footprint. *(3 marks)*

....

Q3: What impact does the plan have on M&S's operations? *(4 marks)*

Research   Go online

Choose a large company and go online to investigate their environmental policy.

Produce a report (about 500 words) outlining what the company does regards environmental issues and how it affects the organisation both positively and negatively.

Share your findings with the rest of the class. A suggested answer is provided at the end of this topic using the example of Tesco.

7.2 Government influence

A main aim of the UK Government is to ensure there is sustainable economic growth within the economy. This means increasing the monetary value of goods and services produced and sold in the UK (the Gross Domestic Product (GDP)) by reducing unemployment, increasing employment, stabilising **inflation** rates and growing new industries.

The main polices that governments use in its approach to managing the economy are:

- **Fiscal policy** which involves changes in taxation and spending within the economy. This impacts on businesses because if business taxation increases it means less profit for the business and may curtail its growth plans. Main taxes affecting business are income tax, corporation tax, VAT and capital gains tax.
- **Monetary policy** is designed to control the amount of spending in an economy by altering interest rates, the money supply and exchange rates. Responsibility for this control lies with the Bank of England to administer and is decided by their Monetary Policy Committee (MPC). When interest rates go up the cost of borrowing increases for both businesses and consumers. This impacts on businesses as it can have an adverse affect on its cash flows, increases business costs as the cost of borrowing increases and it will likely reduce turnover as consumers now have less **disposable income** than before.
- **Regional policy** aims to redress the balance in terms of employment, income and wealth between areas of the UK. A variety of incentives, such as grants, rent-free and rate-free premises, providing training programmes for employees, providing cheaper loans etc, are given to companies who locate in less affluent areas in order to create employment and wealth in these areas.
- Fluctuations in the **Exchange rate** alter the value of UK sterling against other currencies. Governments often try to manipulate exchange rates in an effort to maintain business competitiveness. It can influence the exchange rate by using its gold and foreign currency reserves held by its central bank to buy and sell its currency or it can use interest rates through its monetary policy.

A rise in the value sterling against other currencies e.g. £1 = €1.3 to £1 = €1.5, means exports are harder to sell abroad as the customers have to use more of their currency to buy UK goods therefore the export price rises for them. However, it reduces the cost of imports for UK businesses as buyers in UK now use less sterling than before to pay for goods purchased from abroad.

Government influence Go online

Q4: Exchange rates have been held at 0.5% for another month.

a) Fiscal policy
b) Monetary policy
c) Regional policy

....

TOPIC 7. GOVERNMENT INFLUENCE / TECHNOLOGICAL DEVELOPMENTS

Q5: Stirling Council are offering three months free rent to any business taking a unit on High Street.

a) Fiscal policy
b) Monetary policy
c) Regional policy

....

Q6: The value of the pound has strengthened against the euro in recent months.

a) Fiscal policy
b) Monetary policy
c) Regional policy

....

Q7: The Conservative government have passed legislation capping VAT at 20% for the next five years.

a) Fiscal policy
b) Monetary policy
c) Regional policy

....

Q8: Corporation tax was first introduced in 1965.

a) Fiscal policy
b) Monetary policy
c) Regional policy

....

Q9: Grants are available for new business in areas of high deprivation.

a) Fiscal policy
b) Monetary policy
c) Regional policy

7.2.1 Government influence on business activity

Governments will use various tactics which attempt to influence the business environment as part of its overall economic strategy. This involves providing a suitable framework within which businesses, large or small, can operate efficiently whilst simultaneously putting in measures to ensure both employees and consumers are not disadvantaged by business actions.

Government influences business activity through their **political** and **economic** measures (see table below).

As a regulator (measures to ensure equality and fairness exist in the marketplace)	As a promoter (measures to ensure business success)
Competition and Markets Authority (CMA) - investigates proposed mergers to ensure they do not act against the public interest.	**Research & development** - encourages innovation through direct grants and reduced taxation.
Regulatory bodies - organisations set up to oversee certain industries e.g. energy (Ofgem), telecommunications (Ofcom), financial services (FCA), advertising (ASA).	**Small firms assistance** - in gaining access to loan capital, giving tax allowances and grants, offering advice, training and support via enterprise partnerships, e.g. Scottish Enterprise.
Health and safety laws - to ensure a safe working environment, adequate safety equipment and training.	**International trade** - CMA prevents restrictive practices which reduce competition between firms.
Labour laws - minimum wage, Working Time Directive, various discrimination acts, parental leave.	**Regional policy** - giving assistance to firms who set up in certain underdeveloped areas.
Consumer laws - various laws which protect the consumer from shoddy goods, short measures, false or misleading claims, unhealthy products.	

Government influence on business activity

Some of the ways in which government influences business activity today are:

- through **taxation** and spending, as governments can finance new initiatives and give grants to promote Scottish businesses as well and encouraging multinationals to set up in Scotland;
- through laws, directives and regulations such as the change to shared parental leave and other flexible working practices;
- by encouraging business activity through subsidies;
- by providing advice and support through government agencies such as Skills Development Scotland and Princes Trust;
- by working closely with new business start-ups to provide them with advice, partners and trade opportunities. Government ministers often visit foreign countries to negotiate new trade partnerships;
- by providing a suitable infrastructure to deal with transportation of goods, services and people such as duelling the A9 road between the North of Scotland and the Central Belt to increase exports to other parts of the UK;
- by providing grants and emergency loans when a business is in crisis or facing liquidation. The Scottish Government will often intervene to find new buyers or to provide cash injections to ensure continuing employment for workers. For example, the Scottish Government bought Prestwick Airport to ensure its survival.

TOPIC 7. GOVERNMENT INFLUENCE / TECHNOLOGICAL DEVELOPMENTS

Government influence on business activity Go online

Q10: Which act is used to ensure employees and employers are provided with a safe working environment?

a) Consumer Rights Act 2014
b) Health and Safety at Work Act 1974
c) Telecommunications Act 1974

....

Q11: Mothers and fathers can share paid parental leave. This is an example of a:

a) labour law.
b) consumer law.
c) parental law.

....

Q12: Small firms can be given assistance from:

a) The Prince's Trust
b) The Princess's Trust
c) The King's Fund

7.3 Other external influences

Businesses do not operate in a vacuum. When making any strategic decisions or plans, as well as considering their own internal operations and constraints, they must also take into account how external factors may influence any decisions or actions they take.

As well as competition from rivals, businesses need to consider many other influences. Some of these we have already touched on in previous subjects - some other external influences on business are outlined below:

- ***Social*** - relates to changes in society and social structures. e.g. changes in demographics, changes in patterns of demand, e.g. greater choice of organic foods, growth in health clubs, etc.
- ***Political*** - relates to ways in which changes in government and government policies affect businesses, e.g. competition policy.
- ***Technological*** - provides opportunities for businesses to adopt new innovations and invention to cut costs and develop new products/services.
- ***Legal*** - relates to changes to laws and regulations and how they impact on the ways in which businesses operate.
- ***Ethics*** - following ethical decisions may involve turning down lucrative contracts but can bring rewards of increased sales if a business is perceived as an ethical one by consumers.
- ***Economic*** - relates to changes in the wider economy. A growing economy provides

businesses with greater opportunities for growth while one in recession does the opposite. Therefore changes in interest rates, exchange rates, inflation, unemployment and trade cycles may impact on a firms strategic plans.

- **Environmental** - relates to what businesses are doing to protect the environment and is often part of their CSR policy. It can also refer to the influence of pressure groups such as Green Peace.
- **Stakeholder** - particularly to external stakeholders such as banks, local community and customers. Relates to actions the business may have to take to ensure these stakeholders' needs are met.
- **European Union** - this relates to issues such as enlargement and EU directives and regulations.

7.3.1 Case study - Starbucks

Starbucks

Coffee was first imported into Europe in the 17th century but the high street coffee shop phenomenon is a fairly recent thing. Costa, the UK's largest coffee house, opens approximately three new stores a week, including over 300 in China. They sold more than 400 million drinks last year and overtook Starbucks to become the UK's largest coffee shop chain in 2010. This coincided with Starbucks's first drop in operating profit for 16 years.

Costa would like to think that their brand and marketing strategies was to blame for the decline in Starbucks's fortune, but other external factors were to blame. Starbucks's turnover fell by over £13 million in 2013 as it struggled to combat a negative public perception when it was revealed that the American company had been minimising its UK tax bill. Despite healthy sales and operating profits, Starbucks declared a £30 million loss in 2012 to avoid paying tax in the UK.

This led to public protests and a series of negative press coverage. A poll showed a third less people rated the brand as their number one preference as a result of the news. People were turning against the company in droves, forcing them to change their strategy. The company has had to close unprofitable stores, reduce their planned expansion strategy and transfer its EU headquarters from Amsterdam to London in an effort to increase consumer confidence. It has also declared its first ever profits in the UK and announced that it will no longer be looking to minimise its tax bill.

Q13: What external factor involves setting taxation in a country?

a) Political
b) Social
c) Environmental

....

Q14: Consumer pressure groups held protests outside of Starbucks stores. What external factor does this exemplify?

a) Political
b) Social
c) Environmental

....

Q15: What is the method whereby a company moves profit from one country to another to lower its tax bill?

a) Price fixing
b) Transfer pricing
c) Transfer fixing

....

Q16: Describe the benefit of moving profits from one country to a subsidiary in another country.

7.3.2 Case study - AG Barr

AG Barr

The soft drinks market in the UK is worth £15.6 billion per year in retail sales and is growing. A.G.Barr plc is the UK's leading independent manufacturer of branded carbonated soft drinks. It produces a large range of soft drinks including IRN-BRU, Tizer, D'N'B, Findlays Spring Water and Orangina (produced by Barr under licence from brand owner Cadbury Schweppes). It has four production sites, at Cumbernauld, Mansfield, Atherton and Pitcox, supported by distribution centres covering the whole of the UK. Barr's share of the total carbonated drinks market is 3.8% while Coca-Cola has over 30%.

Most of its production sites have recently been updated with more advanced production facilities. The Atherton site produces a variety of brands in 330ml cans and Orangina in the famous bulby bottle. The Cumbernauld and Mansfield sites produce drinks in several sizes of plastic (polyethylene teraphthalate (PET)) bottle. The Cumbernauld site has a 750ml returnable glass bottle line which was the first to be installed in the UK for many years. Barr are the biggest distributor of this environmentally friendly pack.

Findlays Spring Natural Mineral Water is a wholly owned subsidiary of Barr's with its source at the foot of the Lammermuir Hills, at Pitcox near Edinburgh.

Barr's has a workforce of over 900 staff. Over half of the workforce have worked for the business for more than 20 years. One former driver, now a sales executive, received an award for 50 years' service. By the end of January 2006, 448 of its workforce had received an award to mark 15 years' service with the company.

The company run a 12-week programme with young people in conjunction with the Princes Trust as well as sustainable partnerships with local primary and secondary schools.

Source: http://www.agbarr.co.uk - March 2015

Q17: Analyse the influence that external factors may have on Barr's activities.

(6 marks)

7.4 Technological factors

In recent years the growth in the use of information and communications technology has brought many benefits and challenges to businesses. In the longer term it is believed that new technological advances will provide one of the main drivers of business growth. This is evident in the exponential spending in this area by the worlds biggest multinationals. For example, Amazon are investing in drones for making deliveries. Amazon said: "from a technology point of view, we'll be ready to enter commercial operations as soon as the necessary regulations are in place." This will reduce the need for labour and see great savings being made in the future.

These technological advances affect both the processes used by businesses in all their functional areas, whether that be in production, finance, human resources or marketing and the products being offered to consumers in conjunction with the way in which they are offered.

Technological developments include:

- more advanced and sophisticated computers;
- the internet - in 2014 over 38 million households in the UK (76%) had internet access (the comparable figure in 2006 was 15 million households). 91% of all UK households with internet access have a broadband connection;
- many business transactions are now carried out using the internet;
- fourth-generation (4G) mobile phones - phones turned into small personal computers that have access to the internet and can download music, games and short films;
- access to the Internet on mobile phones doubled between 2010 and 2014 to 58%;
- **Computer-aided design** (CAD) and **computer-aided manufacture** (CAM), e.g. many architect firms now specialise in computer generated virtual reality views of the proposed exterior and interior of their projects This enables non-technical clients to experience and comment upon the project during the design stage;
- **Video conferencing** - many more sophisticated PC's are being bundled with video conferencing software; this means that businesses can easily communicate with clients and suppliers across the globe without the need for expensive software. Potential job applicants can use video conferencing software to complete an interview rather than travelling to another county. Software such as Skype and Microsoft Lync offer this service for free;
- **Internet banking** - all major banks now offer this service although there is still some concern over its security.
- Websites such as Office 365 and Dropbox mean that businesses can securely store all content in the cloud. This means that files can be accessed from anywhere with internet access whilst

TOPIC 7. GOVERNMENT INFLUENCE / TECHNOLOGICAL DEVELOPMENTS 83

still remaining secure.

Increased competitiveness through ICT Go online

Use of the internet can improve communications between companies and their customers through continuous access. This enhances customer services. It can provide links so that customers can buy and pay online and have access on the status of their orders whilst simultaneously providing customer advice and support. Having access to customers' personal details allows the company to email information to them about new products and services that may be of benefit to them, satisfying their needs more fully.

Online surveys and market research can be carried out to ensure current products and services meet customer expectations. Use of the internet will also help companies scan their environment and keep up to date with developments within their own industry.

Companies can set up their own internal intranet to manage email and video conferencing which enables swift communication between all parts of the organisation, wherever they are located. This helps maintain an efficient communication system within the company and can co-ordinate projects or developments that are taking place in different locations within the company.

Q18: From the passage above identify nine ways in which ICT can enable a firm to be more competitive in world markets.

7.4.1 Costs and benefits to businesses of technological change

Use of ICT can bring many benefits to businesses including cutting costs, expanding markets, increased turnover and increased competitiveness. If used appropriately it can help a business become more successful by enhancing its levels of customer satisfaction. However, care must be taken to ensure compliance with the Data Protection Act and Computer Misuse Act. Businesses will also have to develop new ways of offering customers a personal touch to retain their loyalty in light of the loss of face to face contact that trading over the internet brings.

Costs and benefits to businesses of technological change Go online

State whether the following are costs or benefits to firms using ICT.

Q19: New products can be developed relatively cheaply.

a) Cost
b) Benefit

....

Q20: Staff training and investment in, and renewal of, ICT equipment.

a) Cost
b) Benefit

© HERIOT-WATT UNIVERSITY

Q21: Average cost per unit can be reduced.

a) Cost
b) Benefit

Q22: Faster communications between suppliers and customers.

a) Cost
b) Benefit

Q23: Employees can access data readily to enable them to work from home.

a) Cost
b) Benefit

Q24: E-security breaches from fraud, hackers, viruses.

a) Cost
b) Benefit

Q25: Loss of face to face customer contact minimising the personal touch.

a) Cost
b) Benefit

Q26: Complying with the General Data Protection Regulation (GDPR) and Computer Misuse Act (1990).

a) Cost
b) Benefit

7.4.2 Legislation

The General Data Protection Regulation (GDPR) aims to protect the rights of the individual by providing legislation to govern the collection, storage and use of information that is held in electronic or paper file systems.

The Data Protection Registrar holds a list of businesses that are registered under the Data Protection Act and it is the responsibility of the individual business to register their interest with the Registrar. This means that if you are running a business and you hold information on third parties, it is your responsibility to register your business under the Act and follow the rules of the law.

There are seven basic Data Protection Principles which all organisations holding personal data must follow:

1. Lawfulness, fairness and transparency
2. Purpose limitation
3. Data minimisation
4. Accuracy
5. Storage limitation
6. Integrity and confidentiality (security)
7. Accountability

The Data Protection Principles apply to organisations in both the public and private sectors and also information held about children.

The Information Commisioner's Office (ICO) exists to oversee the enforcement and application of the rules of the Act. The ICO has the authority to have inaccurate records corrected and erased. The ICO also deals with complaints by members of the public. A complaint may be raised by an individual where there is a failure to allow access to records or where there has been a breach of one of the data protection principles.

In cases where there has been a serious breach, the individual concerned may be entitled to compensation if it can be successfully proven that they have suffered a loss or damage as a direct result of incorrect information being held by the organisation.

Find out more information about data protection at https://ico.org.uk/for-organisations/guide-to-data-protection/guide-to-the-general-data-protection-regulation-gdpr/.

The Computer Misuse Act was passed in 1990 and is of importance to business and individuals alike.

It created three new offences:

- Unauthorised access to computer material
- Unauthorised access with intent to commit or facilitate commission of further offences
- Unauthorised modification of computer material.

It is generally accepted as good business practice nowadays to issue IT Guidelines to all employees. This document should make reference to the provisions of the Computer Misuse Act 1990.

The Freedom of Information Act 2000 is "challenged with the task of reversing the working premise that everything is secret, unless otherwise stated, to a position where everything is public unless it falls into specified excepted cases" (Lord Chancellor's first Annual Report on the implementation of the Freedom of Information Act 2000; November 2001). The Freedom of Information (Scotland) Act 2002 gives everyone two specific separate rights:

- the right to know whether information exists,
- the right to access that information (subject to exemptions).

The individual right of access was introduced on 1 January 2005. The main features of this are:

1. Every written request for information including emails will be considered to be an access request under the Freedom of Information Act. There is no set format, nor is there any requirement to justify the request. There are no citizenship or residency restrictions and the only requirement is that applicants provide a name and address.
2. Access requests must be dealt with within 20 working days.
3. If the information is not available or the information is not supplied the applicant must be told why.
4. In cases where either the precise information covered by the request is unclear or where the scope is so wide as to make it likely that the request would be refused on the grounds of cost, public bodies are encouraged to discuss with the applicant the nature of their request to see whether it can be redefined to lead to a positive outcome.
5. The Act requires public bodies to set up an appeals procedure to review refusals at the request of the applicants, and if the applicant remains unhappy at the refusal there is an avenue of recourse to the Information Commissioner.

To date, the Act has mostly been used by those in the media wishing to find out information about companies and public bodies.

7.5 E-commerce

E-commerce refers to business transacted using electronic media, primarily the internet. It is a massive growth area as many more consumers and businesses now have access to the internet via broadband, therefore it can open up many new opportunities for businesses. UK household internet access is well above the EU-28 average (89% compared to 76.5%) whereas businesses internet access is almost identical to the EU-28 at 95%. In 2014, the UK had the second highest proportion of enterprises receiving orders over the internet in the EU (Germany had the highest). With regard to sales over the internet as a proportion of total turnover, the UK once again ranked very highly.

E-commerce can take various forms:

- **B2C** - Business to Consumer

    Consumers order direct from the business and the goods are delivered to their homes. Large businesses have little advantage over smaller ones in this area.

- **B2B** - Business to Business

    Companies order direct from their suppliers, receive invoices and make payments.

- **B2G** - Business to Government

    Government orders direct from the business.

TOPIC 7. GOVERNMENT INFLUENCE / TECHNOLOGICAL DEVELOPMENTS

The volume of B2B transactions is much higher than the volume of B2C transactions. This is because businesses have adopted electronic commerce technologies in a greater percentage than households. Also in a typical supply chain there will be many B2B transactions but only one B2C transaction, as the product is retailed to the consumer. Retailers are more predominantly involved in B2C transactions while manufacturers are more predominantly involved in B2B transactions.

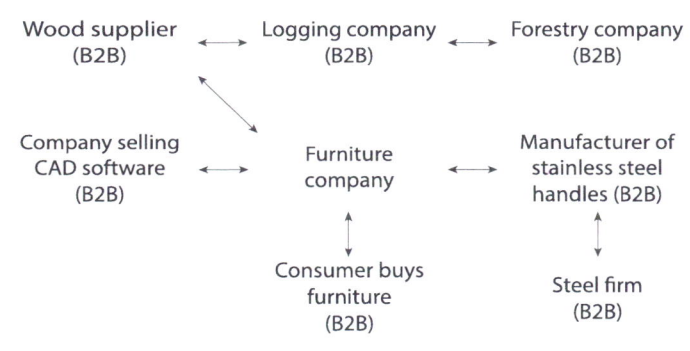

```
Wood supplier  <--->  Logging company  <--->  Forestry company
   (B2B)                  (B2B)                   (B2B)
      ^
      |
      v
Company selling                               Manufacturer of
 CAD software   <--->     Furniture    <--->   stainless steel
    (B2B)                  company             handles (B2B)
                             ^                      ^
                             |                      |
                             v                      v
                       Consumer buys            Steel firm
                         furniture                (B2B)
                           (B2B)
```

Diagram showing the flow of business transactions for a furniture company

E-commerce advantages and disadvantages   Go online

Q27: From the following list of advantages and disadvantages of e-commerce place each one under the correct heading in the table below:

- Can find out if products are in or out of stock;
- Can increase global market share;
- Concerns about security when purchasing/banking online;
- Customer data can be used for marketing;
- Delivery problems;
- Fear that retail shops will be replaced by storage warehouses;
- Improved relationship with suppliers;
- Often reduces lead time;
- Saves costs and improves efficiency;
- Shopping is more impersonal and less of a social affair.

Advantage	Disadvantage

© HERIOT-WATT UNIVERSITY

7.5.1 Internet shopping

Internet shopping is already booming and still on the rise as consumers are more confident in using this service. It was estimated that by Christmas 2014 the UK recorded over £100 billion of online sales. Whilst this figure is still less than the sales of on the high street, it will not be long before the internet takes over. Online sales are increasing year on year, whilst the opposite is true of the high street. Consumers find that online shopping is convenient, saves times and costs and gives more choice, customisation and control.

Recent years has seen the emergence of traditional "bricks and mortar" retailers as important players in internet shopping, for example Tesco, Argos and Currys. This combination of "bricks and clicks" has helped them stay successful. The supermarket chain Morrisons, who have yet to enter the world of online sales, have found themselves losing out to the other supermarket chains. Other retailers, such as the technology retailer Comet, have ceased trading, in part as they could not compete online. The spread of broadband internet is also fuelling online shopping as faster browser speeds enable consumers to compare more sites, research product features and place orders more quickly than before.

Internet shopping   Go online

Q28: Give three reasons why internet shopping is booming.

....

Q29: Why have traditional "bricks and mortar" retailers entered the online shopping market?

7.6 Summary

Summary

You should now be able to:

- explain opportunities and threats to an organisation arising from changes in government influence or technological developments;
- build on your understanding and knowledge of external factors affecting business.

7.7 End of topic test

End of Topic 7 test Go online

Q30: Which of the following does the UNFCCC not aim to do?

a) Adapt to climate change
b) Raise finance to enable action on mitigation and adaptation
c) Increase greenhouse gas emissions
d) Promote green development

....

Q31: Reducing your carbon footprint can be achieved by:

a) redesigning products.
b) writing an environmental policy.
c) reducing waste.
d) offering multipacks for sale.

....

Q32: The main legal influences on business are:

a) inflation and interest rates.
b) consumer, competition and conservative laws.
c) consumer, competition and employee laws.
d) competition and employee laws.

....

Q33: The main purpose of government regulatory bodies is to protect:

a) profits of the industry.
b) the economy.
c) consumers.
d) the government.

....

Q34: Fiscal policy refers to:

a) government spending in the economy.
b) changes in the exchange rate.
c) promoting economic growth by offering grants and subsidies to business.
d) taxation and government spending in the economy.

....

Q35: Which of the following statements, referring to reasons for government involvement with business, is false?

a) To ensure equity and fairness exist in the market place.
b) To provide a framework within which businesses can operate more efficiently.
c) To ensure employees get appropriate training.
d) To encourage innovation by offering grants and reduced taxes.

....

Q36: What is the main effect of government involvement on businesses?

a) It adds to business costs and can put constraints on business activity.
b) It offers opportunities to expand globally.
c) It provides opportunities to be dominant in the market place.
d) It adds to business profits.

....

Q37: External factors influencing businesses can be referred to as:

a) swot analysis.
b) pest analysis.
c) force field analysis.
d) break even analysis.

....

Q38: Recent technological changes are beneficial to a firm as:

a) there is less aggravation from customers.
b) new products for consumers can be developed relatively cheaply.
c) new technology never needs updating.
d) integration of the new processes and procedures into existing ones is minimised.

....

Q39: B2B refers to:

a) businesses buying from their suppliers.
b) consumers buying direct from businesses online.
c) businesses buying from their suppliers using electronic media.
d) businesses buying direct from the government online.

....

Q40: Which of the following statements, referring to how ICT helps a firm's competitiveness, is false?

a) Companies can set up their own intranet which allows speedier, more efficient communications between departments/subsidiaries.
b) The financial costs of setting up a sophisticated ICT presence are relatively cheap.
c) ICT helps companies sell to customers continuously all over the world.
d) Cost reductions are achieved through needing less traditional premises.

TOPIC 7. GOVERNMENT INFLUENCE / TECHNOLOGICAL DEVELOPMENTS   91

Q41: Which of the following is a disadvantage of e-commerce?

a) The global market is reduced.
b) The GDPR bars firms from targeting customers with special offers.
c) Buying from suppliers often means lead times are reduced.
d) Concerns about security when purchasing/banking online.

Q42: The expanding use of e-commerce means that:

a) opportunities to expand abroad are eliminated.
b) traditional "bricks and mortar" retailers are no longer needed.
c) it no longer gives businesses a competitive edge.
d) firms will have to develop new ways of offering customers a personal touch.

Q43: Which of the following statements, referring to how an e-commerce strategy helps maintain high levels of customer satisfaction, is false?

a) Customers can receive relevant promotional offers relatively quickly via online means.
b) Customers' feedback on products/services via online surveys are acted upon.
c) Customers are now more confident in placing orders online.
d) Customers can track the progress of orders placed without the aggravation of lengthy phone calls.

Q44: Discuss ways in which government economic policy might influence an organisation to change.

(6 marks)

Unit 1 Topic 8

The external business environment test

The external business environment test

Go online

There are two parts to this test:

- Part 1 comprises of true/false and multiple choice questions;
- Part 2 comprises of two case studies.

Part 1a : True/False

(1 mark for each question)

Q1: Multinational companies (MNCs) may switch production facilities between countries to increase their profits.

a) True
b) False

....

Q2: Creating new facilities in a host country means the MNC can start earning revenue and profits straight away.

a) True
b) False

....

Q3: Joint ventures are created to spread costs and risks.

a) True
b) False

....

Q4: Creating new facilities in a host country means you can gain a competitive advantage in emerging markets.

a) True
b) False

....

Q5: Transfer pricing is determined by market forces.

a) True
b) False

....

Q6: Transfer pricing can reduce a firm's overall tax burden.

a) True
b) False

TOPIC 8. THE EXTERNAL BUSINESS ENVIRONMENT TEST

Q7: More restrictions in financial markets have fuelled globalisation.

a) True
b) False

Q8: When a MNC invests abroad the GNP of the host country decreases.

a) True
b) False

Q9: When a MNC invests abroad it reduces demand in the home country for people seeking college and university places.

a) True
b) False

Q10: The European single market opens up less opportunities for businesses to grow.

a) True
b) False

Q11: The Social Chapter harmonises social legislation within the EU.

a) True
b) False

Q12: Business ethics are the moral principles underpinning business decisions.

a) True
b) False

Q13: Pursuing a CSR policy can lead to increased business costs.

a) True
b) False

Q14: Pursuing a CSR policy can lead to improved PR for the business.

a) True
b) False

Q15: Pressure groups have acted as a catalyst for the government to tighten the law on tax avoiding businesses.

a) True
b) False

Q16: Glocalisation refers to companies who operate globally but locally.

a) True
b) False

Q17: B2B is when consumers order direct from the business and the goods are delivered to their homes.

a) True
b) False

Q18: Advances in technology gives business the ability to track orders from suppliers and to customers.

a) True
b) False

Q19: The use of e-commerce reduces concerns about security when purchasing/banking online.

a) True
b) False

Q20: Governments' influence on business activity is designed to ensure economic growth in the country is sustainable.

a) True
b) False

Q21: Many government regulations reduce business costs.

a) True
b) False

Q22: External influences on businesses are often referred to as PELT analysis.

a) True
b) False

Part 1b: multiple choice

(1 mark for each question)

Q23: A reason for the increasing growth of multinational companies (MNCs) is a reduction in barriers to:

a) world peace.
b) world time zones.
c) world trade.
d) cultures.

....

Q24: Foreign direct investment takes place when businesses expand:

a) into new markets.
b) their facilities in their home country.
c) their workforce.
d) their facilities abroad.

....

Q25: One main reason for joint ventures between businesses is to reduce:

a) the threat of a hostile takeover.
b) the taxation burden.
c) costs and risks.
d) global warming.

....

Q26: Transfer pricing refers to the price charged for goods:

a) transferred between one international subsidiary and another.
b) to consumers in another country.
c) transferred between one subsidiary and another.
d) transferred between EU countries.

....

Q27: Which of the following statements, referring to the 'drivers' of globalisation, is false?

a) Increasing levels of world trade.
b) Convergence of consumer lifestyles and tastes.
c) Accelerating technological innovation.
d) Accelerating use of transfer pricing in business.

....

Q28: A MNC's investment in a host country means:

a) the MNC's profits can be used as a source of revenue for the host country.
b) tax on the MNC's profits can be used as a source of revenue for the host country.
c) tax on the MNC's profits can be used as a source of revenue for the home country.
d) the MNC's profits can be used as a source of revenue for the home country.

....

Q29: Which of the following statements, referring to the main benefits to a firm for its CSR community involvement, is false?

a) It gets positive PR for the firm.
b) It helps gain more customers therefore increases revenue.
c) It increases staff turnover as staff prefer to work for companies involved in community projects.
d) It increases motivation of staff who are directly involved in community projects.

....

Q30: What is a benefit of 'acting locally' as a global company?

a) Business costs increase as more resources are needed to satisfy local preferences.
b) Businesses can respond quicker to investors' needs in the local area, ensuring loyalty.
c) R&D encourages innovation.
d) Businesses can respond quicker to customers' needs in the local area, ensuring loyalty.

....

Q31: Which of the following statements, referring to the increasing use of online shopping as an alternative to traditional retail shopping, is false?

a) Consumers find online shopping gives more choice, customisation and control.
b) Consumers find online shopping to be secure at all times.
c) Faster browser speeds enable greater comparison of sites.
d) The use of broadband internet is increasing.

Part 2a: Case study - Aegon

Aegon is one of the world's largest life insurance and pension companies. It is headquartered in the Netherlands and employs nearly 27,000 people worldwide. Its major markets are in the USA, the Netherlands and the UK. Aegon entered the UK market in 1994 by setting up its own operations and by taking over Scottish Equitable. Its UK operations are headquartered in Edinburgh and it has over 2000 employees. Other countries in which Aegon operate include Canada, China, the Czech Republic, Hungary, Poland, Slovakia, Spain and Taiwan.

Being a global company allows Aegon to gather expertise from around the world and use it to benefit their customers in local markets. This 'local knowledge, global power' means they develop products, designed in line with national tax and regulatory rules, which fit how people in each country live.

TOPIC 8. THE EXTERNAL BUSINESS ENVIRONMENT TEST 99

With €360 billion in assets under management, Aegon places great importance on its responsibilities as a major institutional investor. In the United Kingdom and the Netherlands, Aegon offers special Socially Responsible Investment funds which invest only in companies that have ethically and environmentally sound business practices.

Wherever they are located Aegon become involved in community programmes. These focus on projects in the community, employee volunteering and sharing Aegon resources and skills. For example, in Edinburgh they fund breakfast clubs in primary schools and actively support any staff from the Edinburgh offices who want to get involved in the breakfast clubs on a voluntary basis. They recycle their waste and take part in the employees cycle to work scheme.

Source: http://www.aegon.com

Q32: Suggest two reasons why Aegon became a multinational company. *(2 marks)*

....

Q33: Suggest two reasons why Aegon used a mix of buying over existing companies and setting up their own companies when entering the UK market? *(2 marks)*

....

Q34: What benefits might the UK gain from being a host country to Aegon? *(6 marks)*

....

Q35: Explain how the Social Chapter might affect Aegon's global operations. *(6 marks)*

....

Q36: What are the main benefits to Aegon of becoming involved in local community projects and ethical investments? *(2 marks)*

....

Q37: Explain how 'local knowledge, global power' supports Aegon in focussing on customer service. *(2 marks)*

....

Q38: How might Aegon make use of e-commerce to attract more customers? *(2 marks)*

....

Q39: How might the Financial Conduct Authority (FCA) in the UK affect Aegon? *(2 marks)*

Part 2b: Case study - Aggreko

Background information

Aggreko plc is listed on the London Stock Exchange and is headquartered in Glasgow. It is the global leader in the rental of power, temperature control and oil-free compressed air systems. It helps customers in many industries to improve and safeguard their operations by solving problems, creating opportunities and reducing risk.

Aggreko provides its customers with service support through its 7,700 employees operating from over 100 countries with revenues of approximately £1.5 million in 2014.

Their singular vision is to be the leading global player in the specialist energy marketplace. Their mission statement is "*To offer specialist energy solutions that are delivered by our high-quality people in such a way that we continually grow our global list of satisfied and long-term customers.*"

Strategy

Aggreko's strategy is to drive the growth of their core business of power, temperature control and oil-free compressed air rental in two ways: by organic growth, enabled by fleet investment and geographic expansion, and by judicious acquisitions. To drive organic growth, they opened new service centres in Dubai, Hong Kong, Brazil and the Netherlands. The acquisition of GE Energy Rentals complemented this by adding further geographic reach, with new service centres being added to their network in Europe.

European countries in which they operate include Belgium France, Spain, Italy, Ireland, Germany, Netherlands, Norway, Czech Republic, Hungary, Poland, Serbia, Slovenia and Slovakia. In 2010 they acquired Northland Power Services to enter the US market. A year later then acquired another business in New Zealand and in 2012 in Brazil.

Corporate social responsibility (CSR)

Aggreko is committed to working in a safe, ethical and responsible manner. The nature of their business means they often operate in remote and difficult environments, with equipment and substances that are potentially dangerous to people and harmful to property and the environment. Over time, they have developed a comprehensive range of operating procedures and processes to ensure that they minimise any risk of harm to people or to the environment.

The two major environmental issues they deal with in their business are emissions-to-air from their equipment, the vast majority of which is diesel powered, and the safe handling and disposal of fuel and oil. Aggreko's equipment and solutions are designed to comply with applicable laws, regulations and industry standards wherever they operate in the world. In effect, this means they comply with the laws, regulations and standards of some of the most stringent jurisdictions in which they operate and, therefore, far exceed the levels required in many others.

Markets

From construction and contracting, to events, shipping and utilities, Aggreko have developed a range of industrial rental solutions, backed up by expert engineers who are committed to delivering outstanding service.

Aggreko has extensive experience in providing both heating and chilling equipment to the food & beverage industry. Their services include seasonal or temporary cooling and cold storage of produce, dairy or meat products to dry ice blasting for packaging or processing. Aggreko has the contract for Glastonbury Festival. It created a new 'green area' on site in response to the organisers demand for use of renewable energy.

In January 2008, Aggreko signed a joint venture contract with the Beijing Organizing Committee for the XXIX Olympic Games (BOCOG) for the supply of temporary power generation. They delivered on their promise and worked again with the Olympic organising committee to supply power to the London 2012 games.

Source: adapted from http://www.aggreko.com

Q40: Aggreko's mission statement is very customer-focussed. Using evidence from the case study, evaluate how Aggreko attempts to fulfil this mission statement.

(4 marks)

Q41: Aggreko has pursued a strategy for growth by organic means and by acquisitions. Suggest reasons why this is an appropriate strategy for Aggreko.

(8 marks)

Q42: Assess why having a CSR policy is important for the operations of Aggreko.

(8 marks)

Q43: Aggreko has undertaken to work in partnership with two organising committees for the Olympic Games. What are the benefits of joint ventures such as these?

(6 marks)

Q44: Explain the main features of globalisation and analyse ways in which globalisation can affect how a business operates.

(8 marks)

The internal business environment

1	Management theory	105
	1.1 The role of management	106
	1.2 Mintzberg's management roles	109
	1.3 Stewart's demands, constraints and choices	111
	1.4 Approaches to management thought	113
	1.5 Taylor's classical school	113
	1.6 The human relations school	121
	1.7 Maslow's neo-human relations school	123
	1.8 Systems theory	126
	1.9 Contingency theory	130
	1.10 Summary	132
	1.11 End of topic test	133
2	Leadership	137
	2.1 Management v leadership	138
	2.2 Styles theory	139
	2.3 Trait theory	141
	2.4 Contingency theory	142
	2.5 Summary	149
	2.6 End of topic test	150
3	Teams	155
	3.1 Importance of teams in organisations	156
	3.2 Team roles	158
	3.3 Team influence on organisational effectiveness	160
	3.4 Stages of group development	161
	3.5 Summary	163
	3.6 End of topic test	164
4	Time and task management	167
	4.1 Time and task management introduction	168
	4.2 Principles of time and task management	169
	4.3 Time stealers	169
	4.4 Task management	172

4.5	Good and bad time and task management	172
4.6	Strategies to improve time and task management	175
4.7	Summary	175
4.8	End of topic test	176

5 Managing change — 179

5.1	Managing change introduction	180
5.2	Stages of change	182
5.3	Forces for and against change	186
5.4	Force field analysis	187
5.5	Approaches to managing change	190
5.6	Costs and benefits of the different approaches to managing change	192
5.7	Change agents	195
5.8	Barriers to effective change	196
5.9	Summary	199
5.10	End of topic test	200

6 Equality and diversity — 205

6.1	Equality Act 2010	206
6.2	Examples of discrimination at work	207
6.3	Mitigation against the effects of the Equality Act	209
6.4	Impact on HR as a result of the Equality Act	209
6.5	Summary	212
6.6	End of topic test	213

7 The internal business environment test — 215

Unit 2 Topic 1

Management theory

Contents

- 1.1 The role of management 106
  - 1.1.1 Fayol's management functions 106
  - 1.1.2 Drucker's management functions 108
- 1.2 Mintzberg's management roles 109
- 1.3 Stewart's demands, constraints and choices 111
- 1.4 Approaches to management thought 113
- 1.5 Taylor's classical school 113
  - 1.5.1 Scientific management 114
  - 1.5.2 Time and motion studies 115
  - 1.5.3 Other writers on scientific management 116
  - 1.5.4 Classical organisation theory 118
  - 1.5.5 Relevance of the classical school today 119
- 1.6 The human relations school 121
  - 1.6.1 Criticisms of the human relations school 121
  - 1.6.2 Relevance of the human relations school 122
- 1.7 Maslow's neo-human relations school 123
  - 1.7.1 Herzberg's motivator-hygiene factors 124
  - 1.7.2 McGregor's Theory X and Theory Y 125
- 1.8 Systems theory 126
  - 1.8.1 Case study - Tavistock Institute 129
- 1.9 Contingency theory 130
- 1.10 Summary 132
- 1.11 End of topic test 133

Learning objective

After studying this topic, you should be able to:

- explain what management is;
- explain what different theorists believe the role of the manager to be.

1.1 The role of management

All human activities have to be managed. Decisions have to be made about what to do and how to do it. Although in one sense all individuals are 'managers', because everyone makes decisions about courses of action, the term 'management' usually applies to those who have the authority to affect the activities of others as well as themselves.

Mary Parker Follet (1868-1933) described as management as "the art of getting things done through people". The manager's role is vital in ensuring that the objectives of an organisation are met effectively, and managers achieve this by making decisions about how to use the resources available to them.

Managers are given responsibility for achieving their objectives and are held accountable for their actions. Their responsibilities include developing appropriate organisational structures, specifying objectives, deploying resources and evaluating performance. Managers are required to make decisions in all the areas for which they are responsible. Managers are given authority over those below them in the chain of command.

There are many theories about what is involved in the manager's role.

1.1.1 Fayol's management functions

The best known writer about management functions is probably Henri Fayol. He based his research on his experience as an engineer in a French mining organisation at the beginning of the twentieth century, although his ideas did not become widely known until the late 1940s. The basic framework he outlined, which you studied at Higher level in Understanding Business, is still relevant today and is the basis on which many modern management theories have been built.

Fayol identified five functions of managers:

- *planning* - developing future activities to secure success through meticulous planning and not leaving anything to chance;
- *organising* - recruiting and retaining the best employees, ensuring a mix of operational and strategic labour, as well as ensuring the organisation of resources;
- *commanding* - supervising employees to ensure the company reaches its potential;
- *co-ordinating* - ensuring that all departments and tasks complement one another to result in an efficient workflow, reduce waste and increase efficiency;
- *controlling* - to ensure that all managers and employees are working towards achieving the common goal, on time and within budget.

Fayol's management functions   Go online

Identify which of the five functions relates to each statement.

Q1: Giving instructions to those responsible to carry out the work.

a) Planning
b) Organising
c) Commanding
d) Coordinating
e) Controlling

....

Q2: Dividing work into units and allocating them to different departments/people.

a) Planning
b) Organising
c) Commanding
d) Coordinating
e) Controlling

....

Q3: Deciding what needs to be achieved and developing action plans.

a) Planning
b) Organising
c) Commanding
d) Coordinating
e) Controlling

....

Q4: Setting targets, ensuring they are met and correcting failure to achieve targets.

a) Planning
b) Organising
c) Commanding
d) Coordinating
e) Controlling

....

Q5: Harmonising all the different activities of the organisation.

a) Planning
b) Organising
c) Commanding
d) Coordinating
e) Controlling

Fayol's functions in action

Here are four managers:

1. a marketing manager of a large manufacturing company;
2. a football club manager;
3. a human resources manager;
4. the head teacher of your school.

Q6: Write down an example of an activity each of these managers might do to carry out each of Fayol's five functions.

1.1.2 Drucker's management functions

There are many other writers who have described the different types of activity carried out by managers.

For example, writing in the second half of the 20th century, Peter Drucker identified five different functions of managers:

- **setting objectives** - ensuring that employees are aware of the direction of travel for the business and that all decisions made are helping to meet the organisations objectives. Drucker argued that these communicating the objectives to employees was as important as setting them in the first place;
- **organising** - an organised business runs more efficiently and makes better decisions. By classifying the work into manageable activities, groups of workers were able to perform better;
- **motivating and communicating** - Drucker believed in the power of teamwork. He believed that employees needed to be motivated and empowered to perform better and that communicating success improved performance;
- **measuring** - Drucker believed in analysing and appraising performance by measuring success. Communicating the measurement of success further motivated employees to work harder;
- **developing people** - Drucker valued workers and believed that employees should be encouraged to develop their skills and develop others.

Drucker also believed in **management by objectives** - an idea he developed this technique from his study of General Motors, a large car firm in the USA in the 1950s. According to this idea, the best way to manage is to set clear objectives for each person at every level of the organisation. Once the strategic objectives have been decided, tactical objectives are set for each department and then each employee is given individual objectives (targets).

Drucker stressed the motivational importance of involving employees in deciding their personal objectives. Regular appraisal interviews are held to assess performance and adjust targets or set new ones.

Management by objectives (MBO)

Go online

Q7: Decide which of the following MBO statements is an advantage or a disadvantage:

- Everyone's focus is on the main objectives of the organisation.
- Employees may be tempted to take excessive risks in order to ensure they meet targets.
- Failure may undermine confidence and demotivate employees.
- MBO helps to identify training needs.
- Areas where specific objectives have not been set may be seen as less important and ignored.
- Basing rewards and promotion on the achievement of targets rather than the subjective view of managers is likely to be seen as fairer by the workforce.
- Striving to reach targets may put stress on employees, leading to absenteeism and illness.
- Individual targets act as motivators.
- Employees may cheat and cut corners e.g. leading to quality problems in order to achieve their targets.
- MBO increases each employee's awareness of responsibility for their own work.

Advantages	Disadvantages

Q8: Describe how a manager would set carry out an appraisal if they were following the principles of management by objectives.

1.2 Mintzberg's management roles

Henry Mintzberg closely observed the work of the chief executives of five different American companies in the 1970s. He found that, although all the executives agreed that in theory their role was to plan, organise, command, etc., in practice they spent much of their day to day working time on activities which did not fit neatly into these categories. Mintzerg thought that much of a manager's daily working life consisted of "firefighting" - dealing with frequent interruptions, unforeseen events requiring quick decision making, and an ever increasing pace.

Mintzberg concluded that, in spite of the wide variety of activities managers engaged in, all managerial relationships had certain common characteristics. He divided these characteristics into three categories:

- *interpersonal relationships* - mainly have to do with relationships with people.

- *informational relationships* - mainly have to do with handling and passing on information.
- *decisional relationships* - mainly have to do with the manager's choice of course of action.

Mintzberg further subdivided each of these categories into ten roles that managers carry out:

- *Interpersonal roles*
    - figurehead, e.g. representing the business abroad or during a conference;
    - leader, e.g. motivating staff through the appraisal process;
    - liaison e.g. co-ordinating with other departments.
- *Informational roles*
    - monitor, e.g. checking the organisations sales figures;
    - disseminator, e.g. producing the monthly production report for directors;
    - spokesman, e.g. speak about new product development at board meeting.
- *Decisional roles*
    - entrepreneur, e.g. identify new markets;
    - disturbance handler, e.g. resolves conflicts amongst staff;
    - resource allocator, e.g. allocates budget to departments
    - negotiator, e.g. represents department during union talks.

Mintzberg's roles Go online

Q9: Match the following ten roles with each description in the table below:
- Leader;
- Figurehead;
- Negotiator;
- Disseminator;
- Entrepreneur;
- Liaison;
- Disturbance handler;
- Resource allocator;
- Spokesperson;
- Monitor.

TOPIC 1. MANAGEMENT THEORY

Description	Role
Describes the organisation to those outside	
Represents the organisation	
Passes data on to other people in the organisation	
Chooses how to use resources such as money and people	
Deals with unusual situations and unforeseen problems	
Keeps track of what is going on inside and outside the organisation	
Acts as a link between the organisation and external organisations	
Mediates in, and helps to resolve, internal and external conflicts	
Harmonises the needs of the individuals with the needs of the organisation	
Initiates and plans how to exploit opportunities and solve problems	

Note that, in the case of lower level managers, we could substitute the word 'department' for 'organisation'. For example: in the liaison role the middle manager would act as a link between her/his department and the rest of the organisation, as well as between the department and firms outside the organisation altogether.

1.3 Stewart's demands, constraints and choices

Writing in the 1980s, Rosemary Stewart said the manager's role had three features:

- **demands** - the expectations placed on the manager by the organisation - what he/she *must* do;
- **constraints** - internal and external limiting factors;
- **choices** - the options available to the manager - what he/she *can* do.

Demands, constraints and choices

Go online

Q10: Categorise the following list of scenarios for a middle manager under the correct heading in the table below:

- Buying a new machine will go over budget;
- Deciding which workers should be given overtime;
- Working Time Directive limits workers to a 48-hour week.
- Managing Director needs budget projections by Monday;
- Negotiating a further discount from a supplier;
- Scheduling double shifts;
- Senior management need workers to increase output;
- The cheapest supplier has closed down;

Demand	Constraint	Choice

The balance of constraints, choices and demands varies from manager to manager. Some managers may spend most of their time trying to meet the demands of senior management, while others have plenty of scope to make their own choices. Skilful managers may be able to increase their area of choice by reducing constraints.

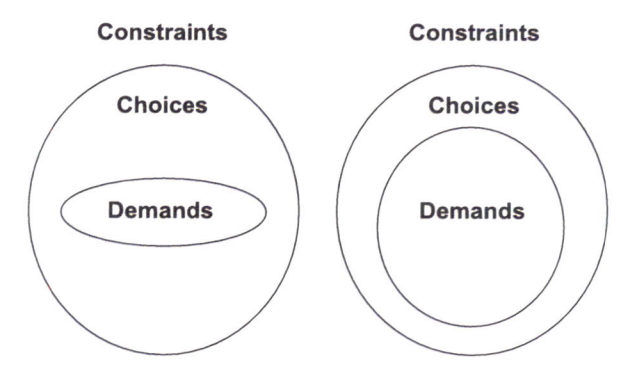

Role A and Role B

Role B may be easier for the manager because there is less danger of making mistakes if she/he is simply carrying out the wishes of senior management. Role A is likely to be more fulfilling though also more risky!

TOPIC 1. MANAGEMENT THEORY

Head Teacher

Try and make an appointment with your Head Teacher to ask them the demands, choices and constraints they face everyday. Ask them about the different roles according to each theorist.

Classroom manager Go online

Q11: What are the constraints, choices and demands of your business management teacher's role as classroom manager?

1.4 Approaches to management thought

The need to develop theories about management was largely a result of the **Industrial Revolution** in the 18th and 19th centuries. Before this, most people worked in agriculture. Goods were produced by people working from home and there was no large-scale production. There was little need for 'management' as we know it today. Then the Industrial Revolution brought mechanisation and large-scale manufacturing. Production and workers moved into factories whose owners had to find effective ways of managing large numbers of workers.

We will be looking at four schools of management thought:

- The classical school;
- The human relations school;
- Systems theory;
- Contingency theory.

1.5 Taylor's classical school

The earliest theories of management were largely based on the same scientific approach which had led to the Industrial Revolution in the first place. The classical school of management is based on the ideas of scientific management and classical organisation theory.

It focuses on formal hierarchical structures, as studied in the Higher Business Management course, and purports to their being 'one best way' of working. It focuses on increasing productivity and increasing the performance of workers by paying them "a fair days pay for a fair days work".

Management thought - revision Go online

Choose which of the following statements are true or false.

© HERIOT-WATT UNIVERSITY

Q12: Fayol and Drucker both included organising as one of their five functions of management.

a) True
b) False

....

Q13: Only Fayol included motivating and developing people.

a) True
b) False

....

Q14: Piece rates and commission are both financial methods of motivation.

a) True
b) False

....

Q15: Piece rates are likely to lead to better quality work than time rates.

a) True
b) False

1.5.1 Scientific management

Frederick Taylor is seen by many as being the founder of the scientific management movement. Taylor wanted to develop a science of management so that the best method for doing each task could be determined. He based his ideas on **Adam Smith**'s theory that division of labour, or specialisation, was the best way to organise the workforce. He developed his five principles of scientific management by studying workers at the Bethlehem Steel factory in the 1890s.

Taylor's five principles   Go online

Put the following words into the sentences below:

- monitored;
- efficiency;
- procedures;
- scientifically;
- thinking;
- efficient;
- trained.

TOPIC 1. MANAGEMENT THEORY   115

Q16: Managers are responsible for ....; workers are responsible for carrying out managers' instructions.

....

Q17: Scientific methods should be used to find the most .... method of doing a job.

....

Q18: Managers should select workers .... allocating each to the specific job for which he or she is best suited.

....

Q19: Workers should be .... to improve their ....

....

Q20: Performance should be .... to check that workers follow .... and perform to the best of their ability.

1.5.2 Time and motion studies

Taylor's research was based on time and motion studies. He timed the best workers and studied the movements they took when completing a task.

Each job was then divided into small tasks; 'one right way' of doing each task was established, and each worker specialised in doing one task. Taylor argued that reducing the number of movements necessary to complete a task would reduce worker fatigue and hence improve morale.

Workers were paid different rates according to their efficiency (piece rates). Taylor believed that this was the only way to motivate employees, as they would see a tangible reward for working hard. He discouraged initiative and employees communicating ideas as he believed workers were purely motivated by money.

Scientific management   Go online

Q21: Explain, in one paragraph, how you could improve efficiency using the ideas of scientific management. *(6 marks)*

Include the following words in your paragraph:

- manufacturing;
- specialised;
- piece rate;
- training;
- supervision;
- procedures;
- efficient;
- incentives;
- time and motion studies.

© HERIOT-WATT UNIVERSITY

Results of scientific management

Go online

Choose which of the following results of scientific management being put into practice apply to the scenarios in the questions below:

a) Efficiency grew.

b) Training costs were reduced.

c) Wage costs went down.

d) Groups of unskilled workers protested because they feared there would not be enough work for everyone.

e) Henry Ford used Taylor's ideas to produce the Model T Ford.

N.B. Some results may apply to more than one scenario.

Q22: Each worker became highly specialised in their job.

....

Q23: Having each worker specialise in only one process made it easy to introduce machinery, leading to mass production techniques.

....

Q24: Each worker needed to be trained for only one process.

....

Q25: Having each worker responsible for a single step in the production process meant that craftsmen could be replaced by unskilled workers.

....

Q26: Productivity went up dramatically so fewer workers were needed to produce the same output.

1.5.3 Other writers on scientific management

Max Weber was a German politician who coined the term **bureaucracy**. He believed in rules, process, authority and power. He believed workers needed expert training and that employees should be tested with only those showing technical knowhow being able to progress in an organisation. The words 'bureaucracy' and (the adjective) 'bureaucratic' are still used today, though often not in the way Weber intended.

Henry Gantt was an American engineer and management consultant. He suggested that giving a bonus to supervisors and the workers who completed the work assigned to them for the day would be a more acceptable way to motivate the workforce. Gantt also invented many charts, including **Gantt charts**, still in use today, to schedule production. You will learn more about Gantt charts in **Researching a business**.

Frank and Lilian Gilbreth filmed workers laying bricks and observed that it took 18 individual micro-

TOPIC 1. MANAGEMENT THEORY

movements (or 'therbligs' as they called them) to lay a brick. They reduced the number of therbligs to four - the number of movements still used by bricklayers today. They wrote books on 'motion studies', similar to Taylor's idea of scientific management. However, they felt that Taylor fell short on managing the human element of the workforce, and spent much of their time and research watching and interacting with workers.

Mary Parker Follett was an American social worker who also influenced organisation theory and behaviour. She raised the importance of **organisational objectives**, saying that organisations were more productive when they had shared processes in place. She did, however, stress that the workforce were more important than any process. She also introduced ethics into business thought.

Criticisms of scientific management

Criticisms of scientific management are that:

- the theory does not take into account social needs of workers;
- the theory treats workers as machines;
- it states that workers are only motivated by money which is not always the case, e.g. nurses and teachers;
- it cannot be applied to creative jobs like architects where piece rate would not be an acceptable form of payment.

Classical school theorists   Go online

Q27: Match the following classical school theorists with their associated management thought in the table below:

- Frank and Lillian Gilbreth;
- Frederick Taylor;
- Henri Fayol;
- Mary Parker Follett;
- Max Weber.

Management thought	Theorist
Believed managers have five roles	
Introduced the term 'bureaucracy'	
Pioneered motion study using 'therbligs'	
Raised the importance of organisational objectives	
The 'father' of scientific management	

1.5.4 Classical organisation theory

Classical organisation theory was based on scientific management. It concentrated on the formal structure of organisations. Classical writers believed that the best form of organisation was structured and orderly with a clear hierarchy and discipline.

Fayol, whose functions of management you have already studied, is one of the best-known classical writers. He described 14 principles of management which he believed were essential to the smooth running of an organisation.

Fayol's 14 principles of management Go online

In each of the following questions, select the principle which matches the description.

Q28: Managers use this principle to produce more work from the same effort.

a) Scalar chain
b) Division of work
c) Discipline
d) Unity of command
e) Subordination of individual interest to general interest

....

Q29: Managers decide what to do if subordinates disobey orders.

a) Scalar chain
b) Division of work
c) Discipline
d) Unity of command
e) Subordination of individual interest to general interest

....

Q30: Each subordinate should be directly responsible to one superior only.

a) Scalar chain
b) Division of work
c) Discipline
d) Unity of command
e) Subordination of individual interest to general interest

....

Q31: The line of authority running from top to bottom of an organisation.

a) Scalar chain
b) Division of work
c) Discipline
d) Unity of command
e) Subordination of individual interest to general interest

....

TOPIC 1. MANAGEMENT THEORY

Q32: Individuals and groups should put the organisation's interests above their own.

a) Scalar chain
b) Division of work
c) Discipline
d) Unity of command
e) Subordination of individual interest to general interest

Bureaucracy   Go online

Q33: Which of the following words would you associate with the word "bureaucratic"? Use a dictionary if you need to.

a) Hierarchy of authority
b) Impersonality
c) Inefficiency
d) Red tape
e) Specialisation
f) System of rules
g) Time wasting

1.5.5 Relevance of the classical school today

Classical writers assumed there was a common set of principles you could apply in all situations. Classical writers shared a **mechanistic** view of human nature which treated workers as if they were parts of a machine. People were seen as rational and motivated only by self-interest. The classical school ignored social and psychological factors.

Nowadays the word bureaucracy often has negative connotations. Modern writers refer to "bureaucratic dysfunction" where rules come to be seen as more important than goals, initiative is stifled and the organisation is unresponsive to the needs and unique characteristics of individual people.

Many organisations still manage using the principles of the classical school. Organisations such as McDonald's split tasks into small chunks and workers concentrate on becoming good at individual tasks. Many organisations who have factories, particularly in countries where the minimum wage does not apply, still pay piece rate. Offices, such as call centres, can use time and motion studies to measure the optimum length of tasks and they measure employee performance accordingly.

The world has changed considerably since the days of the writers on classical theory, e.g. there has been a huge increase in tertiary sector industry and a huge decline in the secondary sector on which many of Taylor and Fayol's findings were based. This **deindustrialisation** makes classical theory less relevant to modern organisations.

Classical structures are rigid and unchanging. It is argued that organisations need to be more flexible nowadays because of influences such as rapid changes in the external environment, new management techniques such as delayering and empowerment, and a more educated workforce.

It is argued that the emphasis on division of labour led to boring, repetitive jobs, the loss of autonomy for workers, and "worker alienation" (a feeling among workers that they were unimportant and uninvolved in any meaningful way).

Criticisms of the classical school

Go online

Q34: From the following list, put the words that are sometimes used about the classical school of management into place in the paragraph below:

- boring;
- bureaucracy;
- deindustrialisation;
- ignored;
- mechanistic;
- rigid;
- self-interest;
- stifled;
- unchanging;
- unimportant;
- unresponsive.

Classical writers shared a .... view of human nature, with people motivated only by .... The classical school .... social and psychological factors. Nowadays, the word .... often has negative connotations of initiative being .... and an organisation being .... to people's needs.

Classical theory is less relevant to modern organisations due to .... Classical structures are .... and ...., when compared with the modern flexible workplace and management techniques. Division of labour arguably led to .... , repetitive jobs and a feeling among workers that they were ....

Scientific management

Scientific management is still relevant today in any situation requiring the production of a standardised product or service. Many organisations continue to benefit from the routine processes where standardised output is required. Highland Spring, producing bottled water of the Blackford hills in Perthshire, manufacture to strict timelines using the scientific management approach.

It is used in secondary sector organisations where the work involves carrying out routine tasks in a precisely specified way, e.g. in assembly lines used in mass production.

The ideas of scientific management can even be used in the service sector, e.g. in McDonalds, where workers are trained in great detail about the tasks they must do and the phrases they must use when speaking to customers, so that the service is identical in every branch.

Newer system approaches, such as just-in-time stock management techniques are derived from scientific management.

Bureaucratic organisation is still relevant to organisations which demand **uniformity** of treatment and regularity of procedures, such as the Civil Service.

TOPIC 1. MANAGEMENT THEORY

The biggest change from Taylor's day is the wealth of the workforce. Although, with the economic conditions and pay freezes of recent years we may again see money being the driver for improvement in UK businesses.

1.6 The human relations school

The human relations school recognised the importance of non-financial methods of motivation. It was based on the findings of Elton Mayo. He carried out his research at the Western Electric Hawthorne plant in Chicago from 1927-1932.

Mayo conducted many research projects, later termed the **Hawthorne effect**. In one such project Mayo formed a group of six workers with a friendly supervisor in charge and experimented to see if changes in working conditions, such as varying the lighting, could improve their productivity. Before his experiments he had assumed that productivity would increase when working conditions improved and worsen when conditions got worse. To his surprise that did not happen. No matter what Mayo and his team did to the working conditions, output continued to improve.

Mayo concluded that:

- belonging to a group which appreciates you is a stronger motivator than money;
- the social support offered by informal (unofficial) groups has a strong influence on motivation;
- people are motivated by feeling specially selected by management;
- the positive effect of being made to feel valued and part of a team is called the Hawthorne Effect.

What motivated the workers? Go online

Q35: Which of the following list of things that might motivate a person to work harder affected the workers at the Hawthorne plant?

a) An autocratic management style;
b) Feeling oneself to be part of a team;
c) Feeling singled out as special by management;
d) Threats of punishment;
e) Wage increases.

1.6.1 Criticisms of the human relations school

Mayo has been criticised for not taking enough notice of environmental factors, e.g. the members of the group whose output increased were all young women - most of whom lived at home. In the 1930s this would have meant they were probably used to obeying male authority. Hence, it is argued, results were bound to be good.

Whereas the classical school tended to ignore people's feelings, the human relations school has been accused of thinking only of people's feelings and ignoring the needs of the organisation.

The human relations school

Discuss with another student whether Mayo would have seen the same outcome if he had experimented with a similarly aged group of young women today.

If you think he would not, what has changed?

1.6.2 Relevance of the human relations school

The unique insight of the human relations school was that people's behaviour at work is motivated not just by money, but by a wide variety of needs and wants to do with factors both inside and outside the organisation. This still remains relevant today.

The fact that large organisations have human resources departments today is largely due to the findings of the human relations school.

Many organisations use the principles of the human relations school to motivate workers today. They provide cafeterias, social clubs, sport clubs and leisure facilities on site or as perks. Google and other technology firms embrace this strategy. Facebook provide daily barbeques on-site, chess pods and a dry cleaning service among other things. These perks, although valuable, can encourage employees to never leave the office!

The human relations school showed the importance of informal as well as formal organisation, i.e. it acknowledged that workers are affected not just by the organisation's demands but also by the views of colleagues with whom they identify and whose values they share.

Relevance of the human relations school   Go online

Q36: Mayo discovered that people are more motivated by money than conditions.

a) True
b) False

Q37: The human relations school was a reaction to the work of scientific management.

a) True
b) False

Q38: The Hawthorne study would get the same result today.

a) True
b) False

Q39: The study proved that woman work harder than men.

a) True
b) False

TOPIC 1. MANAGEMENT THEORY

Q40: Human relations believe that factors such as working conditions are important.

a) True
b) False

1.7 Maslow's neo-human relations school

'Neo' means 'new'. Neo-human relations writers such as Abraham Maslow and Frederick Herzberg published their findings 40 years after Mayo. They shared his belief that **socio-psychological** factors must be taken into account when deciding how to manage effectively.

Abraham Maslow was an American psychologist who developed the 'hierarchy of needs'. He said that people are motivated to satisfy five different needs:

- *physiological needs* - for food, sleep, etc.;
- *safety needs* - for security and freedom from threats;
- *social needs* - for love and friendship;
- *self-esteem needs* - for respect from oneself and others;
- *self-actualisation needs* - for self-fulfilment.

If you are using this model to understand what motivates an individual you first need to look at where they are on the hierarchy. If they are only having their physiological needs met then you could motivate them by providing them with 'safety'. If they are getting a lot of self esteem from their job then you could motivate them by helping them to fulfill their potential.

You will have studied Maslow at Higher level. However, at Advanced Higher level you be asked to evaluate the impact of the theory, e.g. what is good and bad about using it?

Maslow's hierarchy   Go online

Q41: Maslow arranged these needs in a pyramidal hierarchy. Which order in the pyramid should you place Maslow's five needs (below)? Remember, Maslow said people look to satisfy their needs in order, starting with the lowest level.

- Physiological;
- Safety;
- Social;
- Self-esteem;
- Self-actualisation.

Maslow argued that managers should adjust their approach according to the level of need motivating their subordinates.

© HERIOT-WATT UNIVERSITY

Hunger — Go online

Q42: According to Maslow what would be the effect of offering the chance to work in a group to someone who is hungry? Give a reason for your answer.

1.7.1 Herzberg's motivator-hygiene factors

In the 1960s Frederick Herzberg interviewed accountants and engineers to find out what gave them satisfaction or dissatisfaction at work.

He found that some things satisfied workers and motivated them to work harder. He called these motivators; another name for them was satisfiers. They are similar to Maslow's growth needs. They are factors that have to do with the *content* of a job.

Motivators (satisfiers) include:

- being given the chance to increase your skills;
- achieving work goals;
- management recognising the worker's efforts;
- the chance of getting promoted;
- being given responsibility.

On the other hand Herzberg found that the things that made workers positively unhappy were different. He called these hygiene factors, or dissatisfiers. Workers were demotivated if hygiene factors were poor but did not work any harder if they were particularly good. These are similar to Maslow's deficiency needs. They are factors that have to do with the context of a job.

Hygiene factors (dissatisfiers) include:

- poor working conditions;
- low wages;
- low status;
- lack of job security;
- bad relationships with managers and colleagues;
- feeling too closely supervised.

Herzberg concluded that managers first of all had to ensure that all the hygiene factors were adequate before they could even begin to motivate staff.

Criticisms of Herzberg are that:

- he studied only skilled workers, so it is argued that his theory may not apply as much to unskilled or semi-skilled workers;
- his theory ignored the motivational effects of teamwork.

Despite these criticisms, Herzberg's theory pointed the way towards a number of non-financial motivational techniques still in use today.

Herzberg's motivator-hygiene factors Go online

Q43: Match the following hygiene factors with their associated motivators in the table below:

- Fair pay;
- Job security;
- Machines that work;
- Supervision;
- Working conditions.

Motivators	Hygiene factors
Challenging work	
Empowerment	
Profit sharing schemes	
Promotion	
Target setting	

1.7.2 McGregor's Theory X and Theory Y

Douglas McGregor argued that managers had two different ways of looking at their subordinates. He named these Theory X and Theory Y. Whether the manager would take a classical or a human relations approach to managing his/her subordinates would depend on which theory they believed in.

If you believe in **Theory X**, you believe that people:

- naturally dislike work and will try to get out of it if they can;
- have to be threatened with punishment and supervised to get tasks done;
- want to be told exactly what they have to do;
- have security as their greatest need.

If you believe in **Theory Y**, you think that people:

- think work is fulfilling and natural;
- are able to use self-discipline to achieve their objectives;
- want to be given responsibility and decision making power;
- have self-actualisation as their greatest need.

Theory X and Theory Y

Discuss the following questions with another student before answering.

Q44: Which of these theories do you tend to believe in? Is it is possible to believe in both? Hint: think of different types of workers, different types of job.

....

Q45: If a manager held a Theory X view would she/he be more likely to use a classical or a human relations approach?

a) Classical approach
b) Human relations approach

....

Q46: If a manager held a Theory Y view would he/she be more likely to use a classical or a human relations approach?

a) Classical approach
b) Human relations approach

1.8 Systems theory

This school developed in response to the failings of the classical and human relations schools. It was argued that the classical school ignored the needs of individuals and concentrated on organisational structure and procedure, while the human relations approach did not look at organisation as a whole, just at the needs of individuals within it.

Systems theory tried to consider the needs of both the organisation and the individual employees.

A business organisation is an *open system*. It operates in an environment that contains many other systems, e.g. supplying firms, the government.

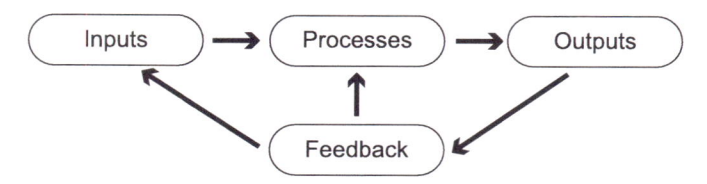

Inputs → Processes → Outputs → Feedback → (loops back to Inputs and Processes)

Diagram showing the four main features of an open system

TOPIC 1. MANAGEMENT THEORY

An open system has four main features:

- It receives inputs or energy from the environment.
- It converts inputs to outputs.
- It discharges outputs into the environment.
- It gets feedback from its environment which may make it decide to change its inputs or processes.

A business system Go online

Q47: Put the following inputs, processes and outputs of a business system under the correct heading in the table below:

- Finance;
- Goods;
- Machinery;
- Marketing;
- People;
- Planning;
- Production;
- Research & Development;
- Services;
- Waste.

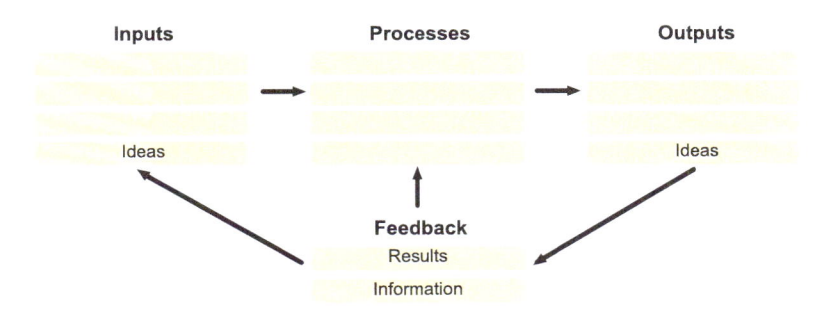

Inputs	Processes	Outputs
Ideas		Ideas

Feedback
Results
Information

Systems theorists study the effects of changes in one system or subsystem on other systems and subsystems.

Systems theory can get quite complicated and many writers have suggested different names for the subsystems which are common to all organisations. For our purposes the classification below summarises the main sorts of subsystems in an organisation:

1. *Human/social* - to do with motivation, leadership etc.;
2. *Administrative/structural* - to do with lines of authority;
3. *Informational/decision making* - to do with the decisions and information that are essential to keep the organisation in business;
4. *Economic/technological* - concerned with how work will be done and how costs will be minimised.

The systems approach looks at the organisation as a whole and considers all aspects of its relationships within and outside the firm. Managers should focus on the role each part of an organisation plays in the whole organisation, rather than deal with each part separately. Managers need to anticipate the effects that changes in one part of the system will have on other parts.

Advantages and disadvantages of a business system

Advantages:

- a holistic approach which views the organisation as a set of sub goals and the systems which work together;
- takes into account the organisation's goals and the external business;
- understands that a change in one part of the organisation can impact another;
- suits environments which are constantly changing;
- can suit customer focused organisations as takes into account the business environment.

Disadvantages:

- more a way of looking at work flow rather than a management theory;
- complicated as it involves analysing lots of sub systems.

Systems theory today

Go online

Q48: Complete the summary of the ideas of the systems school below using the following list of words:

- feedback;
- information;
- interaction;
- open;
- PEST;
- processed;
- resources;
- subsystems;
- synergy.

TOPIC 1. MANAGEMENT THEORY

The systems school sees organisations as systems made up of several .... (individual parts) which are all connected to each other.

In a system, ... and .... flow through and are .... into goods and services. The success of the system is monitored through the process of .... Businesses are .... systems because they interact with their environment. They affect and are affected by happenings in the outside world (............... factors).

The idea that departments and units in a business are more productive when they work together than when they operate separately is termed .... This approach calls for a lot of .... between departments.

1.8.1 Case study - Tavistock Institute

Any change in a system will affect the other systems with which the system interacts. In the 1940s researchers from the Tavistock institute of human relations studied coal extraction in British pits to see what effect introducing new technology had on the social and work organisation at the coalface.

Before the change the men worked in close-knit teams. Each team did all the tasks needed. Team members relied upon each other but each team was completely independent of other teams.

After the change the teams were broken up and each shift of workers specialised on a single task.

The researchers concluded that changes to the technological system had not taken account of the changes they would cause to the social system. They suggested a compromise. All the basic operations would be carried out on any one shift, workers themselves would decide who would do what and payment would include a group bonus. After the compromise was adopted productivity went up and accidents and absenteeism went down.

Tavistock institute research results   Go online

Which of the following statements applied to the miners after the change?

Q49: They worked much harder.

a) True
b) False

....

Q50: They began to argue with each other.

a) True
b) False

....

Q51: They were absent more often.

a) True
b) False

Q52: They socialised much more with each other.

a) True
b) False

Q53: Productivity went up.

a) True
b) False

Q54: They blamed other shifts for things that went wrong.

a) True
b) False

1.9 Contingency theory

Where the classical school looked at structure and the human relations focused on people, the **contingency theory** suggests that there is no one single approach to getting the best out of people. A manager's best choice of behaviour depends on the particular contingency, or situation, that she/he faces. Every contingency has different variables. In each situation there will be a different mix of external factors, technological factors and human factors.

Thus, the most effective method of management varies according to circumstances.

Different ideas

Pair up with another student.

Imagine that one of you is a manager of 100 workers on a mass production assembly line and the other the owner of a small boutique employing one other person.

Think about the approach to management that you would adopt. How far would you follow the ideas of the classical, human relations or systems schools?

Summarise your thoughts on paper. Swap your answer with your partner and read each other's ideas. Do they differ? Why?

TOPIC 1. MANAGEMENT THEORY

Different management approaches Go online

In the 1960s two writers called Burns and Stalker researched different management approaches that were used in situations where the work demands were routine and unchanging, as opposed to those where the work was non-routine and constantly changing. Their discoveries were similar to what you probably found in your discussion.

Advantages and disadvantages of different management approaches

Advantages:

- no single method is best;
- lots of variables need to be taken into account, e.g. size, type, technology, staff, finance, skill of staff, management experience, market environment and information;
- takes into account external business environment;
- helps organisation change to adapt to different PESTEC environments.

Disadvantages:

- no single approach works so managers must be very flexible;
- not all managers are able to adapt their approaches.

Q55: Match the following ways in which managers might relate to their subordinates with the type of work in the table below:

- Complete obedience and loyalty of subordinates to management are stressed;
- Decisions are made by managers and communicated down the hierarchy;
- The manager encourages lateral communication;
- The manager encourages subordinates to use their initiative;
- The manager mainly offers advice and information;
- The manager supervises employees closely to ensure they follow procedures.

Routine and unchanging	Non routine, constantly changing

1.10 Summary

Managers are constantly taking decisions to ensure that they and their subordinates contribute effectively to the achievement of organisational objectives. We have analysed the manager's role according to the views of some of the best-known writers about management. These views are not mutually exclusive; they all highlight aspects of the manager's role.

Writers such as Fayol and Drucker proposed a list of functions that managers typically carry out. Drucker also devised the theory of Management by Objectives. Mintzberg subdivided the manager's role into interpersonal, informational and decisional areas.

By now you should be able to explain different theories about the role of management and apply them to specific situations. You should also be able to explain how Management by objectives might be used in an organisation and the benefits and drawbacks of this technique.

Management thought has played a tremendous role in shaping the modern workforce, which is a great testament to the work carried out between 1900 and the 1940s.

The classical theorists included Frederick Taylor, Max Weber, Henri Fayol and the Gilbraiths. They all based their theories on scientific management. Motion studies allowed the work of employees to be scrutinised. They believed in efficiency and the 'one best way'. This school of thought is useful in low paid, monotonous jobs, or ones were process is important, like a surgeon's operating room.

Some years later the human relations school was born. This approach says that workers needs are important and that organisations who fail to motivate workers will not be as successful. It also looks at the importance of groups and non-financial and financial motivators.

During the late 1940s a new school of thought emerged. The neo-human relations school acknowledged the work of the human relations theorists but believed that it did not go far enough, and that organisation structure was needed in addition to motivating the employee.

More recently, systems theory has emerged, suggesting that all previous theories were too narrow and that the whole organisation, its processes and people need to be looked at together before improvements can be seen.

It suggests that the system - input, process, output - should look at skilled labour, quality raw materials and top of the range machinery, as well as a systematic approach to design and production methods.

Finally, the contingency theory argues that every organisation is different, and that every problem requires a unique solution. It suggests there is no 'one best way'.

Summary

You should now be able to:

- explain what management is;
- explain what different theorists believe the role of the manager to be.

1.11 End of topic test

End of Topic 1 test Go online

Q56: The system of paying workers per item made is known as:

a) flat rate.
b) piece rate.
c) time rate.
d) basic rate.

....

Q57: One of the main ideas put forward by contingency theory is that:

a) motivation is always increased by democratic management.
b) managers need to vary their approach according to the situation.
c) motivation is never increased by autocratic management.
d) dividing workers into teams always increases motivation.

....

Q58: An advantage of the classical approach to management is that it:

a) stresses the importance of group interaction.
b) takes into account needs of both managers and workers.
c) sets out exactly how work should be done.
d) is flexible in adapting to changing conditions.

....

Q59: The four parts of a system in order are:

a) inputs, processes, feedback, output.
b) inputs, processes, output, feedback.
c) inputs, feedback, processes, output.
d) inputs, output, processes, feedback.

....

Q60: One possible drawback of the classical approach is that it:

a) decreases productivity.
b) ignores the needs of the organisation as a whole.
c) makes an organisation hard to control because of its stress on teamwork.
d) tends to cause a "carrot and stick" approach to motivation.

....

Q61: Which theory is associated with the idea that you cannot change one part of an organisation without it affecting other parts?

a) Systems theory
b) Contingency theory
c) Human relations theory
d) Classical theory

....

Q62: Which theory or school is scientific management part of?

a) Systems theory
b) Contingency theory
c) The human relations school
d) The classical school

....

Q63: Which theory or school is the Hawthorne effect associated with?

a) Systems theory
b) Contingency theory
c) The human relations school
d) The classical school

....

Q64: Which of the following is a feature of a bureaucracy?

a) Structure based on hierarchy
b) Structure based on team working
c) Decentralised decision making
d) More lateral than vertical communication

....

Q65: According to Theory X, workers:

a) are keen to be given responsibility.
b) can motivate themselves.
c) naturally avoid having to work.
d) always prefer financial to non-financial methods of motivation.

....

Q66: One of Fayol's principles of management is:

a) perfection of effort.
b) separation of management.
c) unity of command.
d) managers think; workers obey.

....

TOPIC 1. MANAGEMENT THEORY   135

Q67: The researchers from the Tavistock Institute concluded that the reason miners became less effective after the introduction of technology was that changes had been made to the:

a) social subsystem without anticipating the knock-on effects on the technological subsystem.
b) technological subsystem without anticipating the knock-on effects on the social subsystem.
c) economic subsystem without anticipating the knock-on effects on the social subsystem.
d) technological subsystem without anticipating the knock-on effects on the economic subsystem.

....

Q68: Two examples of Maslow's higher level needs are:

a) physiological and self-actualisation needs.
b) safety and self-esteem needs.
c) safety and social needs.
d) self-esteem and self-actualisation needs.

....

Q69: Systems theory views organisations as open systems. An open system:

a) is self-contained.
b) is always willing to change.
c) allows everyone in it to participate equally.
d) interacts with its external environment.

Three hours in the life of Sam Bacon, Production Manager

Read the following extract from Sam's diary and answer the question at the end.

> 7.30 am Arrive in the office early to put the finishing touches to my report on the new automated production system and exactly why we need to install it. Email report to my PA, Mavis, who has an eagle eye for spotting errors.
>
> 8.10 am Joe Wood, one of the three supervisors, appears in my office in an agitated state. One of his machines is down and a big order has to be ready for dispatch by noon today. Maintenance told him last night they have a backlog from the Bank Holiday weekend and won't be able to fix the machine till next Monday.
>
> 8.15 am Phone Arnold, Maintenance Supervisor, and manage to persuade him to prioritise us; say I'll buy him a pint sometime. Pass the good news on to Joe who reminds me that I said I'd have a word with Lucy about her habit of taking an excessively long lunch hour on Fridays. Tell him to send her to me and give Joe a copy of the Health and Safety Inspectors' Report - apparently they spotted trailing flexes and cans of cola perched on the edge of one of the machines on their recent visit. Tell Joe to get it sorted.
>
> 8.20 am Mavis asks me if I'm available to open the local Gala on Saturday. The MD was going to do it but her daughter's getting married in Zambia this weekend. Agree to stand in for her.

© HERIOT-WATT UNIVERSITY

8.25 am Lucy puts her head round the door and says Joe said I want to see her. When I bring up her over-long lunch hours, she vigorously denies Joe's allegations. Arrange to meet both of them at noon to try to sort things out.

8.40 am Walk down to the production floor to check that all the lines are flowing and someone from Maintenance has arrived to fix the broken machine.

9.00 am Mavis hands me the printed report for my signature. She reminds me I have a meeting with Marketing at 10 am to discuss production schedules to support their new sales campaign.

9.05 am Approve for publication the advertisement Mavis has keyed in for two new assembly line workers for Dan's team. Phone HR to arrange date for interviews. E-mail Rosie telling her she is to switch from Joe's team to Dan's team temporarily.

9.15 am A-Z calls to discuss the training programme they are running for us tomorrow. They have just remembered to tell us we need to split staff into three training groups on the basis of experience.

9.20 am With Mavis's help, work out who's going to be in which group.

9.45 am Have a look at the breakdown of last week's production figures. Note that, for the third week running, Dan's team is the worst. Get Lucy to set up appointment with Dan to discuss ways to get the figures up.

10.00 am Meeting with Marketing. They reckon their campaign will increase demand by 50%. I tell them the most we could achieve if we increased overtime would be 40% and Finance would not be pleased. Marketing says if we agree to a 50% increase they will stop pressuring senior management to introduce a new line for children. I say I'll think about it; a new line at this stage would cause us a lot of hassle.

10.30 am Coffee!

For each of the following write down as many examples as you can.

Q70: What different management functions did Sam use? *(5 marks)*

....

Q71: What different management roles did Sam play? *(3 marks)*

....

Q72: What managerial skills does Sam need to use? *(3 marks)*

....

Q73: What are the demands, choices and constraints affecting Sam? *(3 marks)*

Q74: Describe the classical school of management and the contingency school of management and assess their relevance to modern business practice. *(10 marks)*

Unit 2 Topic 2

Leadership

Contents

2.1 Management v leadership 138
2.2 Styles theory 139
2.3 Trait theory 141
    2.3.1 Criticisms of trait theory 142
2.4 Contingency theory 142
    2.4.1 Task or relationship orientation (Fiedler) 144
    2.4.2 Situational leadership (Hersey and Blanchard) 145
    2.4.3 Action centred leadership (Adair) 146
    2.4.4 Path goal theory (House) 148
2.5 Summary 149
2.6 End of topic test 150

Learning objective

By the end of this topic you should be able to:

- explain differences between management and leadership;
- explain and evaluate the style theory of leadership;
- explain and evaluate the trait theory of leadership;
- explain and evaluate the contingency theory of leadership.

2.1 Management v leadership

Leadership differs from management in significant respects. A leader has the ability to persuade others to follow them whereas a manager is given authority to make other people follow them. A leader is an innovator, someone who is not afraid to try new ideas and challenges others to join them. They have a vision and they inspire others to join them to make that vision a reality. They inspire trust from those who follow them.

A manager follows procedures and adheres to policy whereas a leader takes calculates risks to enable the organisation to improve. A manager relies on others to carry out tasks, by telling them what and how to do. There are established guidelines and everyone works within a structure.

Many of the descriptions of management and leadership will overlap, as both want the organisation to be successful. Where managers may delegate, leaders will devolve responsibility. The difference may be subtle, but an employee working under a leader should feel a greater sense of responsibility and trust.

Managers are given positional power (authority) to require people to follow their lead, but an effective leader motivates people to want to change their own behaviour.

Differences between managers and leaders Go online

Choose which of the following words are most associated with managers or leaders.

Q1: Sets the pace

a) Manager
b) Leader

....

Q2: Inspires

a) Manager
b) Leader

....

Q3: Controls

a) Manager
b) Leader

....

Q4: Attracts loyal followers

a) Manager
b) Leader

....

TOPIC 2. LEADERSHIP

Q5: Organises

a) Manager
b) Leader

Q6: Follows procedure

a) Manager
b) Leader

Q7: Creates

a) Manager
b) Leader

Q8: Coordinates

a) Manager
b) Leader

Q9: Has a vision

a) Manager
b) Leader

Q10: Initiates change

a) Manager
b) Leader

2.2 Styles theory

In the last topic you learned that different leaders have different styles. You studied McGregor's Theory X and Theory Y and the difference between autocratic and democratic leadership styles. Use the next two activities as revision to check your understanding of leadership styles and the advantages or disadvantages associated with them.

Leadership styles (1)

Go online

Q11: Match the following six adjectives describing styles of leadership with each of the phrases that a manager might say to their subordinates in the table below:

- Autocratic;
- Consultative;
- Democratic;
- Laissez-faire;
- Participative;
- Persuasive.

Management phrase	Style of leadership
"I know best. I'll make you do as I decide."	
"I know best. I'll persuade you that what I decide is right."	
"I'll ask you what you think before I decide."	
"I'll take your views into account and let you help me decide."	
"I'll let you decide within certain limits."	
"You know best - you can decide."	

Leadership styles (2)

Go online

Q12: Put the following adjectives in order from *more manager-centred* to *more subordinate-centred*:

- Autocratic;
- Consultative;
- Democratic;
- Laissez-faire;
- Participative;
- Persuasive.

Advantages and disadvantages of autocratic and democratic styles

Go online

Q13: Some advantages and disadvantages of different leadership styles are listed. Place each statement into the appropriate place in the table.

- In an urgent situation there may not be time to allow employees to discuss options.
- More responsibility motivates employees.

TOPIC 2. LEADERSHIP

- Supervision can be expensive and time-consuming.
- Employees know exactly what they are required to do.
- Managers will have a better view than employees of the needs of the organisation as a whole.
- Better decisions can be made with input from those actually carrying out the work.
- The initiative and knowledge of employees is not fully used.
- Decisions are made by managers without discussion with employees so time is saved

	Autocratic	Democratic
Advantages		
Disadvantages		

2.3 Trait theory

Many theories exist that try to explain leadership; one is the trait theory. Trait, meaning quality or characteristic, suggests that only a few have what it takes to be a successful leader.

Trait theory is based on the idea that leaders are special. The ability to lead is something you are born with. It depends on traits such as intelligence and personality and cannot be learned. According to this theory leadership has nothing to do with the job and everything to do with the person.

Some believe that these qualities can also be physical in appearance, e.g. tall people make better leaders or people who look after their bodies are more likely to be successful.

Leadership traits

Think of two good leaders you know.

Write down the characteristics they have in common that make them effective.

Join up with two other students and compare your lists.

Did you all identify the same characteristics?

Discuss the reasons for any differences.

How certain can you be that your group has definitely identified the traits that make a good leader?

Assessment of trait theory

Go online

Q14: Rearrange the following sentence endings in relation to trait theory to match the first half of the sentence in the table below:

- but there is no general agreement about which are most important.
- it may still be possible to train them to improve their effectiveness.
- such as self-confidence, initiative, intelligence and self-belief.
- therefore it is impossible to identify a common pattern of traits.
- therefore objective assessment of the traits needed is impossible.

First half	Second half
A long list of traits that leaders are born with has been developed	
Different people have different ideas about what makes a good leader	
Even if leaders are born with certain traits	
Most leaders do seem to share certain general characteristics	
Part of the success of being a good leader seems to come from being unique	

2.3.1 Criticisms of trait theory

Many writers believe trait theory to be flawed. There are too many exceptions in real life to accept that this theory is correct. The theory is subjective as it focuses on what followers believe the traits are rather than the managers. Some will argue that many of the characteristics of a leader already mentioned can be learned, and improved, and that a person does not need to be born with these characteristics to become a successful leader.

The list of characteristics is so long and diverse that it is not possible for one person to display them all. Different roles may require different traits. It can also be argued that the need for a specific is subjective, as is the objective itself.

Employers who define trait characteristics by physical appearance are contravening the Equality Act 2010, that states all employees must be treated equally.

2.4 Contingency theory

The idea that the most effective management or leadership style depends on circumstances is known as contingency theory.

Contingency theorists argue that leaders must adapt their style if they are to be successful. They

TOPIC 2. LEADERSHIP

believe that leaders should show authority at times whilst allowing for democracy when appropriate. They suggest that leaders who have many characteristics can used these characteristics to their advantage depending on the situation.

Different leadership styles Go online

For each of the following situations that a manager might face, identify the most appropriate leadership style.

Q15: The building is on fire.

a) Autocratic
b) Democratic

....

Q16: Creative ideas are needed to solve a problem.

a) Autocratic
b) Democratic

....

Q17: The subordinates are young and inexperienced.

a) Autocratic
b) Democratic

....

Q18: The manager is new and wants to make use of the expertise of her subordinates.

a) Autocratic
b) Democratic

....

Q19: The manager has to do something which is bound to be unpopular with employees.

a) Autocratic
b) Democratic

....

Q20: The organisation uses a matrix structure, creating project teams as necessary.

a) Autocratic
b) Democratic

Contingency theory

Q21: Put the following words into the appropriate places in the paragraph below:

- autocratic;
- external;
- human;
- situation;
- technological;
- unchanging;
- variables.

A 'contingency' is a particular .... faced by a manager. Each contingency has different .... These include different ...., ... and .... factors. For example, when a job is routine and ...., the management style is likely to be more .... than in a job which presents workers with constantly changing demands.

Many different writers have devised theories to explain the relationship between leadership style and different situations or people. We will look at four of these below.

2.4.1 Task or relationship orientation (Fiedler)

Writing in the 1970s Fred Fiedler said that managers are either task-oriented (concentrating on the job) or relationship-oriented (concentrating mainly on the people involved).

Fiedler argued that, since it was impossible for a manager to change their style, an organisation needs to choose the right manager for each situation to ensure a leadership match.

Whereas his people-oriented approached is more consistent with McGregor's Theory Y - it states that there must be high trust between the leader and team members.

Task or relationship orientation

Determine which of the statements in the following questions might be made by a task-oriented manager or a relationship-oriented manager.

Q22: "Never mind your domestic issues, this order has to go out by midnight!"

a) Relationship-oriented manager
b) Task-oriented manager

....

Q23: "Never mind the order, go home and sort things out."

a) Relationship-oriented manager
b) Task-oriented manager

2.4.2 Situational leadership (Hersey and Blanchard)

Writing in the 1980s, Paul Hersey and Ken Blanchard suggested four leadership styles based on the level of maturity of the followers. The more mature workers are the less they require support or instructions from management. From least to most mature the styles are:

- **telling** - the lowest in terms of maturity. The leader defines the role of the group and it is mainly one-way communication, i.e. top down. Tasks are simple in nature and the leader takes an autocratic approach;
- **selling** - the leader is still setting the direction of travel here, but the communication is more two-way. A useful approach for workers who are enthusiastic about their work but lack the skills or abilities to work independently;
- **participating** - at this level, decision making is shared between the leader and employee. There is more focus placed on the relationship than the task and workers are encouraged to think for themselves. Leaders need to ensure this happens are the employee may be reluctant;
- **delegating** - the highest in terms of maturity. The leader has the confidence to fully delegate responsibility onto the employee and simply has an overview of the work being carried out.

Situational leadership   Go online

Which of the situational leadership styles would be appropriate in each of the following situations?

Q24: Will be used when subordinates are very mature.

a) Delegating
b) Participating
c) Selling
d) Telling

....

Q25: Will be used when subordinates are maturing.

a) Delegating
b) Participating
c) Selling
d) Telling

....

Q26: Will be used when subordinates are immature or new.

a) Delegating
b) Participating
c) Selling
d) Telling

....

Q27: Will be used when subordinates are at their highest level of maturity.

a) Delegating
b) Participating
c) Selling
d) Telling

Which of the situational leadership styles would be appropriate in each of the following features?

Q28: High relationship, low task-oriented.

a) Delegating
b) Participating
c) Selling
d) Telling

....

Q29: Task-oriented and autocratic.

a) Delegating
b) Participating
c) Selling
d) Telling

....

Q30: High task-oriented and high relationship-oriented.

a) Delegating
b) Participating
c) Selling
d) Telling

....

Q31: Low task-oriented and low relationship-oriented.

a) Delegating
b) Participating
c) Selling
d) Telling

2.4.3 Action centred leadership (Adair)

John Adair said that in any situation a leader has responsibilities for three overlapping elements:

- the task;
- the team;

TOPIC 2. LEADERSHIP

- the individual.

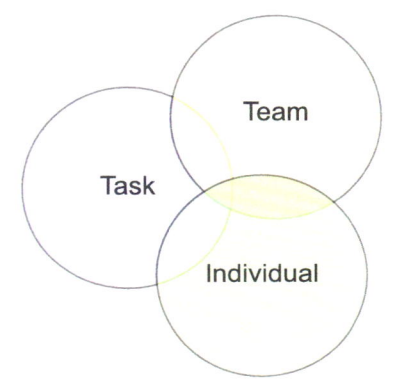

John Adair's action centred leadership model

The leader has to devise courses of action that will ensure that the task is done and at the same time the needs of both teams and individuals are met. The importance of the different elements will vary from one situation to another.

Action centred leadership   Go online

Determine which of the following responsibilities that leaders might have are task, team or individual elements.

Q32: Understanding employees' personalities, needs and fears.

a) Task
b) Team
c) Individual

....

Q33: Ensuring effective group communication.

a) Task
b) Team
c) Individual

....

Q34: Establishing objectives.

a) Task
b) Team
c) Individual

....

Q35: Resolving group conflict.

a) Task
b) Team
c) Individual

Q36: Training and developing each subordinate.

a) Task
b) Team
c) Individual

Q37: Monitoring performance.

a) Task
b) Team
c) Individual

2.4.4 Path goal theory (House)

Path goal theory suggests that the best leader shows followers how their performance will result in them being rewarded, i.e. the leader shows the path to the goal.

Robert House described four styles of leadership:

- *Supportive leadership*

    A leader should consider the needs of the employee, both in terms of their personal welfare and their friendly working environment. (Interesting that this theory was written prior to the establishment of the Health and Safety at Work Act that incorporated this in legislation). This style includes improving the employee's self-esteem and making their job more interesting. It works best when the work being undertaken is stressful, boring or dangerous.

- *Directive leadership*

    This leadership style involves telling employees what needs to be done at every step. Specific tasks should be described and time frames provided. Rewards may be introduced to support this process. It works best when the task is unstructured and complex and the employee lacks experienced.

- *Situational leadership*

    This involves consulting with employees and taking their ideas into account when making decisions. Leaders and employees can then work together to define the environment. This approach is best when the employees are experts.

- *Achievement-oriented leadership*

    This leadership style involves setting challenging goals, both in work and in self-improvement. High standards are demonstrated and expected by the leader. The leader shows faith in the capabilities of the employee to succeed. This approach is best when the task is complex.

Path goal theory

Q38: Match the following four leadership styles with each description in the table below:

- Achievement-oriented;
- Directive;
- Situational;
- Supportive.

Description	Leadership style
Developing friendly relationships with followers	
Fitting in with subordinates' characteristics or with environmental factors	
Setting challenging goals and helping followers to achieve them	
Telling people what to do	

It does not matter which approach the manager adopts as long as he or she can convince subordinates that they will get the reward.

2.5 Summary

Summary

You should now be able to:

- explain differences between management and leadership;
- explain and evaluate the style theory of leadership;
- explain and evaluate the trait theory of leadership;
- explain and evaluate the contingency theory of leadership.

2.6 End of topic test

End of Topic 2 test　　　　　　　　　　　　　　　　　　　　Go online

Q39: A .... follows procedures.

a) manager
b) leader

Q40: A .... relies on discipline.

a) manager
b) leader

Q41: A .... inspires trust.

a) manager
b) leader

Q42: A .... innovates.

a) manager
b) leader

Q43: A .... has vision.

a) manager
b) leader

Q44: A .... administrates.

a) manager
b) leader

TOPIC 2. LEADERSHIP

Q45: Trait theorists believe that leadership qualities are things you are born with.

a) True
b) False

....

Q46: Trait theory is often criticised because:

a) everyone has the same traits.
b) real life is not taken into account.
c) measuring traits objectively is impossible.
d) trait theory does not focus on the perception of others.

....

Q47: A leader who makes a decision but takes the time to explain is described as:

a) autocratic.
b) democratic.
c) consultative.
d) persuasive.

....

Q48: Fiedler believed that managers were task or people orientated and could change to suit the situation.

a) True
b) False

....

Q49: A selling style will be used when subordinates are immature or new.

a) True
b) False

....

Q50: A participating style is high relationship, low task.

a) True
b) False

....

Q51: A leadership style that involves telling employees what needs to be done at every step can be described as:

a) directive.
b) supportive.
c) achievement-oriented.
d) situational.

Read the following passage and answer the questions.

It was going to be a busy morning, Trudi thought as she pushed through the swing doors into the office block. Jim was chatting to Ron beside the coffee machine. "Jim! Hurry up; I need the stats about the new product launch." Jim started to say something but Trudi swept on to her office. Thank goodness her PA was already there. "Good morning Sean. Did you book my flights for Paris?" As Sean nodded Trudi glanced over at the diary in front of him. "I see I've got a space now," she said. "Can you ring Helen and ask her to bring the sales figures for last month right away?" Sean nodded again as he lifted the phone.

Trudi just had time to make herself a cup of coffee before Helen arrived. Right away Trudi quizzed her about the sales figures from last month; did Helen realise that a 5% increase really wasn't good enough given that a major competitor had just closed last month? "I want to see at least a 10% increase next month," Trudi announced firmly. Helen blinked but didn't say anything. After she left, Trudi set off for her 10am appointment upstairs with the Managing Director. As she passed Sean's desk she thought he was looking a bit depressed but she didn't have the time to stop and investigate. "I'm off upstairs," she called to him as she passed. "Don't leave that phone!"

It was going to be a busy morning, Greg thought. He paused to ask his PA if there were any messages for him. Anil handed them over with a sad smile. "What's wrong Anil? You don't seem your usual happy self." Anil explained that his wife was ill and he was worried about leaving her at home all day with two toddlers. "Don't be silly, Anil," Greg exclaimed. "Go home and look after your family. We can manage here without you for a day or two." Anil brightened up immediately and left promising to come back as soon as he could.

At 9 o'clock Joseph brought the new sales figures. "Hello Joseph," Greg said. "How are you feeling? That was a nasty bout of tonsillitis you had." Greg listened while Joseph told him about how the antibiotics prescribed by his doctor had done the trick. "Now, what about those sales figures?" Joseph explained that they had gone up by 5%, but added that he and the team realised that the increase would be less than Greg would want. So they had met after work and come up with a great new advertising scheme. "That sounds brilliant," said Greg. "I really appreciate all the effort you and the team have put into this." "No problem Mr Coull," replied Joseph. "We're all happy to go an extra mile for a manager who treats us so well."

Q52: What are the differences between Trudi and Greg's management styles? *(2 marks)*

....

Q53: In what situations would Trudi's management style be appropriate? *(2 marks)*

....

Q54: In what situations would Greg's management style be appropriate? *(2 marks)*

....

Q55: Using examples from the passage, suggest possible drawbacks of Trudi's management style. *(2 marks)*

....

Q56: Using examples from the passage suggest possible drawbacks of Greg's management style. *(2 marks)*

Q57: Using at least two theories of leadership, examine the extent to which each is relevant to managers in the UK today. *(10 marks)*

Unit 2 Topic 3

Teams

Contents

- 3.1 Importance of teams in organisations 156
- 3.2 Team roles 158
- 3.3 Team influence on organisational effectiveness 160
- 3.4 Stages of group development 161
- 3.5 Summary 163
- 3.6 End of topic test 164

Learning objective

After studying this topic, you should be able to:

- explain the role of teams in organisations;
- explain the characteristics of effective teams;
- explain the stages of group development;
- evaluate the impact of teams on organisational effectiveness.

3.1 Importance of teams in organisations

Businesses today could not function without successful teams. Teams are needed to allow leaders to develop, to allow shared goals to be shaped and successes to be sought. Different ideas can be shared and solutions found more easily when teams are formed.

Formal teams can be both permanent and temporary. In a traditional structure, teams will exist at all stages in the hierarchy. Ad hoc (autonomous) teams can be formed as the need arises, e.g. to complete a one-off project or to complete a piece of research and development. Matrix structures, consisting of employees from across the business, will form from time to time when a complex solution to a problem is sought.

Informal teams also add value to an organisation. Many motivation writers talk about the importance of interpersonal relationships. Informal teams allow for these relationships to flourish.

Permanent, temporary or informal teams   Go online

Decide whether the following are examples of permanent, temporary or informal teams.

Q1: A focus group looking at a new build development.

a) Permanent
b) Temporary
c) Informal

....

Q2: Marketing subordinates meeting a new head of department.

a) Permanent
b) Temporary
c) Informal

....

Q3: IT department introducing new infrastructure to support the network.

a) Permanent
b) Temporary
c) Informal

....

Q4: Social fund organising a celebration event after the business is awarded a new contract.

a) Permanent
b) Temporary
c) Informal

Advantages and disadvantages of teams

Go online

Although teamwork is found in most modern businesses, there can also be drawbacks. Decide which are advantages and disadvantages of teams from the following list.

Q5: Social needs are met by being part of a team.

a) Advantage
b) Disadvantage

....

Q6: Decision-making can be slow.

a) Advantage
b) Disadvantage

....

Q7: Tasks may be done more quickly when people work together.

a) Advantage
b) Disadvantage

....

Q8: A low-performing team member can drag the whole team down.

a) Advantage
b) Disadvantage

....

Q9: Being given responsibility for making decisions motivates team members.

a) Advantage
b) Disadvantage

....

Q10: Conflict could arise within the team.

a) Advantage
b) Disadvantage

....

Q11: Each member can learn from others in the team.

a) Advantage
b) Disadvantage

....

Q12: Some people prefer working on their own.

a) Advantage
b) Disadvantage

....

Q13: Modern workers are much more highly educated than previous generations and expect to be allowed to make more decisions.

a) Advantage
b) Disadvantage

....

Q14: Team members may be able to swap jobs, providing more variety.

a) Advantage
b) Disadvantage

....

Q15: Close-knit teams might develop their own norms (beliefs and values) that conflict with those of the organisation.

a) Advantage
b) Disadvantage

What makes an effective team?

Write down five features you think you would see in a team that was operating effectively. Swap your paper with another student. Add any different ideas you had to the end of their list.

Continue swapping papers until everyone has had a chance to add to all the lists.

3.2 Team roles

We discovered in the last activity that having a variety of team members performing different roles helps a team to be effective. Meredith Belbin specified nine (initially eight) different roles that are necessary for a team to be effective.

Belbin stated that the optimum team should have a mix of talents and should be between six and eight people.

Belbin's team roles:

- ***Coordinator*** - a confident, decisive person who listens to others. This person is a natural leader who delegates appropriately;
- ***Plant*** - an ideas person; a problem solver. This person is needed but may not be able to

communicate their ideas well;

- **Implementer** - an enthusiastic team player who is focused on results. This person is disciplined and turns ideas into a reality;
- **Teamworker** - a supporting player, with strong interpersonal skills. This person avoids confrontation and supports others;
- **Completer-finisher** - someone to see the task through to the end, to make sure everyone completes their job. This person solves problems and encourages others;
- **Resource investigator** - the research, the person who finds the necessary facts;
- **Shaper** - a determined person who enjoys a challenge. This person is not afraid of upsetting others if it means getting their way;
- **Specialist** - a highly competent individual who will bring expert knowledge to a task;
- **Monitor-evaluator** - this person is logical and has clear objectives. They inspire others and bring out the teams strengths.

Team roles   Go online

Q16: Identify one of Belbin's team roles for each of the following descriptions.

Team role	Description
	Checks details, makes sure the team meets deadlines
	Checks the value and feasibility of the team's ideas and proposals
	Comes up with new ideas about how to achieve team goals
	Draws up schedules and plans to turn ideas into actual tasks
	Ensures harmony in the team by getting along with and supporting everybody
	Expert in their field, others can go to them for advice on particular issues
	Finds new contacts and opportunities for the team
	Natural leader who delegates appropriately
	Sparks life into the team, pushes other members into action

The optimum make up of a team are influenced by factors such as:

- nature of the task;
- clarity of the task;
- team members.

3.3 Team influence on organisational effectiveness

Teams can influence organisational effectiveness both positively and negatively. Effective teams can increase motivation and efficiency. This means the business will increase customer satisfaction and reduce costs, leading to profit increases and a positive ethos amongst employees. Staff can learn from each other to improve skills.

The impact of this can be seen in the increased work rate and motivation of staff. Higher quality goods and services are produced as a result. Tasks can be completed to a higher standard when a mix of staff are involved as everyone brings different skills and talents to the team.

However, conflict may arise if team members do not feel that the workload is being shared fairly. It is possible that some team members may rely too heavily on others. Teams can also become stale if the membership is not refreshed regularly. A team without an effective leader may lose direction and focus and not be able to thrive.

Influence of teams   Go online

Q17: Place each of the following ways in which teams might influence organisational effectiveness into the appropriate column in the table below:

- By offering mutual support teams improve motivation and hence performance;
- Competition between teams could be divisive and lead to inter-group conflict, harming the achievement of organisational objectives;
- Group decision-making is time consuming; time is money;
- 'Groupthink' may develop where everyone in a team ends up thinking in the same way, so they are not open to new ideas that could generate more profit;
- Healthy competition between teams can improve performance;
- If a team member is absent the work still gets done if work is allocated to teams rather than individuals;
- 'Parochial self-interest' - teams may become unable to see the viewpoint of other teams or management so that they are pursuing their own team goals rather than organisational ones;
- 'Risky shift' may occur, where people in teams may take ill-advised risks that they would not take if they were acting on their own;
- Teams combine the expertise of many people, allowing members to learn from each other and become more multi-skilled;
- Teams increase the loyalty of employees as they develop relationships within the group; not wishing to let their fellow team members down will motivate them to work hard;
- Teams may operate as cliques against management and prevent the achievement of organisational goals;
- Team members contribute many more ideas, leading to more efficient production and better quality products.

Positive influences	Negative influences

3.4 Stages of group development

Effective teams must go through four stages, according to Bruce Tuckman, an American university psychology professor.

Tuckman published his stages of group development in 1965:

- **Forming** - the initial stage were a new group is first formed. A leader has not yet emerged and the team have little focus or purpose;
- **Storming** - the second stage where team members compete for position. Group purpose increases as ideas emerge;
- **Norming** - in the third stage roles are agreed and the team have a shared vision. The leader is established and the group begin to carry out their task;
- **Performing** - in the final stage the individual members of the team feel knowledgeable and confident enough to work independently of leader support. Tasks are completed and the team are motivated to achieve.

The following table shows what managers could do to support teams at different stages.

Stage	Manager role
Forming	organise social events, clarify roles, set goals
Storming	mentor members, help find compromise, promote team goals, help resolve conflict
Norming	monitor communication, reaffirm goals and vision, confirm roles and boundaries
Performing	light touch management, give praise, provide realism

What managers could do to support teams at different stages of group development

Tuckman later added a fifth and final stage, adjourning, to take account of the fact that many teams will have a finite life span. If the team have performed to a high standard and achieved their goals then the team can dissolve knowing they have increased their skills set and can learn from their experience in the future.

Place in group development

Go online

Q18: Think of a team or group you are in and, with that in mind, answer the 12 questions in the table below.

For every statement give yourself:

- 2 marks if it is generally true of your group;
- 1 mark if it is occasionally true of your group;
- 0 marks if it is never true of your group.

	Statement	Score
Q1	Team members are shy about asking others for help.	
Q2	We are very critical of each other and often argue.	
Q3	We share our problems with each other.	
Q4	We all share responsibility for the team's success or failure.	
Q5	We allocate specific roles to each member.	
Q6	Some of us think the goals we have set are totally unrealistic.	
Q7	We have developed procedures for sorting out our disagreements.	
Q8	We achieve an amazing amount of work.	
Q9	We don't trust each other fully yet.	
Q10	We tend to reject each other's ideas without really listening to them.	
Q11	We criticise each other constructively.	
Q12	We thoroughly enjoy working productively together.	
Q13	We are trying to define our goals and what we need to do.	
Q14	Our leader has to referee a lot of arguments.	
Q15	We all share the same understanding of our team's goals.	
Q16	Each team member feels really close to all the others, accepting their strengths and weaknesses.	

Enter your marks on the grid below to work out your total score.

Forming	Score	Storming	Score	Norming	Score	Performing	Score
Q1		Q2		Q3		Q4	
Q5		Q6		Q7		Q8	
Q9		Q10		Q11		Q12	
Q13		Q14		Q15		Q16	
Total		**Total**		**Total**		**Total**	

3.5 Summary

Summary

You should now be able to:

- explain the role of teams in organisations;
- explain the characteristics of effective teams;
- explain the stages of group development;
- evaluate the impact of teams on organisational effectiveness.

3.6 End of topic test

End of Topic 3 test — Go online

Q19: Ad hoc teams are well-planned and form every year.

a) True
b) False

Q20: Matrix structures involve employees from across the business, regardless of their role.

a) True
b) False

Q21: Belbin organises six different team roles.

a) True
b) False

Q22: Good communication is important because:

a) it means managers can be more autocratic.
b) it allows teams to share goals.
c) it allows time rate payments to work.

Q23: Which answer is the odd one out?

a) Forming
b) Conforming
c) Norming
d) Performing

Q24: Examine the characteristics that teams should have if they are to operate effectively. *(10 marks)*

Read the case study below and answer the questions which follow.

Many firms nowadays organise their workforce in autonomous, or self-directed, teams. Teams make workers happy by helping them to feel that they are shaping their own jobs. Managers no longer have to pass orders downwards which saves time. The firm can draw on the skills and imagination of everyone rather than rely on managers to spot mistakes and suggest improvements.

TOPIC 3. TEAMS 165

Teams are given responsibility for organising the flow of work - many American manufacturing firms are trying out cell manufacturing, where teams of workers make entire products. Teams can also devise ways to improve quality and efficiency. Some teams are given responsibility for hiring and firing workers. Teams often elect their own leaders. Teams bring together a variety of different workers. One computer manufacturer includes lawyers and marketing managers along with engineers and shop floor workers in its teams.

Not all teams are successful though. One Swedish car manufacturer introduced team working to some of their factories in the 1990s to add interest to the work - the employees enjoyed working in teams but the costs were so high that eventually the manufacturer disbanded the teams and rearranged workers on a traditional assembly line.

Good management is essential to the effective introduction of teams in an organisation. Managers need to give teams clear objectives; otherwise they will be unclear about the tasks they should be undertaking. Managers need to adjust the appraisal and rewards systems in the organisation to ensure that they are based on group rather than individual performance. Employees are unlikely to support other team members if by doing so they risk sacrificing their own rewards, such as piece rate or commission.

Introducing team working is expensive. Managers need to ensure that employees receive training on matters such as self-management and how to handle conflict within the team. Empowering teams of workers can result in lengthy team meetings about what to do which detract from time spent in carrying out actual tasks. Ideally team members should be interchangeable, so that if one member is absent any other member can substitute for them, but "cross-training" to equip workers with all the skills for this can take years.

Middle managers often see teams as a threat to their authority. Managers may also fear that their own jobs may be at risk. Workers may see teams as an organisation's way of making them work harder, with peer pressure replacing pressure from managers. Some team members may not want responsibility, while others may come to dominate, stifling the creativity of quieter members.

Q25: Identify four things that self-directed teams may be allowed to decide. *(4 marks)*

....

Q26: Give three advantages of teams. *(3 marks)*

....

Q27: What three things should managers do to increase the chance of teams working effectively? *(3 marks)*

....

Q28: Give three reasons why workers might not like team working. *(3 marks)*

....

Q29: Give three reasons why managers might not like team working. *(3 marks)*

....

Q30: Give one example of a situation where team working was unsuccessful. *(1 mark)*

© HERIOT-WATT UNIVERSITY

Unit 2 Topic 4

Time and task management

Contents

4.1	Time and task management introduction	168
4.2	Principles of time and task management	169
4.3	Time stealers	169
4.4	Task management	172
4.5	Good and bad time and task management	172
4.6	Strategies to improve time and task management	175
4.7	Summary	175
4.8	End of topic test	176

Learning objective

After studying this topic, you should be able to:

- explain how the principles of time management can help to increase effectiveness;
- describe the range of time and task management techniques used by managers;
- suggest strategies to improve time management.

168   UNIT 2. THE INTERNAL BUSINESS ENVIRONMENT

4.1 Time and task management introduction

People are the most expensive resource to a business and wasted time is one of the biggest costs that a business suffers. Managers who can minimize time wasting and maximise productivity will see huge gains not only in output but also in staff motivation, turnover and profit.

Think back to the roles of management as advocated by Fayol and Mintzberg. Each of these roles highlight skills or applications designed to improve efficiency by enabling a workforce to work better. If a manager plans well then there should be less down time, an organised manager will minimise time stealers, a manager who monitors will be aware of time issues, a resource allocator will ensure time is not lost by employees having a poor workflow.

The saying goes that "time is money" and when a manager or employee is not working due to poor time or task management then they are not making any money.

Roles of management   Go online

Can you remember what roles of management were defined by which management theorist?

Q1: Put the following roles into the correct column in the table below:

- commander;
- controller;
- coordinator;
- disseminator;
- disturbance handler;
- monitor;
- negotiator;
- organiser;
- planner;
- resource allocator.

Fayol function roles	Mintzberg roles

© HERIOT-WATT UNIVERSITY

4.2 Principles of time and task management

Pareto's Law (named after Vilfredo Pareto, an Italian economist) and Parkinson's Law (named after Cyril Northcote Parkinson, a British naval historian) are two laws that have been applied to time and task management.

Pareto's 80/20 principle can be applied to many areas of life: he noted that 80% of Italy's land was owned by 20% of the people and that 80% of the world's GDP was generated by 20% of the world's countries. As regards time management, he suggested that 80% of a manager's time tends to be spent on 20% of what really needs to be done and only 20% of their time on the other 80% - i.e. managers waste a lot of time on unimportant matters.

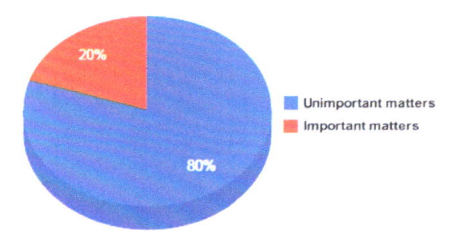

Pareto's Law

Parkinson's Law says that work tends to expand to fill the time available to complete it. Employees - or students - who are given a deadline months ahead for a piece of work rarely finish it early; they may even be rushing to complete it at the end. This is because once they know the end date they simply reschedule their activities to fill all the time available. On the other hand, when time is really short, what has to be done is done.

Both these laws point to the importance of managing time wisely.

Time and task management

Take a note of everything you need to achieve in the next 24 hours. For example, what work do you need to complete, what homework do you have, what other plans do you have?

Keep a brief diary of your activities over the next 24 hours. Record the tasks you planned to do (and those that you didn't) and note how long you spent on each. Share your times with a classmate tomorrow.

Record the times in your jotter, computer or phone - you will need them later in this subject.

4.3 Time stealers

Time stealers is the name given to the things that stop us from achieving our goals, or get in the way of us completing tasks.

We can control many of our time stealers, although not all. Time stealers that we can control include procrastination (checking emails, Facebook and Twitter instead of working), desk stress (tidying your bedroom or desk instead of completing work) and poor prioritising (competing fun or interesting tasks before more important ones). Other time stealers that you have less control over include dealing with emergencies, dealing with visitors and telephone calls and a more senior colleague giving you more work and changing your priorities for you.

Time stealers   Go online

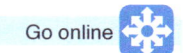

Q2: Choose the most appropriate cause of time stealing from the following list for each of the scenarios and put it in the appropriate row in the table below (please note, there are two scenarios for each cause):

- Delays in making decisions;
- Inability to say "no";
- Interruptions;
- Poor meetings;
- Telephone time stealers;
- Too much paperwork.

Scenario	Cause
Nobody remembers what happened at the last meeting so they discuss the same issues.	
People are confused about the purpose of a meeting so have not prepared for it.	
People call you about trivial matters when you are doing an important task.	
You put things in your pending tray and then forget to deal with them.	
You are worried that people will take offence if you don't help them.	
You are worried you might make a mistake so dither about deciding.	
You find it difficult to get rid of people because you don't want to seem rude.	
You like to be kind to people.	
You like to keep your door open to show you are available to your subordinates.	
You realise that you forgot to mention something in a phone call and have to ring back.	
Your deadline is unrealistic and you need more time.	
Your filing system is disorganised.	

TOPIC 4. TIME AND TASK MANAGEMENT

Whether the time stealer is a direct result of your actions or an external factor such as a colleague, you can plan to minimise the disruption with some planning and focus.

For example:

- if you find your phone is causing you a distraction turn it off or disable your internet connection to avoid checking social media too often;
- only open an email when you know you have time to deal with it;
- maintain a tidy desk or room so that you do not have to face tidying it;
- keep a priorities list and stick to it;
- put a polite but firm notice on your door that says "Deadline to meet - please only disturb if important";
- unhook the telephone for an hour or divert all calls to your voicemail - people who phone without a good reason tend to not leave voice messages;
- take the time to explain to your boss that you are working to a deadline and would prefer not to be disturbed.

Possible solutions to time stealers Go online

For each of the following statements, decide on a solution to the time wasting problem identified.

Q3: People are confused about the purpose of the meeting so nobody has prepared for it.
....

Q4: Nobody remembers what happened last time so they discuss it all again.
....

Q5: You realise after you hang up that you forgot to mention something and have to ring back.
....

Q6: People call you about trivial matters when you are in the middle of an important task.
....

Q7: You are worried you might make a mistake, so dither about deciding.
....

Q8: Your deadline is unrealistic and you need more time.
....

Q9: You are worried that people will take offence if you don't help them.
....

Q10: You like to be kind to people.
....

© HERIOT-WATT UNIVERSITY

Q11: You find it difficult to get rid of people because you don't want to seem rude.
....

Q12: You like to keep your door open to show you are available to your subordinates.
....

Q13: Your filing system is disorganised.
....

Q14: You are putting things in your pending tray and then forgetting to deal with them.

4.4 Task management

In today's fast paced, competitive environment a manager must ensure that all tasks are completed efficiently and to a high standard. This means prioritising and working on multiple tasks at once.

There are a number of tools that a manager has at their disposal to ensure effective task management:

- **Action plans**

    An action plan is a document that is drawn up to organise and prioritise tasks during a project or long-term task. It will include details of the tasks or activities to be completed as well as naming the person responsible for each task. A planned time frame and additional details may also be included.

- **Gantt chart**

    A Gantt chart can be used to graphically represent an action plan. It looks like a horizontal bar graph and shows blocks of actual activity and blocks of planned activity. It will also show where tasks or activities may conflict with each other, or to show at which times workload may increase or decrease. This will allow an employee to see where they can take on other tasks or projects and where they may struggle with their workload.

- **Electronic diary**

    Electronic diaries can be used to help managers to manage tasks. They allow appointments to be scheduled and reminders can be set to alert the diary owner that a task or appointment is due. Colleagues' diaries can be checked online to schedule meetings or reminders and entries can be searched for specific information or dates. This allows for double-bookings to be flagged up to avoid meetings or activities being booked at the same time. An address book facility is included to allow ease of contact with other staff members.

4.5 Good and bad time and task management

Good time and task management will bring advantages to employees and managers as well as the business as a whole and similarly poor time and task management will have a negative effect and impact on the employee and the business.

The benefits of good time and task management may be that:

- deadlines are met;
- work is completed to a good standard;
- the business has increased effectiveness;
- employees are happier, less stressed and more productive;
- employees absence levels are lower, there is less staff turnover and less money needs to be spent on staff training (as less new staff are employed);
- there is less tension between employees and management as work is completed on time;
- customer satisfaction increases as service standards are high and their expectations are met by the organisation.

Consequences of bad time and task management may be that:

- tasks are not completed on time;
- tasks may be completed but may be of poor quality or contain errors;
- costs may increase as additional resources may be required to complete tasks in short timescales;
- deadlines may be missed which means a loss of competitive edge for the business or department;
- customer service may suffer and therefore customer expectations are not met by the organisation;
- employees may suffer from increased levels of stress leading to possible increased levels of absence and resulting in higher costs for the business;
- relationships in the organisation may be poor due to increased stress and lower productivity;
- employees experience poor job satisfaction and may seek employment elsewhere;
- it may be more difficult to recruit quality staff due to a poorer reputation.

Good and bad time and task management

Go online

Decide whether the following are:

- the results of *good* time and task management;
- the consequences of *bad* time and task management;
- *not affected* by time and task management.

Q15: Employees are less stressed when tasks are completed.

a) Good
b) Bad
c) Not affected

....

Q16: Poor job satisfaction as a result of deadlines not being met.

a) Good
b) Bad
c) Not affected

....

Q17: Expenses increase as overtime has to be used.

a) Good
b) Bad
c) Not affected

....

Q18: Motivation increases as employees are well trained.

a) Good
b) Bad
c) Not affected

....

Q19: Managers are motivated by the external constraints placed on the business.

a) Good
b) Bad
c) Not affected

....

Q20: Employees are more productive as they are given clear instructions.

a) Good
b) Bad
c) Not affected

TOPIC 4. TIME AND TASK MANAGEMENT

4.6 Strategies to improve time and task management

Being organised is the best way to improve time and task management, as disorganisation proves to be the biggest block to an effective workforce. The role of the manager is also extremely important. This means regular supervision by a team leader or manager to ensure that the team is on task and able to complete their work to a given deadline.

The following strategies can help improve time and task management:

1. to do lists;
2. setting targets;
3. delegation;
4. using signs on office doors 'busy do not interrupt';
5. effective chairing of meetings;
6. tidy workplaces.

Random and constant checks throughout the project can help greatly. Double-checking a completed task is completed is also a good way of ensuring effective task management. A mentoring system where a senior manager works closely with a junior associate to ensure good practice takes place can give positive results. Similarly, a buddy system with peer or paired working between two employees can result in tasks being completed on time and to a high standard.

Regular meetings between team colleagues and managers can help keep staff on track. Tools such as Gantt charts and action plans can ensure the effective time and task management of the individual and project. Self-evaluation is also a good way of ensuring that targets are met. Regular appraisals can highlight issues or examples of good practice. Understanding time stealers and having the tools to avoid them can ensure an effective and highly organised workforce.

4.7 Summary

Summary

You should now be able to:

- explain how the principles of time management can help to increase effectiveness;
- describe the range of time and task management techniques used by manager;
- suggest strategies to improve time management.

4.8 End of topic test

End of Topic 4 test Go online

Q21: Use the following words to fill in the blanks in the paragraph below:

- a Gantt chart;
- a to-do list;
- an action plan;
- chairperson;
- delegation;
- empowerment.

To ensure effective time and task management an organisation can create .... to give each job a priority so important tasks are done first. Organisations can also make effective use of .... by giving jobs to junior assistants - freeing up time to spend on more important tasks and developing the experience / skill set of the junior, known as ....

It is also important that managers do not allow meetings to overrun. To do this you can set an agenda and time for meetings - appoint a strong .... to manage the items / timing will also help.

Managers can also prepare .... to comment on the task needing done and by when. This provides accountability and allows for prioritising of tasks which is easier for senior management to track progress.

If managers are more visual they may prefer to use .... to show the progress of a medium to long term project. This compares actual and projected time to help managers track progress to ensure deadlines are met.

Q22: Read the short case study below and suggest ten things Gerry could do to resolve his time management problems, giving an example from the case study of how each suggestion might help. *(10 marks)*

> Gerry looked wearily at his in-tray. He picked up the item on top, an invitation to attend a sales convention in Manchester next month. I'll need to coordinate that with Tom and David, he thought, putting it in the pending tray to deal with later. He was just noticing how full his pending tray was when Alison put her head round the door.
>
> "Good weekend?"
>
> "Yes. You?"
>
> "Oh, we had a great time!"
>
> Gerry hoped Alison would leave but she moved further into the room and spent the next 15 minutes telling him about the hilarious weekend she and her friends had had in Newcastle.

TOPIC 4. TIME AND TASK MANAGEMENT

After Alison left Gerry looked over his to-do list. It had 24 items on it. How on earth was he going to get through this lot? He decided to start by phoning Albert about the arrangements for refreshments at the new product launch next week. After exchanging pleasantries he discovered that Albert did not in fact have the necessary details. They ended up having a 10-minute discussion about whether vegetarian "sausage" rolls would be needed as well as meat ones. Gerry ended the phone call, only to realise he had forgotten to ask a crucial question about numbers expected to attend. No time to call again - he had to finish two reports and the staff holiday rota before lunchtime.

It was only 10am but already Gerry felt pangs of hunger and weariness as he loaded up the document and put the finishing touches to the all important conclusions that would mean the difference between success and failure in persuading senior management to approve the next new project.

....

Q23: Provide a brief analysis of six time management techniques. *(6 marks)*

Unit 2 Topic 5

Managing change

Contents

5.1	Managing change introduction	180
	5.1.1 Common barriers to change	181
5.2	Stages of change	182
	5.2.1 The manager's role in the change process	185
5.3	Forces for and against change	186
5.4	Force field analysis	187
	5.4.1 Force field analysis conclusions	188
	5.4.2 Usefulness of force field analysis	189
5.5	Approaches to managing change	190
5.6	Costs and benefits of the different approaches to managing change	192
5.7	Change agents	195
5.8	Barriers to effective change	196
5.9	Summary	199
5.10	End of topic test	200

Learning objective

After studying this topic, you should be able to:

- describe stages of changes, such as Kurt Lewin's theory;

- explain approaches to managing change, such as top-down, participative, negotiated, piecemeal, and action-centred;

- analyse factors affecting the success of change management, such as organisational culture.

UNIT 2. THE INTERNAL BUSINESS ENVIRONMENT

5.1 Managing change introduction

All organisations exist in an environment that is constantly changing. Pressures to change may come from inside or outside an organisation.

You looked at some of the external factors that might cause change in the Higher course. Political, economic, social, technological, environmental and competitive factors (PESTEC factors) can all affect the activities of organisations.

Change can also be affected by internal changes, such as changes to employees and management, decisions a business makes, money made available to spend on research and development, advertising and promotion or the internal culture of the business.

Internal and external factors Go online

Q1: Put the following factors that might cause change in an organisation into the correct column in the table below:

- Appointment of new managers;
- Changes in the economic framework;
- Changes in the law or government policy;
- Changes in the market;
- Changing staff skills and backgrounds;
- Financial problems;
- New management techniques in the media;
- New organisational objectives;
- R&D creating new products;
- Resignations of managerial staff;
- Social and demographic changes;
- Technological changes.

External	Internal

© HERIOT-WATT UNIVERSITY

TOPIC 5. MANAGING CHANGE

External pressures and change Go online

Q2: Put the following types of change next to the appropriate external factor in the table below:

- competitive;
- economic;
- environmental;
- political;
- social;
- technological.

External factor	Type of change
More firms entering a market for a product	
A new law	
A rise in the average age of the UK population	
The development of e-commerce	
Increasing media pressure to recycle	
Economic growth increasing	

5.1.1 Common barriers to change

Organisations and employees may be reluctant to change which can often bring uncertainty and risk. Some of the more common barriers to change are:

- *Employee fear*

    Employees can fear change as they believe it may lead to job losses. Improvements in technology may result in job losses as businesses become more automated. As technology improves some employees may feel that they are unable to keep pace with the change and that they will not understand or be able to work the new machinery. Older employees can often feel pressured as young employees appear to have more energy and a different approach.

- *Resource limitations*

    Sometimes a business wants to change but does not have the necessary capital to enable the change to take place. Bringing in new investors may not be ideal as they may want to take the business in a different direction and loans may not be feasible due to the resulting cash flow problems that repayment plans can bring.

- *Uncertainty*

    The fear of the unknown can be enough to stop change from occurring. Businesses, like people, can get into their comfort zone too easily and be weary of making changes in case the result backfires.

UNIT 2. THE INTERNAL BUSINESS ENVIRONMENT

- *Resistance*

    Change is difficult for everyone. A business wishing to change needs to ensure that enough of the workforce are behind the change as ultimately they are the ones who will be driving the change forward daily.

Barriers to change   Go online

Q3: Read the following extract from a speech made by a Trade Union official at a meeting with factory managers about their decision to change the method of production.

Arthur thumped his fist on the desk. "The workers won't accept this; you're going to have a strike on your hands. You don't have enough new machines and anyway half of them can't work them. They're already talking about job losses. Nobody knows what's going on and it's three months since the last staff meeting. There's no way you can get them all trained up by the start of the year. In any case we've just heard our biggest customer is on the verge of going bust; what will you do if that happens?

From the passage identify each example of a barrier to change and put it into its correct position in the table.

Barrier	Example
Communication problems	
Fear of redundancy	
Impact of other changes outside the firm's control	
Lack of skills in the workforce	
Resistance from apathy to revolt	
Resource limitations	
Uncertainty causing anxiety	
Unrealistic time scales	

5.2 Stages of change

One of the best known description of the stages of change was put forward by Kurt Lewin. He based his description on a block of ice, and the names he gave to the stages reflect this.

A man has been asked to create a round shape from the block of ice. What will happen if he tries to put the cube of ice into the mould?

TOPIC 5. MANAGING CHANGE

Ice problem diagram

The cube of ice resists the change. How can it be made to fit? Through brute force?

Attempting to solve the ice problem diagram (using a chisel and hammer)

No, it will need to be unfrozen, put in the mould, then refrozen.

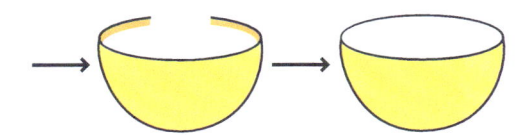

The solution to the ice problem diagram

Lewin said that an organisation is like a block of ice. It has to unfreeze the old ways of doing things before it brings in the changes it wants. Once it is satisfied with the changes then it must refreeze the organisation, or part of the organisation affected by the change, to ensure that the change stays in place.

Two more stages - preparation and evaluation - can be added to Lewin's three.

The five stages of change are:

- **Preparation**

    Preparation is similar to Fayol's planning role. Change is a big thing that should not be rushed in to. Employees and stakeholders should be consulted to ensure that everything has been thought through. Why is the change happening? What is driving the change?

- *Unfreezing*

    Breaking down the beliefs and assumptions that currently exist and opening up an acceptance of the need for change. At this stage the forces that are resisting the change must be confronted - this could be staff who are unsure of the change, or historic policies that need be evaluated.

- *Changing (transforming)*

    At this stage the business implements the process of change required to achieve the desired outcome. Policies are changed, staff are briefed and the culture of the business is changed.

- *Refreezing*

    Consolidation of the new state begins once changes have been successfully implemented. It is possible to see the new structures, polices and processes in place. Referred to as the new equilibrium state.

- *Evaluation*

    Evaluation is just as important. Has the change had the desired affect? Are further adjustments required?

The five stages of change Go online

Q4: Match the following five typical stages of change with the correct description in the table below:

- Changing;
- Evaluation;
- Preparation;
- Refreezing;
- Unfreezing.

Description	Stage of change
Bringing in the necessary alterations to the organisational structure, culture and processes	
Checking that the change is happening as planned and whether further adjustments need to be made	
Planning the change	
Reducing the forces maintaining the organisation's behaviour in its current state (resistors or restraining forces)	
Stabilising the organisation in its new equilibrium state with new structures, culture and processes, i.e. making sure there is no going back to the old ways of doing things	

TOPIC 5. MANAGING CHANGE

5.2.1 The manager's role in the change process

Throughout this process it is important that management are driving change forward, with the support of employees and external stakeholders. It is the role of the manager to adequately plan for change, to ensure that the business objectives are known and met, to ensure that appropriate and timely feedback is gathered and analysed and that those involved in the process are in receipt of the feedback.

The manager's role in the change process   Go online

Q5: The questions below include examples of things a manager might do when bringing in a change. For each one of the following examples, choose the stage of change and put them into the correct column in the table below:

- Reassure employees that management will support them through the change;
- Decide on the objectives for change;
- Make sure those involved receive regular feedback on the results of the change;
- Ensure feedback is quick and up to date;
- Identify driving and restraining forces;
- Involve employees in planning the change;
- Identify the resources needed;
- Show the workforce how the change will benefit them;
- Set timescales;
- Remove opportunities to go back to the old way of doing things;
- Explain the reasons for change to the workforce;
- Set a deadline for corrective action to be completed and subsequently assessed;
- Ensure that all the resources needed are available;
- Threaten redundancy if the change does not happen;
- Offer appropriate training;
- Make minor adjustments to plans if necessary;
- Treat mistakes as learning opportunities;
- Offer positive affirmation for continuing to do things in the new way;
- Analyse the new situation and identify what further changes are needed;
- Be supportive, enthusiastic and positive;
- Offer incentives;
- If possible, implement the change gradually;
- Give employees opportunity to practise the new working practices.

Preparation	Unfreezing	Changing	Refreezing	Evaluation

© HERIOT-WATT UNIVERSITY

5.3 Forces for and against change

Some of the forces pushing for and against change are summarised in the diagram below.

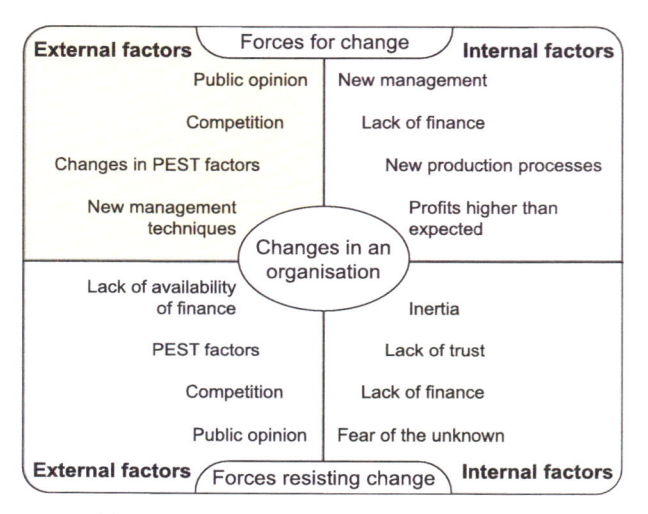

	Forces for change	
External factors		**Internal factors**
Public opinion		New management
Competition		Lack of finance
Changes in PEST factors		New production processes
New management techniques		Profits higher than expected
Lack of availability of finance	*Changes in an organisation*	
		Inertia
PEST factors		Lack of trust
Competition		Lack of finance
Public opinion		Fear of the unknown
External factors	Forces resisting change	**Internal factors**

You can see that many of the same factors may act as forces for change or forces resisting change. For example, not having enough money might make a firm change production methods to cut costs. On the other hand, not having enough money might stop a firm from making the change it wants.

Forces for and against change

Q6: Give examples of circumstances in which each of the four factors in the table below might act as a force for change or a force resisting change. The first one is done for you.

	Force for change	Force against change
Anti-discrimination laws	A new law, e.g. ending age discrimination may force a firm to change its HR policies.	The cost of complying with legislation, e.g. the cost of creating disabled facilities may prevent a firm from expanding.
Environmental protesters		
New competition		
Shortage of money		

5.4 Force field analysis

In addition to his five stages of change model, Lewin also developed **force field analysis**. Force field analysis summarises the factors that will help or hinder the introduction of a particular change.

The forces that will help the change (forces for change in the activity above) are called **drivers**. The forces that will hinder the change (forces against change in the activity above) are called **resistors**. Drivers and resistors are sometimes referred to as driving forces and restraining forces respectively. Drivers and resistors push against each other.

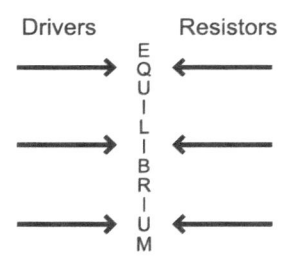

```
     Drivers        Resistors
                E
  ———————→     Q      ←———————
                U
                I
                L
  ———————→     I      ←———————
                B
                R
                I
  ———————→     U      ←———————
                M

           Assets for change
```

Force field analysis diagram

Note from the diagram above that:

- equilibrium is the current position - usually equilibrium is shown as a vertical line dividing drivers and resistors as in the example that follows;
- **assets for change** are organisational strengths that will help a firm when it tries to change but do not cause it to change, e.g. a strong corporate culture or an experienced management team;
- arrows of different lengths are used to show the strength of the different forces;
- arrows point inwards;
- for change to happen drivers must be greater than resistors;
- to get to the desired situation you need to strengthen the driving forces or weaken the restraining ones.

The following is an example of a force field diagram for a firm which wishes to move production to China.

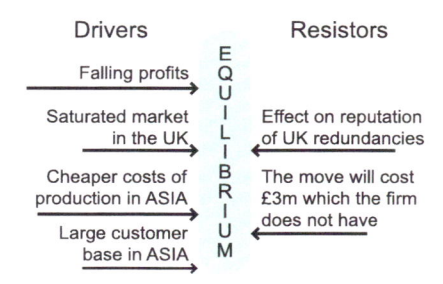

Drivers and Resistors Diagram

```
           Drivers                         Resistors
                              E
      Falling profits  →      Q
                              U
      Saturated market        I    Effect on reputation
         in the UK    →       L  ← of UK redundancies
                              I
      Cheaper costs of        B    The move will cost
      production in ASIA →    R  ← £3m which the firm
                              I    does not have
      Large customer          U
        base in ASIA   →      M
```

Assets for change
The MD worked in China for many years and is bilingual in Mandarin and English

Force field analysis diagram for moving production to China

5.4.1 Force field analysis conclusions

After you have drawn up your force field diagram you are usually asked to analyse it critically. This means you need to add some conclusions, e.g. explain why certain drivers or resistors are important, why some are more important than others, or suggest ways in which drivers might be strengthened or resistors weakened.

Force field conclusions

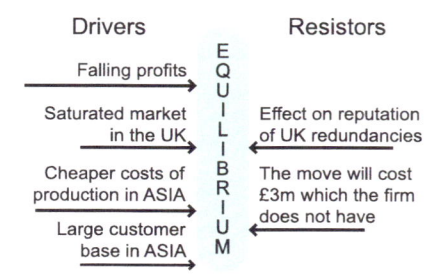

```
           Drivers                         Resistors
                              E
      Falling profits  →      Q
                              U
      Saturated market        I    Effect on reputation
         in the UK    →       L  ← of UK redundancies
                              I
      Cheaper costs of        B    The move will cost
      production in ASIA →    R  ← £3m which the firm
                              I    does not have
      Large customer          U
        base in ASIA   →      M
```

Assets for change
The MD worked in China for many years and is bilingual in Mandarin and English

Write a paragraph of conclusions to the force field diagram above. Six marks are allocated and the first two marks are done for you (below).

Falling profits coupled with a saturated market mean that the firm must look abroad to capture new customers. *(1 mark)* Entering China will give faster and lower cost access to other world and European markets in which the firm already has customers. This is an important driver because the reduction in distribution cost will increase profit. *(1 mark)*

Force field analysis

Q7: A business has decided to introduce a new production process that will enable it to cut staff costs and increase productivity and quality. Create a force field diagram using the following drivers, resistors and assets for change:

- Accountants have warned the firm may go out of business if the change is not made.
- None of the staff knows how to work the new machines.
- One third of customers have been lost to a rival firm owing to complaints about quality.
- Staff are worried about losing their jobs and are threatening to go on strike.
- The firm has a long history of good employee relations.
- The firm has enough retained profit to finance the new machines without any borrowing.
- The new machines will help to reduce pollution, saving the firm £10,000 a year in costs.

Q8: Once you have completed the diagram, analyse it critically by writing a paragraph of conclusions. This could include an explanation of which are the most significant drivers and resistors and why. You could also suggest ways in which drivers might be strengthened or resistors weakened.

5.4.2 Usefulness of force field analysis

It is always a worthwhile exercise to critically examine all avenues when proposing a change. A force field analysis allows a business to identify the drivers for change and any resistors opposing a change. Completing the analysis, and more importantly, critically analysing the analysis, will help a firm weigh up the pros and cons of any change. It allows the business to gather all the necessary information and identifying any constraints early can help the process of eliminating or reducing them.

Like any structured decision making model, it takes time to gather and analyse information. This delay may lead to some of the drivers or resistors being out of date by the time the decision is made. Managers may only concentrate on the factors identified in the analysis and may miss new information as it becomes available. A force field analysis is not detailed nor is it specific which could lead to confusion or an important decision being made based only on broad statements. It is also subjective.

Usefulness of force field analysis

In each question decide whether each statement is an advantage or a disadvantage of using force field analysis.

Q9: Summarising the forces for and against change allows firms to gather information.

a) Advantage
b) Disadvantage

Q10: A firm can identify constraints and take action in advance to reduce them.

a) Advantage
b) Disadvantage

....

Q11: The relative strengths of the factors may be overestimated or underestimated.

a) Advantage
b) Disadvantage

....

Q12: Drivers and resistors may change in importance or disappear over the time.

a) Advantage
b) Disadvantage

....

Q13: Identifying drivers and resistors allows a firm to amend its strategy.

a) Advantage
b) Disadvantage

....

Q14: Managers may ignore factors not identified in the force field analysis.

a) Advantage
b) Disadvantage

....

Q15: Giving each force a weighting helps the firm evaluate strategic factors that must be in place.

a) Advantage
b) Disadvantage

5.5 Approaches to managing change

The past four decades have been a period of huge change in the business world. Trading patterns, technology, markets and society itself are all constantly changing at an ever accelerating pace. This means that all organisations have to learn to manage change effectively. There are many approaches a business can use to deal with and manage this change. It should be noted that a mixture of approaches will be required, as no single approach on its own can deal with change.

TOPIC 5. MANAGING CHANGE

Some of the approaches are listed below.

- *Action-centred*

    This is a practical approach to change that is driven by finding a solution to a problem. Once a problem is identified possible solutions are discussed. Businesses will pilot one solution in a targeted small area and, depending upon its success, either implement that solution on a more widespread basis or pilot an alternative solution until success is achieved.

- *Negotiated*

    The opposite of top-down, change is reached through a bargaining process between employees, employers and other stakeholders. Communication flows both ways with managers making use of employees' ideas and opinions. Trade unions may be involved to ensure the voice of all employees is heard or change may be directed as a result of works councils.

- *Participative*

    Similar to negotiated, this change is the result of discussion and consensus among all those involved. This is shown by complete confidence and trust between managers and employees. Employees are free to discuss their jobs and their ideas are welcomed. There is a lot of communication and co-operation within the team. Feedback of information is used for problem solving and so the people who participate will be committed to implementing the change. Motivation increases as employees feel empowered through their part of the process.

- *Piecemeal initiatives*

    Change can also be implemented in a piecemeal fashion, which means small incremental changes being made over time. This can build confidence within the business as taking small steps is seen as less risky. If a change is not working out it can be reversed before the whole change is complete.

- *Top-down*

    This approach is achieved when management decide what to do. It is imposed on the business and its employees and is therefore associated with an autocratic management style. Communication is directed from the top and little or no attention is paid to the ideas of employees. This strategy is normally used for large, one-off changes, in response to an emergency or when change needs to be brought in quickly, e.g. in response to a change in legislation.

Different approaches to managing change

Go online

Q16: Match the following five different approaches to managing change with the correct description in the table below:

- Action-centred;
- Negotiated;
- Participative;
- Piecemeal;
- Top-down.

Description	Approach to managing change
Change is brought in gradually through a series of small alterations.	
Change is made by running through a list of potential solutions to a problem until the best one is identified.	
Changes are the result of a bargaining process between managers and employees, often represented by trade union representatives.	
Employees are invited to contribute to decisions about change and the change incorporates their ideas.	
Those at the top of the organisation make decisions about change and impose them.	

5.6 Costs and benefits of the different approaches to managing change

Each approach to managing change comes with its own advantages. There are also disadvantages to each approach. For this reason, successful businesses will use more than one approach, depending in the size and rate of change, and the number of staff involved in the process.

Top-down

Advantages:

- Top level management have a holistic overview so can make the change in line with the businesses objectives;
- This method works best in a crisis as decision making time is short and the survival of the business may be at risk;
- If a change is inevitable this is an efficient method of implementation; this is especially true

when the main drive to change is an external factor, such as a political or economic decision made by government.

Disadvantage:

- Staff resistance can be high if they feel they are being overlooked, undervalued or not listened to;
- Employees' working on the ground have the skills, knowledge and experience but this method does not take these views into account;
- This may result in high levels of staff turnover or absenteeism if motivation is low;
- In turn this may create a culture of low morale.

Negotiated/participative

Advantages:

- The change is more likely to be successful as everyone has been involved;
- This fosters trust between management and employees;
- Reduces staff resistance and improves morale;
- Allows for staff skills, knowledge and experience to contribute to the strategy in the hope for a more effective and competitive change.

Disadvantage:

- These methods are time consuming as they involve lengthy discussions and consolation through the use of focus groups and quality circles;
- Trust can be easily damaged if either management retract the empowerment or employees abuse it;
- Not effective in a situation of urgency/crisis or where there is an unnegotiable outcome as too many people need to be consulted and they all might have differing views.

Action-centred

Advantages:

- Allows a business to try out possible solutions on a small scale for a limited time before making a permanent change;
- Explores many different options and therefore contingency strategies are often formed;
- Allows employees to have an input and pilot aspects of change which leads to better decisions being made.

Disadvantage:

- This methods does not work when the change is being driven by an external factor, such as a change in government legislation;

- Piloting ideas can be a lengthy and expensive process;
- Often used as part of continuous improvement and may not be suitable for large changes.

Piecemeal

Advantages:

- Employees become accustomed to the change as it is gradually introduced which can build confidence for the future;
- Smaller changes are less likely to result in staff resistance;
- Gradual change is easier to manage and control so reduces risk.

Disadvantage:

- A sense of overall direction may be lost as the change is 'bitty';
- The smaller components of the changes may be in conflict with each other;
- Decentralised changes may not be fairly rolled out across the firm upsetting staff in different departments.

Benefits of the different approaches to managing change   Go online

Q17: Match the following five advantages of different approaches to managing change with the correct description in the table below:

- Action-centred;
- Negotiated;
- Participative;
- Piecemeal;
- Top-down.

Description	Approach to managing change
Changes can be implemented quickly as employees are not consulted.	
Employees can have an input into the pilot which improves motivation and confidence.	
Involving all employees throughout the process leads to better decisions being made.	
Mistakes can be rectified as they happen and everyone can learn from the process when changes are gradual.	
Negotiations empower employees to believe that their voice matters; this leads to an improved corporate culture.	

TOPIC 5. MANAGING CHANGE

Costs and benefits of the approaches to managing change   Go online

Q18: Put each of the following costs and benefits of the approaches to managing change in the appropriate column in the table below:

- Changes are carried out swiftly and exactly as management wants.
- Change will be quicker to implement as workers already know what they will get out of it.
- Employees may resist changes if they have not had an input.
- Getting everyone accustomed to constant small changes makes it easier to introduce large changes later.
- Negotiations can be time consuming; some things may be non-negotiable, e.g. redundancies.
- Some changes may conflict with others.
- This method avoids the cost of full scale implementation of a change that doesn't work.
- Trying out a succession of different changes can be time-consuming.
- Workers may lack expertise to make good decisions about change.
- Workers will "own" the change and be highly motivated to make it a success.

	Costs	Benefits
Action-centred		
Negotiative		
Participative		
Piecemeal		
Top-down		

5.7 Change agents

Change agents are the people responsible for bringing about change. They can be individuals, groups of employees, external experts or a combination of the above.

Change agents can be instrumental in ensuring that the change takes place. They take the lead in working out what the issues are (the potential drivers and resistors to change). They manage employees expectations and set realistic goals. They can also inspire and educate colleagues and ease their concerns through the process.

They may be responsible for groups of colleagues if using the negotiated or participative approach or can be key to choosing the correct pilot if using an action-centred of piecemeal approach. Where a lack of expertise is evident, change agents are responsible for buying in expert consultants. They then coordinate with management to ensure the process is smooth.

© HERIOT-WATT UNIVERSITY

Change agents may be tasked with getting others on board and can be given a budget to introduce incentive or recognition schemes to identify and share best practice. They monitor and control the change process, ensuring all interested parties are kept fully briefed throughout.

Change agents — Go online

Q19: A change agent must be internal to the organisation.

a) True
b) False

Q20: A change agent manages the change process.

a) True
b) False

Q21: Change agents can be given a budget that is used to eliminate some of the resisters to change.

a) True
b) False

Q22: Change agents can hire and fire staff to help the change process.

a) True
b) False

Q23: Change agents can have line manager responsibility for groups of employees.

a) True
b) False

5.8 Barriers to effective change

The role of the change agent is an important one. It is vital that the change agent has the correct experience in managing change, especially if the project is large. Internal change agents, whilst the may not have managed large scale change in the past, will at least be familiar with the organisational policies and hierarchy. External change agents are more likely to have expertise in dealing with a variety of situations but will take time to get to know the organisation and are expensive.

The change agent, whether they are internal or external, must work well with all staff. Staff resistance is a sizeable resister to change and a change agent must work hard to ensure they have the support and the backing of all staff in the process.

TOPIC 5. MANAGING CHANGE

Organisation culture is often deep routed and may be particularly difficult to overcome. An effective change agent must ensure that the culture is in line with the change that needs to take place.

The change agent must also ensure that they have the resources required to make the change. Lack of finance is often noted as the largest resister to change. The quality and quantity of staff required to ensure the change process is smooth can also be a limiting factor. Availability of information and technology can also result in a change not taking place.

Barriers to effective change   Go online

Q24: Decide whether the following factors are internal or external to the business and put them in the correct column in the table below:

- Staff resistance;
- Changes to legislation;
- Availability of information;
- Bank agreeing further finance;
- Organisational culture;
- Quality of specialist.

Internal	External

Corporate culture can also improve or delay the change process. An organisation's culture can be seen as its personality. Just as individuals may have very different personalities, so organisational culture varies from one organisation to another. Organisational culture is important to a business and can define the change process and its success.

Organisational culture definition   Go online

An organisation's culture exerts a major influence on its ability to change.

Q25: Put the following words into place in the paragraph below:

- acting;
- attitudes;
- beliefs;
- goals;
- history;
- size;
- thinking;
- time;
- values.

The culture of an organisation is its customary way of .... and .... : its shared ...., ... and .... It can take a long .... to change an organisation's culture. Some of the factors that might influence the type of culture an organisation has include its ...., ... and ....

Corporate culture and the change process   Go online

Q26: Place each of the following scenarios, identifying whether it would be easier or harder for an organisation to introduce change, in the appropriate column in the table below:

- Adaptive cultures show trust in their workers and reassure them of their support;
- An organisation may have several subcultures which may conflict with each other;
- An organisation with a strong culture and past achievements may not see the need to do anything different;
- Cultures such as the net (matrix structure) stress teamwork based on expertise and empower workers to make their own decisions.
- Many organisations with a strong culture have operated in much the same way over many years
- People in an organisation with a strong culture are sometimes blind to its failings;
- Rigid cultures such as the temple have a hierarchical structure and strictly defined roles and procedures so that people always know what to expect in their jobs;
- Some cultures involve employees in decisions about change;
- Some organisations encourage workers to take risks and treat mistakes as learning opportunities;
- Where a strong culture has developed, employees may be loyal to the organisation and eager to help it overcome problems.

TOPIC 5. MANAGING CHANGE

Easier to introduce change	Harder to introduce change

5.9 Summary

Summary

You should now be able to:

- describe stages of changes, such as Kurt Lewin's theory;
- explain approaches to managing change, such as top-down, participative, negotiated, piecemeal, and action-centred;
- analyse factors affecting the success of change management, such as organisational culture.

5.10 End of topic test

End of Topic 5 test

Choose the approach to change that applies to each statement in the questions below.

Q27: Resistance is lessened because the change is decided through a process of give and take between managers and workers.

a) Action-centred
b) Negotiated
c) Participative
d) Piecemeal
e) Top-down
f) Use of change agents

....

Q28: Workers are inspired by the visionary leadership of someone who is experienced in change.

a) Action-centred
b) Negotiated
c) Participative
d) Piecemeal
e) Top-down
f) Use of change agents

....

Q29: Put the following stages of change into the correct order.

1. Evaluation
2. Refreezing
3. Preparation
4. Unfreezing
5. Changing

Choose the most appropriate stage of change for each of the following questions that a manager might ask.

Q30: What can we do to help our workers accept this change?

a) Preparation
b) Unfreezing
c) Changing
d) Refreezing
e) Evaluation

....

TOPIC 5. MANAGING CHANGE

Q31: How do we need to change?

a) Preparation
b) Unfreezing
c) Changing
d) Refreezing
e) Evaluation

....

Q32: Has the change achieved what we wanted it to?

a) Preparation
b) Unfreezing
c) Changing
d) Refreezing
e) Evaluation

....

Q33: What procedures do we need to put in place to keep everyone committed to the new system?

a) Preparation
b) Unfreezing
c) Changing
d) Refreezing
e) Evaluation

....

Q34: Will all employees please follow their new job descriptions from today?

a) Preparation
b) Unfreezing
c) Changing
d) Refreezing
e) Evaluation

Q35: Read the case study below. Using a force field diagram, critically analyse the forces for and against change. *(10 marks)*

Four large supermarkets operate within a particular area. The local council wishes to implement a scheme to address the problem of abandoned supermarket trolleys. Abandoned trolleys have been blamed for five accidents over the past six months, and the local council has received many complaints about the detrimental effect they have on the environment. One of those injured sued the council and was awarded £3,000 in damages. The council plans to fine anyone caught abandoning a trolley and to round up all abandoned trolleys once a week and return them to the supermarkets they came from. The scheme would be financed by the revenue from fines and by charging supermarkets 0.001% of their turnover plus £1 for each trolley collected. A further benefit of the scheme is that it would create 20 new jobs for trolley collectors.

The newly appointed Chief Executive of the council has a history of handling many changes successfully in her previous job as a Managing Director of a large US firm. She recently gave a presentation to the council about the success of similar schemes in North America, and pointed out that they have usually more than covered costs. Other councillors, however, pointed out that it would be difficult to catch people abandoning trolleys, or to prove that they were doing so. Also, some trolleys might be hard to locate as people sometimes leave them in very unusual places.

Two of the supermarkets are against the idea because they claim they very rarely have to retrieve their trolleys. The other two supermarkets welcome the scheme as it would cost them much less than placing homing devices in each trolley. A local newspaper survey found that 50% of the public disapproved of the scheme because they felt collecting trolleys once a week was too infrequent.

....

Q36: Read the case study below.

Mining company Marvel Minerals plc plans to take over its largest competitor, San Romano. Margaret Blyth, Chief Executive of Marvel, said that *Marvel's investors had expressed approval of the deal at a recent meeting.* Ms Blyth said that *more than half of San Romano's shareholders had written to say they were in favour of the deal.* However she admitted that *San Romano's Board of Directors had expressed opposition to the planned takeover.* About 60-70% of Marvel's shareholders already hold stakes in San Romano and are keen to see the takeover go ahead.

Innes Black, the San Romano Chief Executive, says that Marvel's offer is too low in light of the fact that *combining the two groups would create a natural resources giant worth more than $500 billion.* It would also mean that *Marvel would become market leader in the iron ore, copper and coal mining.*

The proposed takeover is likely to meet a series of regulatory challenges in the UK, where it has been *referred to the Competition and Markets Authority (CMA).* Marvel claims that *the deal would create cost savings of $3.7 billion annually.* San Romano is thought to be looking at potential *'white knight' deals with other mining companies.*

Ms Blyth was responsible for the successful *acquisition of three soft drinks companies in her previous job at Premier Beverages.*

Now test your understanding by identifying whether the phrases from the passage in italics above are drivers, resistors or assets for change. Put the phrases into the correct column in the table below.

TOPIC 5. MANAGING CHANGE

Drivers	Resistors	Assets for change

....

Q37: As businesses adapt to a changing environment they are likely to face some resistance from parts of their workforce. Discuss the methods which could be used to encourage employees to embrace change. *(8 marks)*

Unit 2 Topic 6

Equality and diversity

Contents

 6.1 Equality Act 2010 206
 6.2 Examples of discrimination at work 207
 6.3 Mitigation against the effects of the Equality Act 209
 6.4 Impact on HR as a result of the Equality Act 209
   6.4.1 Recruitment and selection 209
   6.4.2 Training, transfers and progression opportunities 210
 6.5 Summary 212
 6.6 End of topic test 213

Learning objective

After studying this topic, you should be able to:

- analyse the impact of the Equality Act 2010 on organisations;
- describe training, transfer and progression opportunities.

6.1 Equality Act 2010

The Equality Act 2010 consolidates and simplifies previous anti-discrimination legislation in the UK. The act applies to businesses of all sizes within the UK.

The main areas of legislation that have merged were the Equal Pay Act 1970, the Sex Discrimination Act 1975, the Race Relations Act 1976, the Disability Discrimination Act 1995, the Employment Equality (Religion or Belief) Regulations 2003, the Employment Equality (Sexual Orientation) Regulations 2003, the Employment Equality (Age) Regulations 2006, the Equality Act 2006 Part 2 and the Equality Act (Sexual Orientation) Regulations 2007.

These acts are now redundant, with the Equality Act 2010 superseding them.

The Equality Act contains nine protected characteristics, namely:

- age;
- disability;
- gender reassignment;
- marriage and civil partnership;
- pregnancy and maternity;
- race;
- religion and belief;
- sex;
- sexual orientation.

The act prohibits any business from discriminating against, harassing or victimising any current or future employee on the basis of any of these nine protected characteristics.

Protected characteristics   Go online

Decide whether or not you think the Equality Act is being met in the following examples.

Q1: I am *wheelchair bound* and applied to work on a construction site. I was refused an interview on the basis of my disability. Was the employer wrong?

a) Yes
b) No

....

Q2: I am *partially deaf* and applied to work in a music store. I was refused an interview on the basis of my disability. Was the employer wrong?

a) Yes
b) No

....

TOPIC 6. EQUALITY AND DIVERSITY

Q3: I am *a gay woman* who applied to work for a rape counselling service for woman. I was refused an interview because of my sexuality. Was the employer wrong?

a) Yes
b) No

....

Q4: I am *a gay man* who applied to work for a rape counselling service for women. I was refused an interview because of my sex. Was the employer wrong?

a) Yes
b) No

....

Q5: I am *a Muslim* and applied to work in a café. I was refused an interview as a result of my religion. Was the employer wrong?

a) Yes
b) No

....

Q6: I am *17 years old* and applied to work as a bar tender. I was not given an interview as a result of my age. Was the employer wrong?

a) Yes
b) No

6.2 Examples of discrimination at work

Discrimination comes in many different guises. Five common forms of discrimination are listed below:

- *Direct discrimination*

    This is when an employee or candidate feels that they are being treated less favourably than another person because of one of the nine protected characteristics. For example, a job description that states a preferred age range for prospective candidates.

- *Discrimination by perception*

    This is discrimination against someone because they associate with another person who possesses a protected characteristic, for example a business treating an employee differently because of the jewellery that they wear.

- *Indirect discrimination*

    This discrimination occurs when a business has a rule or policy that applies to everyone but disadvantages a particular protected characteristic, for example insisting that prospective candidates must be able to drive (where driving is not implicit in the job description).

© HERIOT-WATT UNIVERSITY

- **Harassment**

  Harassment can take the form of jokes, negative stereotyping, hostile acts or simple thoughtless comments.

- **Victimisation**

  This is where someone is treated badly because they have made/supported a complaint or grievance under the Equality Act.

Employees have the right to complain about behaviour they feel discriminatory or in the case of unfair harassment. If they do not feel that their complaint has been taken seriously or dealt with they have the right to make a claim in an Employment Tribunal. An employment tribunal can be a lengthy and expensive process for all concerned.

Under the Equality Act, employees can complain of behaviour they find offensive even if it is not directed at them. In addition to the costs associated with legal liability, harassment has a profound negative effect on individuals stress and productivity at work.

Discrimination

Go online

Q7: Match the following types of discrimination with the examples in the table below (note that not all types of discrimination may be used and some may be used more than once):

- Direct discrimination;
- Discrimination by perception;
- Harassment;
- Indirect discrimination;
- Victimisation.

Example	Type of discrimination
A business hires 20 white males to work in an area populated by ethnic minorities. No job adverts were placed as all positions were filled by word of mouth.	
A business refuses to interview an internal candidate who has just returned from a career break.	
A manager makes an employee feel humiliated by telling jokes about their religion at a staff training session.	
A women is employed in a car garage as an engineer. Many of her male colleagues make lurid sexual remarks to her.	
An employer does not interview a candidate because they have heard the candidate may be pregnant.	
You resigned your job despite winning an age discrimination case against your employer. You apply to a competitor but you do not receive an interview as they heard what happened.	

TOPIC 6. EQUALITY AND DIVERSITY   209

6.3 Mitigation against the effects of the Equality Act

The easiest way for a business to mitigate against the effects of the Equality Act is to firstly treat all employees fairly and equally and to be aware of the contents of the act.

A business can produce an equality policy. This will give applicants and workers confidence in knowing that the business is serious about equality. It will also ensure that the business takes the time to ensure that is it complying with current legislation. This policy will set out the minimum standards of behaviour for all employees and will provide adequate equality training. This is important as the employer is responsible for the actions of an employee under the Equality Act. This means that if an employee victimises or harasses a colleague, and the business can prove that the employee handing out the abuse received adequate training, then the employee is responsible for their own actions and not the business.

A business can work with trade unions to ensure that staff are involved and that grievances are dealt with swiftly. A business can also have a fair and transparent payment spine and benefits scheme and conduct equal pay audits to ensure that men and woman across the organisation are paid the same for the role that they have.

Written policies should be made available to all employees. A shorter code of conduct could be drawn up to remind managers of the importance and contents of the legislation.

6.4 Impact on HR as a result of the Equality Act

A business must think about the requirements of the equality act before selecting a candidate for a job. During the recruitment process, when engaging in staff training or when following disciplinary action the business must take positive steps to ensure that it lives up to the requirements of the act.

6.4.1 Recruitment and selection

The language that the business uses here is important. A business must not directly or indirectly discriminate against a prospect candidate with the language they use. For example, when setting out the job advert, a business cannot use terms that favour one sex over the other, such as "sales girl required" or "postman needed". Age related words should be avoided also, such as "mature, experienced manager needed". It is okay to say the candidate is required to have experience but not to say that they have to be mature as this has connotations of an older person.

Only advertising in magazines that focus on one gender can also be seen as indirect discrimination. Using images of only young people in an advert can be seen as indirect discrimination on the grounds of age.

The format of the advert must be accessible to that is can be read by everyone. Similarly, the format of the application form must be made available in large print if requested. There should be a place on the form for an applicant to say that they wish to be interviewed under the Guaranteed Interview Scheme. This states than any applicant who has a recognised disability is guaranteed an interview as long as they meet the minimum rob requirements as specified in the job description. For example, a disabled applicant who applies for a teaching job but does not hold the necessary qualifications would not need to be interviewed under the scheme. This scheme is not compulsory.

A business should encourage as many applicants as possible. Making it clear that they accept applications from disabled applicants will encourage more people to apply, improve the chance of the business finding the best person for the job and improve the public's perception of the business. Non-legally binding organisations, such as the 'two ticks' symbol on adverts is an effective way of alerting candidates that you are a fair employer.

A business must legally make 'reasonable adjustments' to ensure that is does not discriminate against disabled applicants. This can include practical steps such as moving an office to the ground floor or widening door access.

An employer must only ask questions relevant to the application either on the form or at interview. This means questions about the applicants age, gender, sexual preference or religious beliefs should be avoided, as they bear no relevance to the applicant's ability to complete the job. This information can be asked for separately, for monitoring purposes, as long as it is not seen by those involved in the interview process.

A business does not need to meet someone before offering them a job. They can offer the position after reading application forms or by conducting a telephone interview. However a business decides to do this, it is important that everyone is treated fairly. This means asking all candidates the same questions, for example is would not be fair to ask a woman if she is going to need time off due to family commitments while not posing this question to a man.

Testing is a common method used in the recruitment and selection process in the UK. It is important that the test does not discriminate against the applicant. For example, if the test is given to someone with English as an additional language they may underperform and not compare as well to someone for whom English is their native tongue. This would be an example of indirect discrimination on the basis of race.

Recruitment and selection   Go online

Q8: Highlight any statements in the following advert that discriminate and would not be allowed due to the Equality Act 2010.

Hairdresser required, preferably with long hair. She must be experienced with drive and passion. Being able to drive would be an advantage. We are looking for a young and dynamic person with ambition. We are located on the first floor so may not be suitable for a disabled person. We pay above the minimum wage and have great holiday entitlements. Must be able to work nights and weekends. Call in to apply.

....

Q9: Analyse the advert, commenting on what protected characteristics may be contravened.

6.4.2 Training, transfers and progression opportunities

A business must provide training to all staff on the rights and responsibilities of the employee with regard to equality legislation. Additional training should be offered to all managers or any employee who is in a position to recruit staff to ensure they are aware of the requirements of the law.

Businesses must make reasonable adjustments to any training programme to ensure that it is accessible to all participants. For example, making sure that it takes place in a quiet area, so that all employees can hear, that handouts are available to take away or that there are no physical barriers that could stop an applicant from fully engaging with the training.

Management must also ensure that women on maternity leave are offered training as part of their

TOPIC 6. EQUALITY AND DIVERSITY

'keeping in touch' days.

When offering progression or transfer opportunities the same rules that apply to the recruitment and selection of new staff still apply.

Equality training   Go online

Q10: Fill in the blanks in the following paragraphs.

For workers to understand what equality law means for them, they will need to be informed. This is what is meant by 'equality ....' .

Equality training can be an important part of showing that you are preventing discrimination, harassment and .... in your organisation. If an employee was to treat a colleague or customer unfairly by contravening one of the nine protected characteristics without receiving adequate training, the business would be held jointly liable for any action.

A business might choose to do this:

- as part of an .... process for new starts;
- during regular .... meetings;
- by asking staff to attend specific whole or half day ....;
- by asking staff to complete an .... training package at a time of their choosing.

Whatever the format the business chooses, they should also make sure that workers know about any .... and that anyone who joins the organisation (for example, any new employee who comes in after the training has taken place) knows what is expected of them. For this reason many businesses chose to make equality training an annual event.

Training should include:

- the law covering all the protected .... and what behaviour is and is not acceptable;
- the risk of ignoring or seeming to approve inappropriate behaviour and personal ....;
- how discrimination can affect the way an employer functions and the impact that generalisations, stereotypes, bias, inappropriate language in day-to-day operations can have on people's chances of obtaining work, ..., recognition and respect;
- the business's equality ...., if they have one, why it has been introduced and how it will be put into practice.

© HERIOT-WATT UNIVERSITY

6.5 Summary

Summary

You should now be able to:

- analyse the impact of the Equality Act 2010 on organisations;
- describe training, transfer and progression opportunities.

6.6 End of topic test

End of Topic 6 test　　　　　　　　　　　　　　　　　　　　　　　Go online

Q11: Which of the following is *not* an example of direct discrimination?

a) An applicant is refused an interview because of their ethnic background.
b) A job advert states that the post is 'not suitable for disabled people'.
c) An employee is refused promotion as they are a carer for their wife.
d) A new employee is paid less than her colleagues because she is ten years younger then them.

Q12: An employee racially abuses a co-worker but has not received any equality training. Who can be prosecuted under the Equality Act 2010?

a) The employee only
b) The employer only
c) Both the employer and the employee
d) Neither the employer nor the employee

Q13: You must not treat a person worse than another because you incorrectly think they have a protected characteristic.

a) True
b) False

....

Q14: Harassment and victimisation are covered under the Equality Act.

a) True
b) False

....

Q15: Paying a 25-year-old more than an 18-year-old is against the Equality Act on the grounds of age discrimination.

a) True
b) False

Q16: Describe the impact that the Equality Act can have on a business. *(6 marks)*

Unit 2 Topic 7

The internal business environment test

The internal business environment test

Go online

Q1: The role of management, according to Fayol, is to:

a) plan, organise, command, communicate and control.
b) plan, organise, coordinate, communicate and control.
c) plan, organise, command, coordinate and control.
d) plan, order, command, communicate and control.

....

Q2: Other functions of managers, namely setting objectives, organising, motivating, measuring and developing people, was set out by:

a) Maslow.
b) Drucker.
c) McGregor.
d) Mintzberg.

....

Q3: Rosemary Stewart said that a manager is responsible for the balance of demands, choices and contraints.

a) True
b) False

....

Q4: Mayo, writing from the human relations school of management theory, believes that productivity increases when a worker is paid fairly.

a) True
b) False

....

Q5: Fred Fielder said, "management is about doing the right things, leadership is about doing things right".

a) True
b) False

....

Q6: Trait theorists believe that people are born with leadership qualities.

a) True
b) False

....

TOPIC 7. THE INTERNAL BUSINESS ENVIRONMENT TEST 217

Q7: What are the five needs stated in Maslow's hierarchy?

a) Physiological, safety, social, respect and self-actualisation
b) Physiological, safety, social, self-esteem and self-actualisation
c) Physiological, security, social, self-esteem and self-actualisation
d) Physiological, safety, social, self-esteem and self-fulfilment

....

Q8: Which of the following is *not* a team role, according to Belbin?

a) Implementer
b) Resource investigator
c) Specialist
d) Inspirer

....

Q9: According to Tuckman, the stages of group development are:

a) forming, starring, norming and performing.
b) forming, storming, norming and conforming.
c) forming, storming, norming and performing.
d) forming, starring, norming and conforming.

....

Q10: The stages of change, according to Lewin, are:

a) preparation, unfreezing, process, refreezing and evaluation.
b) introduction, unfreezing, transforming, refreezing and evaluation.
c) introduction, unfreezing, transforming, refreezing and delivery.
d) preparation, unfreezing, transforming, refreezing and evaluation.

....

Q11: A Gantt chart allows a team to monitor the delivery of a project.

a) True
b) False

....

Q12: Staff turnover refers to the number of sickness days an employee takes in one year.

a) True
b) False

....

Q13: A force field analysis uses drivers and .... to evaluate the success of change.

....

Q14: Top-down approach to change occurs when conclusions are reached through collective bargaining.

a) True
b) False

....

Q15: Harassment is covered under the Equality Act 2010.

a) True
b) False

Read the case study and answer the questions that follow.

Trouble at the stables

As Helen passed Angus standing expectantly at the fence, she mouthed a "Sorry!" at him. She no longer had time to pamper her favourite horse. The new Head Groom, Greg, had been on her back from the moment she had arrived at 8.36am - Helen knew it was 8.36 because Greg had set up a new scheme which involved Cameron standing at the gate noting the time each person arrived. All right, Helen knew she was late, but she couldn't help it that her alarm had failed to go off. Greg showed no sympathy, however, and even tore her off a strip in front of the other grooms.

Helen noticed Cameron smirking while she got her row. That's the last time I cover for him she thought, remembering the time she had protected him when he borrowed a horse overnight for his little brother's birthday party. The party had been a riot, despite a minor accident to Brimer's fetlock caused by a party popper. Their old Head Groom, Ross, had been puzzled the next day when he had to get a vet out to attend to the injury. Maybe Ross had been a bit too easy going, but all the grooms loved him, and at least you came to work with a smile on your face in the old days. Ross had more or less let Helen and the other experienced grooms get on with things, although he had kept a close eye on Lewis, the newest recruit, during his first few months at the stables. Many of the firm's customers had kept their horses at the stables for over 10 years, and you could tell from the frequent thank you cards the stables used to receive - they hardly got any nowadays - that the care they gave the horses was appreciated.

Everything had changed three months ago when the owner, Mr White, called a meeting of all the staff and told them that two longstanding customers had removed their horses from the stables because they felt they were not being cared for properly. Another customer had arrived unexpectedly at 4pm on a Friday to find that all the grooms had gone home. This not only broke health and safety regulations; it opened the firm to the possibility of being sued and having to pay damages for negligence. Mr White announced that he felt a stricter regime was needed and that Ross had tendered his resignation.

Greg arrived the following Monday and soon put his stamp on the business. He made Cameron Assistant Head Groom, which meant that he got a pay increase and the chance to boss Helen and the others about. After three weeks of watching their every movement, Greg had come up with a scheme he called 'Performance Enhancement'. In reality it was, in Helen's view, a way of subjecting them all to slavery. Their tea break time had been cut to no more than 20 minutes in any one shift and the maximum time they could take to groom a single horse was now limited to 30 minutes. So, no more quality time with Angus for Helen.

TOPIC 7. THE INTERNAL BUSINESS ENVIRONMENT TEST

At lunchtime, Helen chatted to one of the other grooms, Raza, about her feelings. Raza was, as usual, full of common sense and inspirational ideas. "If we all get together," he said, "we could stand up to Greg. Let's ask the others what they think."

Bill, the newest recruit, looked up from his copy of The Sun. "I'm game!" he exclaimed. "Don't ask me to do any of the planning though. I'm quite happy to get hold of anything you need and get messages to people if you want."

Sean put down his sandwich to chip in. "Look, folks, if we're going to do this, let's go about it in the right way. First of all, we need an action plan. Helen, give me a pen, and let's start gathering our thoughts. Right, what do we want to achieve from our protest?"

"Well," mused Helen, "getting treated like human beings might be a start!"

Mr White was astonished when the grooms, led by Sean, put their point of view to him. "But I thought everything was going so well! We haven't had a single complaint from customers since Greg started here," he said. "He is a first rate manager; he came highly recommended after seven years serving with the British Army in the Middle East. I am surprised that he is having problems managing you after being in charge of 100 soldiers!"

"You may not have had any complaints but we haven't had any thank you cards recently either. We know Greg is very efficient," Helen explained, "but we don't really enjoy our work like we used to. I used to get to decide how to do Angus's mane but now it has to be done exactly the way Greg says, or else."

"Yes, and now he's got Cameron backing up his every word," added Sean, somewhat bitterly. "That's why the seven of us have got together. After all, we've all worked here for years, so surely we must have some good ideas. I hope you don't mind, Mr White, but we've drawn up a list of our recommendations which we hope you'll consider."

As Mr White studied the list Sean put into his hand, Raza smiled at the others. Things were going to change, he was sure.

Q16: Describe the advantages and disadvantages of two different leadership styles using examples from the case study. *(10 marks)*

....

Q17: Describe the main features of the classical school of management. *(4 marks)*

....

Q18: Discuss the advantages and disadvantages of the classical school. Illustrate your answer with examples from the case study. *(6 marks)*

....

Q19: Discuss the factors that can help to make a team effective, using examples from the case study to support your answer. *(10 marks)*

....

Q20: Using a force field analysis, analyse whether the a stricter regime for staff should be introduced. *(10 marks)*

Researching a business

1	**Research**	**223**
	1.1 Importance of referencing	224
	1.2 When must I provide a citation?	224
	1.3 When do I not need to provide a citation?	226
	1.4 Plagiarism	227
	1.5 How to reference	227
	1.6 Verify sources of evidence	230
	1.7 Understand the reasons for using a bibliography	231
	1.8 Reference list for this topic	231
	1.9 Summary	232
	1.10 End of topic test	233
2	**Analytical research**	**235**
	2.1 Decision making	236
	2.2 Force field analysis	237
	2.3 SWOT analysis	239
	2.4 Critical path analysis (CPA)	242
	2.5 Gantt charts	244
	2.6 Summary	246
	2.7 End of topic test	247
3	**Evaluating financial information**	**249**
	3.1 Reported financial information	250
	3.2 Annual reports	254
	3.3 Other information	255
	3.4 Summary	256
	3.5 End of topic test	257

Unit 3 Topic 1

Research

Contents

1.1	Importance of referencing	224
1.2	When must I provide a citation?	224
1.3	When do I not need to provide a citation?	226
1.4	Plagiarism	227
1.5	How to reference	227
	1.5.1 Referencing tips	229
1.6	Verify sources of evidence	230
1.7	Understand the reasons for using a bibliography	231
1.8	Reference list for this topic	231
1.9	Summary	232
1.10	End of topic test	233

Learning objective

After studying this topic, you should be able to:

- understand the importance of referencing when presenting findings;
- give examples of how to reference work;
- discuss issues around plagiarism and acknowledging the work of others;
- verify sources of evidence;
- understand the reasons for using a bibliography.

1.1 Importance of referencing

Some material in this topic is reprinted from the 'Harvard Style Citing & Referencing Student Guide' with kind permission of Heriot-Watt University.

Citing and **referencing** allows you to acknowledge other peoples work. It also allows you to demonstrate that:

- you have gathered evidence to back up your ideas and arguments;
- you have used credible, good quality sources;
- you have read from a large number of sources;
- you have used sources that are appropriate to your level of study.

In addition, it allows your teacher to differentiate between your own work and the work of others and makes it easy for your teacher, and the SQA, to locate and verify the sources you have used.

There are many different ways to reference ideas within a formal piece of work. The SQA stipulate that you can use any referencing style as long as you are consistent throughout your report. In this scholar subject the **Harvard Reference style** will be explained.

1.2 When must I provide a citation?

A citation is an acknowledgement that you have included the research of others within your work. You need to cite your source whenever you:

- use ideas from other people in your work;
- refer to the work of another person;
- quote from a book or journal;
- use market research from government or others.

Direct quotes are needed when you use another person's ideas in their own words. If you include information exactly as it appears in a source you need to indicate this by using quotation marks.

Short quotes can be included within the paragraph of text using quotation marks. Long quotes should be treated as a separate block of text, indented from the left margin, as the example shows. Use p. to indicate a page number and pp. to indicate a range of pages.

TOPIC 1. RESEARCH

For example:

> "60% of those surveyed said that they had never heard of other Highland Spring products besides their bottled still water. This tells me that Highland Spring do not effectively advertise their variety of products. This means that they could lose out on additional profits due to their poor advertising of these other products." (Patterson 2014, p.34)

Paraphrasing is when you present another person's ideas in your own words but without the need for quotation marks as you are not quoting directly. Using the example above, the paragraph below has been paraphrased. Its meaning is the same as the original paragraph and so a citation must be provided:

> More than half of the people surveyed had never heard of other Highland Spring products besides their bottled still water. This could imply that the company does not effectively advertise their full product range resulting in additional products being less profitable. (Patterson 2014, p.34)

Summarising is when you express another person's ideas using less words. The following example shows a passage from a book that has been shortened. Its meaning, however, is the same as the original, requiring a citation.

Original:

> The Homeplus Group started in 1999 as a hypermarket only business and today operates as a multichannel retailer. The Homeplus Group operates online and through 1,075 outlets, of which 140 are hypermarkets, 609 are supermarkets and 326 are convenience stores (the supermarkets and convenience stores being a mixture of directly owned and franchised). It also operates 139 shopping malls adjacent to its hypermarkets, with over 6,500 tenant leases. (Tesco news release (http://www.tescoplc.com/index.asp?pageid=17&newsid=1209) [Last accessed September 2015]).

Summary:

> The Homeplus Group have operated for over 15 years and operate a number of outlets, consisting of hypermarkets, superstores and convenience stores. (Tesco news release (http://bit.ly/1iOauA2) [Last accessed September 2015]).

Asda Go online

The following article extract comes from the Asda press centre (http://bit.ly/1jLoyvc) :

> Speaking at an event in London this morning, Asda President and CEO of Asda, Andy Clarke reiterated his commitment to the company's five year strategy to redefine value retailing in a challenging market.
>
> He stated that while there were signs of 'real and sustainable economic recovery' 2015 was proving to be the most challenging year yet for traditional supermarkets.
>
> Joined by Chief Financial Officer Alex Russo, they spoke about the pace and scale of change in the market and customer behaviours, while highlighting a solid, balanced Asda business.
>
> Clarke commented: "This last quarter has been unprecedented. We have seen deflation in the market and exponential shifts in the industry. Although I still believe that 18 months ago we did a great job of predicting changes, we could not have foreseen what's happened to others and the moves they have had to make in order to restore their business - creating an impact on us in the short-term."

Answer the following questions relating to the above article and include a citation in your answer.

Q1: Provide a direct quote to demonstrate Asda did a good job 18 months ago.

....

Q2: Create a paraphrased version of the extract to demonstrate the job Asda did 18 months ago.

1.3 When do I not need to provide a citation?

You do not need to provide a citation when you are expressing your own ideas, arguments or conclusions or where you have created a survey yourself and are reporting the results.

You should provide a citation when you are including information in your report that you have found in your secondary research, for example:

> Glasgow is in the west of Scotland and has a population of approximately 593,000. (Area profiles on Scotland's Census, available online: (http://www.scotlandscensus.gov.uk/ods-web/area.html) [accessed 28 July 2015])

TOPIC 1. RESEARCH

1.4 Plagiarism

The definition of **plagiarism** is using someone else's work and letting people think that it is your own. If you do not reference other people's ideas or quotes you may be accused of plagiarism. It is the equivalent of stealing, often referred to as academic theft. To avoid plagiarism you should always note accurately and fully the details of all the sources you use.

If you follow the correct referencing methods in this topic then you should avoid allegations of plagiarism. Be careful also that you do not give your work out to others - if they then copy your work you could be accused of plagiarism of their work.

SQA marking

Your teacher is used to your writing style, and can quickly tell if you have taken information from a book or the internet without referencing. The SQA employ teachers to mark your work. They have been marking for a number of years and are used to reading hundreds of Business Management essays. They can quickly spot a source that has not been referenced.

Marking is carried out electronically. SQA have anti-plagiarism software that can highlight any source that has been used but not referenced.

The flyleaf that accompanies your Advanced Higher Business Management report will require that you sign a declaration to say that the work you are submitting is your own. That doesn't just mean that you did all the work yourself, it also means that the work you are submitting contains the appropriate citations.

1.5 How to reference

There are a number of ways to reference your work. Any type of referencing is acceptable in your report as long as you are consistent throughout it. A popular method is Harvard referencing, whose origins come from the American University of the same name. The system traces back to the eminent zoologist Edward Laurens Mark (1847-1946), Hersey professor of anatomy and director of Harvard's zoological laboratory until his retirement in 1921. (Chernin, Eli (1988). The 'Harvard system': a mystery dispelled, British Medical Journal. October 22, 1988, pp. 1062-1063).

Citations can appear within the text, at the end of a sentence or as a footnote at the bottom of the page. The same citation, with more information, should also be included in the bibliography at the end of the report.

In-text citations

In-text citations appear in the body of your work. In-text citations from a book or printed publication must provide the following information in order:

- the name of the author(s) or editor(s) of the source being cited;
- the publication date (year) of the source being cited;
- the page numbers you have taken material from.

The following text includes an example of a in-text citation:

> With reference to capacities, Japan has a range of resources considered 'desirable' (Klein, Nicholls, & Thomalla, 2003, p.34), that contribute to them being one of the pioneers in the prevention of environmental disasters having an impact on the nation.

Bibliography

You must take a note of the name of the book, or publication, and the publisher as this information needs to be added to the bibliography. Remember, the point of referencing is to allow the reader, in your case your examiner, to check your source.

The order of information that you need for a bibliography entry is as follows:

- surname(s) of author(s) and the initial(s) of their first name(s);
- publication date (year);
- book title;
- book edition (where the book is beyond the 1st edition);
- place of publication (town/city);
- publisher name;
- page numbers you have taken information from (if a direct quote or a diagram, picture, etc.).

One example of a bibliography entry is as follows (note that this example does not include a book edition or place of publication):

> Wing, L., & Gould, J. (1979). Severe impairments of social interaction and associated abnormalities in children: epidemiology and classification. Journal of Autism and Developmental Disorders, 9, pp. 11-29.

Website references

Text taken from websites is referenced in a similar way to books, for example:

> Trefis Team (2018, April 26). Core Brands And Healthy Portfolio Drive Growth For Coca-Cola. Retrieved August 1, 2018, from https://www.forbes.com/sites/greatspeculations/2018/04/26/core-brands-and-healthy-portfolio-drive-growth-for-coca-cola/#74a55164380a.

The above example includes the author name, date of publication, page title, date retrieved, and full URL of the website. With websites, it is important to include the date you last accessed the site, as the content of the website could change between you writing your essay and the report being marked.

So, these citations within some text:

> Autism is held to be a "lifelong developmental disability" (The National Autistic Society, 2010), and is considered to be a neuro-developmental disorder (Trevarthen, 2000)...

would be added to the reference list as:

TOPIC 1. RESEARCH 229

> The National Autistic Society (2010). Autism: What is it? Retrieved January 8, 2010, from http://www.nas.org.uk/nas/jsp/polopoly.jsp?d=211.
>
> Trevarthen, C. (2000). Autism as a neurodevelopmental disorder affecting communication and learning in early childhood: Prenatal origins, post natal course and effective educational support. Prostoglandins, Leucotrines and Essential Fatty Acids, 63 (1-2), pp. 41-46.

Much of the information you gather for your assignment is likely to come from online news stories with no author. An example of such as source is referenced as:

> BBC (2015) Monsoon tops minimum wage list of shame [online], available: http://www.bbc.co.uk/news/business-34608028 [accessed 25 October 2015]

You can reference the above citation in your project as, for example, "A BBC report (2015) says..."

Online journals

An increasing number of journals can be freely accessed online. Google Scholar (https://scholar.google.co.uk/) is one way to find online articles or books that you may wish to included as part of your research. They are cited and referenced in the same way as paper book and online web pages. For example:

> Taylor, FW (2004) 'Scientific Management' Routledge [online], available: https://books.google.co.uk/books?id=AuLgsZJgSCsC&dq=scientific+management&lr= [accessed 25 October 2015]

Provide a reference　　　　　　　　　　　　　　　　　　　　　　　　　　**Go online**

Q3: Provide a reference for the ASDA example (http://bit.ly/1jLoyvc) cited in the previous section:

1.5.1 Referencing tips

When referencing authors:

- one author is straightforward as, for example, Klein, A., 2003, p. 34;
- two or three authors are written as, for example, Klein, Nicholls, & Thomalla, 2003, p. 34;
- four or more authors are written as, for example, Klein et al, 2003, p. 34.

It doesn't matter whether you use full stops after initials or write p 34 or p.34 - as long as you are consistent throughout.

Make sure you take a note of all the information you need at the time. Finding a great source is brilliant and will improve your report, but you might not be able to use it if you do not take a note of the information needed for the reference and cannot find the original source again later.

© HERIOT-WATT UNIVERSITY

A big tip is to write the reference list as you write your report. Unlike your National 5 and Higher Business Management reports, that were researched in class and then written up in timed exam conditions, your Advanced Higher report should be written by you throughout the year, with minimum help from your teacher.

Modern Microsoft Word programs allow you to build your reference list (they call it a bibliography) as you write your report and lets you use the Harvard style. Microsoft Office has a helpful guide (http://bit.ly/1viYA49) on its website.

You will not be asked about referencing or plagiarism in your final exam, but you will lose marks in your assignment if you do not follow the advice in this guide. Remember, it is important to reference to acknowledge your source - failing to do this (and as a result implying that a piece of work is your own) could result in zero marks being awarded.

Cold calling   Go online

Q4: Using the Microsoft Word guide and the following three web sources, type up a short paragraph on cold calling:

- The BBC website (http://bbc.in/1jFw6zx)
- The Guardian website (http://bit.ly/1ihFZSr)
- Cold calling techniques (https://bit.ly/2OycZr8)

Use each of the links at least once to create a Harvard Style bibliography. Don't spend too long finding quotes, the challenge here is to create a reference list.

1.6 Verify sources of evidence

As the saying goes, don't believe everything you read in the newspapers. The same is true for the internet; just because it is written down does not mean that it is true. When you find something online, it is worth checking how valid the information is.

Can the source be trusted? Popular news sources, such as the BBC, Guardian and Telegraph have to make sure they conform to press standards. That should mean that they have verified information before putting it online or in print. Be careful, they occasionally get it wrong! Be wary of editorials - these are opinion pieces written by journalists and therefore may be biased.

PLCs, by law, are required to publish accurate information about their sales, profits and future plans. These sources should be trusted. (There are some exceptions - search the internet for the story of the Tesco executes who falsified profit predictions. They got caught and no longer work for Tesco!)

Wikipedia is an increasingly popular website where information is crowdsourced meaning that anyone can add to it. This means that the information is current. It can also mean that false information can be added, but the army of loyal supporters usually catch this and remove it quickly. It is especially useful for your research as good articles will cite where they got their information from (using the Harvard style!) so you can click on the citation to find the original source of the text.

Using good keywords and a popular search engine can also help find useful information. Search engines like Google work by putting the most useful site at the top. The more a website is referenced (linked to) by another website, the higher the Google ranking. When you search, the site at the top are the ones that have been cited lots by others. Just watch out for the paid for adverts!

1.7 Understand the reasons for using a bibliography

A bibliography is similar to a reference list. In fact, the both look exactly the same. A reference list appears first and includes, in alphabetical order of author, a comprehensive list of every source that you have referenced within the text.

A bibliography, if required, would follow. It looks the exact same as the reference list, but includes any texts or websites that you have read, but not directly sourced within the report. It is used to show a wide range of reading.

Both are used to make it easy for the marker to locate the source, if required.

Example bibliography:

> Arayici, Y., Coates, L., Koskela, L., Kagioglou, M., Usher, C and O'Reilly, K. (2011). BIM
>
> Adoption and Implementation for Architectural Practices. Structural Survey. 29 (1), pp. 7-25.
>
> ASHRAE. (2010) An Introduction to Building Information Modeling (BIM). A Guide for ASHRAE Members.
>
> Azhar, Salman. (2011) Building Information Modeling for Sustainable Design and LEED Rating Analysis. Automation in Construction. 20 (2), pp. 217-224.
>
> Bausch, J. (2011). 7 Important Renewable Energy Sources. Available: http://tinyurl.com/4yqbbbv. Last accessed 30th Jan 2012.
>
> Bernstein, P. (2007). Building Information Modeling for Sustainable Design. Environmental Design + Construction. 10 (12), pp. 1-2.

1.8 Reference list for this topic

Earlier in this chapter we referred to the Heriot-Watt citing and reference guide. This guide would be referenced as:

> Heriot-Watt University Information Services (2015). Harvard Style Citing & Referencing Student Guide. Retrieved October 6, 2015 from http://www.hw.ac.uk/is/docs/Harvardguide.pdf.

Please note that the Heriot-Watt web link to the Harvard guide no longer works.

1.9 Summary

Summary

You should now be able to:

- understand the importance of referencing when presenting findings;
- give examples of how to reference work;
- discuss issues around plagiarism and acknowledging the work of others;
- verify sources of evidence;
- understand the reasons for using a bibliography.

1.10 End of topic test

End of Topic 1 test   Go online

Q5: Which of the following is *not* a reason for referencing?

a) It is used to demonstrate that you have gathered evidence to back up your ideas and arguments.
b) It is used to demonstrate that you have used credible, good quality sources.
c) It is used to demonstrate that you have read from a small number of sources.
d) It is used to demonstrate that you have used sources that are appropriate to your level of study.

....

Q6: Presenting your own ideas but using another person's work you should: *(you can choose more than one option)*

a) quote directly.
b) paraphrase.
c) cite.
d) summarise.

....

Q7: Identify the errors in the following references:

1. Aldrich, D. The Crucial Role of Civil Society in Disaster Recovery and Japans Preparedness for Emergencies. Japan akuell, 1-12. (2008).
2. P M Bermejo (2006). Preparation and Response in Case of Natural Disasters: Cuban Programs and Experience. Journal of Public Health Policy, V.27, 13-21.
3. Garrett, L. (2000). Betrayal of the Trust: The Collapse of Global Public Health. New York: Hyperion. ppp

(3 marks)

Unit 3 Topic 2

Analytical research

Contents

2.1 Decision making 236
2.2 Force field analysis 237
2.3 SWOT analysis 239
2.4 Critical path analysis (CPA) 242
    2.4.1 Identifying the critical path for a strategy 243
    2.4.2 Usefulness of critical path analysis (CPA) 243
2.5 Gantt charts 244
2.6 Summary 246
2.7 End of topic test 247

Learning objective

After studying this topic, you should be able to:

- prepare, describe and analyse a:
    - force-field diagram;
    - SWOT analysis;
    - Gantt chart.
- describe and analyse a critical path.

2.1 Decision making

Businesses must make informed decisions in order to best plan for the future. The more informed a decision, the higher chance of success. Management is about making decisions.

There are processes that managers should go through to make sure that they are making the best decision to achieve the organisational goals. Organisational goals are the targets that have been set by the senior management for the organisation to achieve.

Some decisions are very easy to make and may have little or no impact on anything else, e.g. creating a staff rota or ordering stationery. These are routine decisions that a business wouldn't normally have to spend a long time thinking about.

Some decisions take a little longer to make, e.g. deciding how to pay for new premises. This will involve some budgeting decisions in order that the business can save money. Many decisions will now be influenced by your aim to purchase new premises.

Other decisions may be about what the business wants to do in the future, e.g. deciding on the business's five-year strategy or changing the mission statement. These decisions may take some time to make, and businesses don't make them very often.

Management decisions

Managers are paid to make decisions which influence the running of the business. Some examples of business decisions that managers may have to make include:

- whether or not to recruit more staff. More staff will cost the business money, but a lack of staff could affect customer supplies, and so lose business.
- new product development. Managers have to decide whether the cost of development will be too high, or if the company risk losing customers in the long run by not developing a new product.
- merging with a competitor. A decision to merge two businesses must be carefully considered. Is it the right thing to do? How will customers react? Will the existing cultures clash?
- moving into new markets. This involves great risks, but also great rewards. Is their enough finance in place? Will the business cope with the increase in demand?

Managers must make decisions from a number of different options. Effective decisions are those decisions which will achieve the desired goals or aims of the organisation.

To aid decision making, a business can carry out a number of research techniques, such as:

- **force-field diagram**;
- **SWOT analysis**;
- **critical path**;
- **Gantt chart**.

The purpose of these techniques is to assist with planning and to ensure that the business is fully prepared before making a decision.

Merlin

Go online

Q1: Merlin, owners of Lego Land and Alton Towers, currently has five attractions in China, with Madame Tussauds in Shanghai, Hong Kong, Beijing, and Wuhan, and the Chang Feng Ocean World aquarium in Shanghai.

It plans to open another three in the next year and a half.

Identify the decisions the Board of Directors need to make to ensure further openings are successful.

2.2 Force field analysis

A business may produce a force field analysis before implementing a decision. We looked at force field diagrams in detail in the previous subject, *The internal business environment*. You may wish to reread the force field analysis section in Topic 5 ('Managing change') before attempting the following revision activity.

Advantages of force field analysis:

- lots of evidence is used so that an informed decisions can be made;
- assets for change are included so it useful to see what the organisation already has that can enable the decision to happen.

Disadvantages of force field analysis:

- it is a static tool;
- it is out of date as soon as it is produced;
- it is subjective.

Force field analysis   Go online

Q2: Put the following headings into the correct area (red box) in the force field analysis diagram below:

- Assets for change;
- Drivers;
- Equilibrium;
- Resistors.

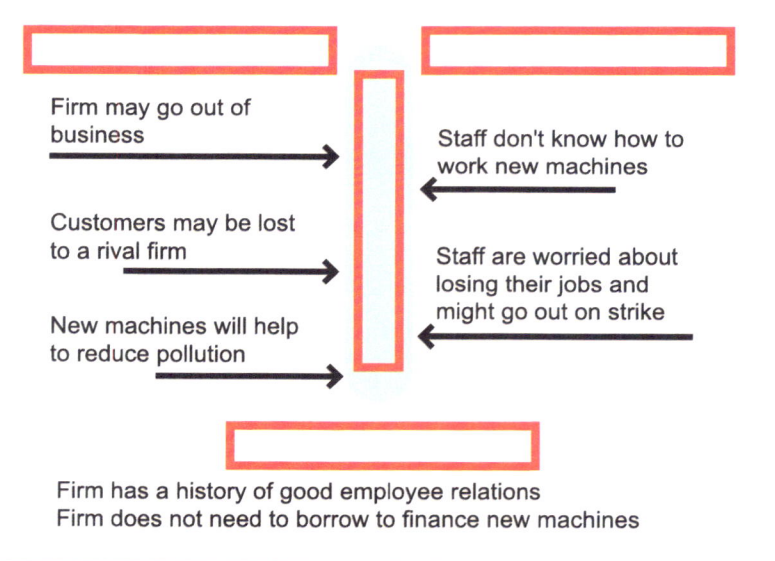

[ ]

Firm may go out of business →

Customers may be lost to a rival firm →

New machines will help to reduce pollution →

← Staff don't know how to work new machines

← Staff are worried about losing their jobs and might go out on strike

[ ]

Firm has a history of good employee relations
Firm does not need to borrow to finance new machines

Dairy Crest - case study

Britain's biggest dairy firm Dairy Crest is to sell its diaries operations to European giant Muller before the end of 2015, dependent on approval from competition authorities. The agreement between Dairy Crest and Müller is for Dairy Crest to sell its dairies operations, in its entirety and with its supporting overhead structure to Müller for £80 million, payable in cash, on completion.

On 26 June 2015 the CMA (Competition and Markets Authority) announced that there were reasonable grounds for believing that undertakings offered by Müller may address the CMA's competition concerns and has invited comments from third parties on its proposal to accept. Dairy Crest had just reported its half-year results showing revenue at the firm was up £10 million on the same period last year to £682 million.

Mark Allen, chief executive of Dairy Crest, said:

"This proposed sale is a great opportunity for our two companies, our farmers, our staff, our customers and consumers. The combination of our Dairies operations with those of Müller Wiseman Dairies will create efficiencies and economies of scale that will help to create a more sustainable UK dairy sector that is better placed to compete on the global stage.

"The disposal will allow Dairy Crest to focus on continuing to grow our successful and innovative branded cheese and spreads operations. We are confident that this focus will deliver further medium term profit growth for our shareholders."

Dairy Crest will retain full ownership of some previously closed dairies and will continue to consult with employees on the site's future. The two companies will also enter into a supply agreement whereby Müller Wiseman Dairies will sell bulk butter to Dairy Crest for five years. In addition, Dairy Crest will provide certain transitional services to Müller Wiseman Dairies.

Dairy Crest has dairies at Frome, in Somerset and at Stonehouse, Gloucestershire, plus a dairy at Chard in Somerset which was already under threat of closure. Dairy Crest will continue to meet the defined benefit pension obligations in relation to the Dairy Crest Pension Scheme.

Source: Western Daily Press, 2015

Q3: Using a force field analysis, justify Dairy Crest's decision to sell its dairies to Muller Wiseman. In your answer you must show at least two drivers, two resistors, one asset for change and arrows of different lengths facing inwards.

2.3 SWOT analysis

SWOT analysis is a tool that management can use to help with decision making. It is used to evaluate where the organisation is now and where it should be in the future. It helps with planning, deciding the way forward for the organisation and looking at strategies which could be used.

SWOT analysis is a tool that can be effectively used for any decision making, however, it is most often used when making strategic and tactical decisions. SWOT analysis should not be seen as a one off exercise; it should be part of the continuing process of evaluating how the organisation is doing now and what it should be doing in the future. It should be considered from the organisation's own point of view and from the point of view of the people they deal with. It is important to be honest and realistic.

A SWOT analysis is often presented in a table such as the one below.

Strengths	Weaknesses
• internal areas where the organisation performs well	• internal areas where the organisations performs poorly
Opportunities	**Threats**
• external areas in which the organisation could be involved in the future	• external areas which pose a threat to the organisation, e.g. competitors, government, changes in the economy

SWOT analysis table

SWOT analysis considers all internal factors (strengths and weaknesses) and external factors (opportunities and threats).

Strengths

The following questions should be considered:

- What advantages do you have?
- What do you do well?
- What relevant resources do you have access to?
- What do other people see as your strengths?

In looking at strengths, the organisation should think about them in relation to its competitors - for example, if all the competitors sell at low prices, then competitive low pricing is not a strength in the market, it is a necessity.

Weaknesses

The following questions should be considered:

- What could you improve?
- What do you do badly?
- What should you avoid?

Again, this should be considered from an internal and external basis.

Opportunities

The following questions should be considered:

- What changes have taken place in technology and markets on both a broad and narrow scale?
- What changes in government policy related to your field?

TOPIC 2. ANALYTICAL RESEARCH

- What changes have there been in social patterns, population profiles, lifestyle changes, etc.?
- What local events are taking place?
- Has there been a positive upturn in the economy?

A useful approach to looking at opportunities is to look at the strengths and ask whether these open up any opportunities. Alternatively, look at weaknesses and ask whether the organisation could open up opportunities by eliminating them.

Threats

The following questions should be considered:

- What obstacles do you face?
- What is your competition doing?
- Are the required specifications for your job, products or services changing?
- Is changing technology threatening your position?
- Do you have bad debt or cash-flow weakness?
- Could any of your weaknesses seriously threaten your business?

SWOT analysis - Dairy Crest   Go online

Q4: Carry out a SWOT analysis of your school with your classmates and then share your findings with your class.

Using a SWOT analysis, you can:

- understand your business better;
- address weaknesses;
- deter threats;
- capitalise on opportunities;
- take advantage of your strengths;
- develop business goals and strategies for achieving them.

Disadvantages of a SWOT analysis include that it:

- is a static analysis;
- doesn't prioritise issues;
- doesn't provide solutions or offer alternative decisions;
- can generate too many ideas but not help you choose which one is best.

© HERIOT-WATT UNIVERSITY

2.4 Critical path analysis (CPA)

Critical path analysis (CPA) is another way of planning and monitoring the implementation of a strategy. CPA starts by:

- identifying each of the activities needed to complete a project;
- calculating the time that will be taken by each activity;
- working out which activities can be done simultaneously;
- identifying which activities cannot start until others have been completed;
- putting the activities in order.

Carrying out a critical path analysis helps keep a project to time. It also allows all members of the team to complete in the planning of the project, and can help identify where time, and therefore financial, savings can be met.

The critical path is the sequence of activities which, when added together, give the total length the project is expected to take. This determines how long a project will last. If there is any delay on the critical path (called "slippage"), the whole project will be delayed.

Businesses who plan will avoid unnecessary delays. For example, completing work simultaneously will shorten the overall length of the project. It may be possible however to delay activities not on the critical path without delaying the final completion of the project.

The critical path is shown in diagrammatic form. The diagram below shows a simple example of a network used for critical path analysis:

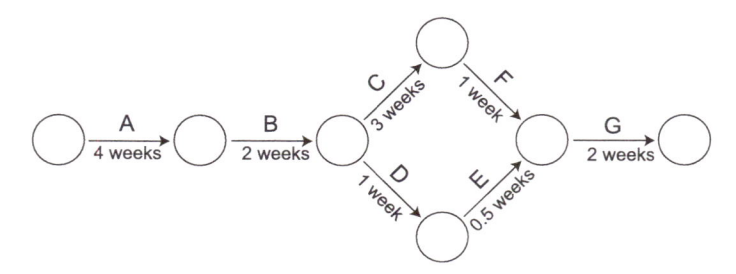

Example of a network used for critical path analysis

Extra time that is available for particular activities not on the critical path is called **float time**. In the diagram above tasks D and E carry 2.5 weeks of float time between them.

Critical path analysis (CPA)   Go online

Q5: In the above diagram, how long is the project expected to last?

TOPIC 2. ANALYTICAL RESEARCH

2.4.1 Identifying the critical path for a strategy

A college's strategy is to build a new extension equipped with computers to accommodate increased demand for IT courses. The college works out that the tasks in the table below are needed need to implement the strategy.

A	Choose a building firm	1 week
B	Erect the new building	12 weeks
C	Install plumbing	4 weeks
D	Install electricity	5 weeks
E	Decorate the building	3 weeks
F	Install shelving for computers	3 weeks
G	Order computers	8 weeks
H	Install computers	2 weeks

Identifying the critical path for a strategy Go online

Q6: Which of these tasks depend on other tasks being completed first?

....

Q7: Which of these tasks do not depend on others being completed first?

....

Q8: Which of these tasks could be done simultaneously?

2.4.2 Usefulness of critical path analysis (CPA)

The advantages of CPA are that it:

- helps reduce the risk and costs of complex projects;
- encourages careful assessment of the requirements of each activity in a project;
- helps spot which activities have some slack ("float") and could lead to reallocation / better allocation of resources;
- provides managers with a useful overview of a complex project.

The disadvantages of CPA are that:

- the reliability of CPA largely based on accurate estimates and assumptions made;
- CPA does not guarantee the success of a project - that still needs to be managed properly.

2.5 Gantt charts

Gantt charts were invented by Henry Gantt, a writer in the classical school of management that you learned about in **The internal business environment**. They are still widely used to schedule projects in modern businesses. They are basically bar charts displaying the different activities involved in a project along with how long they will take. The bars are coloured in as each activity is completed so that progress can easily be checked at any time.

Steps to create a Gantt chart:

1. Identify each different activity that needs to be done to implement the strategy.
2. Decide how much time each activity will take.
3. Decide the order in which the activities must be done.
4. Create a table or a spreadsheet.
5. Key in days, weeks or months as appropriate across the top.
6. Write each activity that will need to be done down the left hand side.
7. For each activity, draw a rectangular box from the start time to the end time.
8. Check that every activity appears on the chart.

Gantt charts are similar to critical path analysis, in that both techniques chart the progress of a project over a period of time. Gantt charts are updated as the project develops, which makes them more helpful to some.

Here is the same project as before, shown as a Gantt chart:

	Week 1	Week 2	Week 3	Week 4	Week 5	Week 6	Week 7	Week 8	Week 9	Week 10	Week 11
Find new suppliers	■	■	■	■	■	■	■				
Identify outlets	■	■	■	■							
Decide on price					■						
Arrange promotion						■	■	■			
Install new equipment								■	■		
Train staff									■	■	
Launch product											◇

Incomplete Gantt chart for project

Some Gantt charts have an actual row below each projected row, to record real progress.

As each activity is completed the relevant part of the chart is shaded in. The chart can be displayed on the wall as a clear indication of what has been done and whether the project is ahead of time or

TOPIC 2. ANALYTICAL RESEARCH

delayed. Managers can then decide how to use any extra time profitably, or identify ways to make up for lost time.

The Gantt chart below shows where the project should be at week 6.

	Week 1	Week 2	Week 3	Week 4	Week 5	Week 6	Week 7	Week 8	Week 9	Week 10	Week 11
Find new suppliers											
Identify outlets											
Decide on price											
Arrange promotion											
Install new equipment											
Train staff											
Launch product											

Gantt chart showing project at week 6

Gantt chart advantages   Go online

Q9: Complete the paragraphs below using the following words:

- activities;
- delay;
- depend;
- focus;
- implement;
- progress;
- simultaneously;
- targets.

Creating a Gantt chart helps managers and employees to .... on the steps necessary to .... the strategy successfully. The charts help managers to see which tasks can be done .... and which .... on other tasks being done first.

Updating the chart by shading in .... as they are completed helps to spot any .... before it becomes serious. They can be displayed on the wall so that everyone involved can see the .... made and what still needs to be done to achieve ....

Gantt chart   Go online

Q10: Imagine you are putting on a concert at school with bands from your year taking part. Create a Gantt chart detailing the planning of the event.

2.6 Summary

Summary

You should now be able to:

- prepare, describe and analyse a:
    - force-field diagram;
    - SWOT analysis;
    - Gantt chart.
- describe and analyse a critical path.

2.7 End of topic test

End of Topic 2 test   Go online

HSBC describes itself as a global investor with local knowledge. Senior managers recently threatened to move its headquarters out of the UK (http://bit.ly/1kQRMZK) amid concerns over excessive tax. Reports suggest that it sees the USA as a more suitable home, with its similar language and business style. According to the Financial Times, the bank is concerned that moving to the Far East could see it end up in the hands of the Chinese.

The systems of banking regulation in the North America appeals to HSBC and the country would easily be able to handle a financial firm of its size - HSBC handles $2.6 trillion worth of assets.

Douglas Flint, HSBC's chairman, told the FT the bank was "about halfway through the process" of looking into moving its HQ and had "prepared the ground by giving presentations to the board on the various aspects, like the regulatory and economic framework, but we have not had any discussion of the relative merits".

In the contrary, Mr Flint recently gave a lecture in London (http://bit.ly/1POLuqf) on the future of banking in China, in which he welcomed the opportunities the country presents for growth as it opens up its markets to the world. Given the size of HSBC's profits from the region and its historic links to the country, Hong Kong is still thought to be the leading alternative to London.

One factor pushing the bank to consider moving is the bank levy, a British tax introduced in 2010 that targets UK-based banks' global balance sheets. As a highly globalised bank, this hit HSBC harder than any of its rivals.

In Chancellor George Osborne's emergency budget earlier this year, he said he would cut back the levy and introduce an 8% corporation tax surcharge on UK profits instead - a move aimed at encouraging HSBC to stay.

"The UK's made some changes to the tax framework which we think are positive to the structure of taxing banks in the UK," Mr Flint said after the changes were announced. But he warned (http://bit.ly/1MpvHOc) that while the change "comes into the mix, it is not determinative".

HSBC is due to make a decision on whether to relocate from the UK by the end of the year.

Source: The Telegraph (http://www.telegraph.co.uk/finance/newsbysector/epic/hsba/)

Q11: Analyse HSBC's decision to move from the UK to the USA or China. Your answer must include a force field diagram. *(8 marks)*

....

Q12: Using the case study and additional internet research, carry out a SWOT analysis for HSBC bank. *(4 marks)*

Unit 3 Topic 3

Evaluating financial information

Contents

3.1 Reported financial information 250
    3.1.1 Ratio analysis 250
    3.1.2 Profitability ratios 250
    3.1.3 Liquidity ratios 251
    3.1.4 Efficiency ratios 252
    3.1.5 Ratio analysis - a worked example 253
    3.1.6 Limitations of ratio analysis 253
3.2 Annual reports 254
3.3 Other information 255
3.4 Summary 256
3.5 End of topic test 257

Learning objective

After studying this topic, you should be able to reach conclusions from:

- reported financial information;
- annual reports;
- government statistics;
- market data;
- customers surveys.

3.1 Reported financial information

Public limited companies are required by law to prepare and publish final accounts at the end of their financial period. This can be the end of the calendar year, the end of the financial year or any time of the business' choosing. The only proviso is that the date must be the same every year.

These final accounts give a historical record for that financial period. The management of the business will be interested in seeing whether the business has improved on last year's performance, has performed better than competitors or what problem areas are there for further investigation.

A wide range of stakeholders will also be interested in the business performance, including prospective investors.

3.1.1 Ratio analysis

To enhance the information given by the final accounts, a business will carry out ratio analysis. Further investigation on the financial performance will be based on the following aspects of the business:

1. **profitability**;
2. **liquidity**;
3. **efficiency**.

Ratio analysis gives further information on the business performance over a financial period. It can also:

- compare a business performance over two time periods;
- compare business performance with that of a competitor;
- compare budgeted and actual performance;
- investigate areas where the business is not performing.

Ratio analysis is a useful tool used by a business to investigate further the financial performance of the business. The ratios in themselves are meaningless unless they are used as a comparison with previous years' figures (inter-firm comparison), the figures of a competitor in the same industry (intra-firm comparison) or as a measure of actual performance against forecasted prediction figures produced by the business. To reach conclusions on the basis of reported financial information a business must analyse the data to draw comparisons, both from one year to the next and with comparable organisations.

3.1.2 Profitability ratios

Profitability ratios will analyse the profit-making capacity of the business and whether the business has met its objectives. We are interested in two profitability ratios:

TOPIC 3. EVALUATING FINANCIAL INFORMATION

- gross profit as a percentage of sales;
- net profit as a percentage of sales.

Gross profit as a percentage of sales is used to calculate the gross profit as a percentage of sales turnover. A high percentage may indicate that the business has an efficient buying policy, or high selling price compared to the purchase price of materials.

Changes in the ratio can be caused by:

- an increase or a decrease in the selling price (usually a deliberate company policy), or;
- a change in the cost of goods sold (usually outwith the company's control).

The formula used is *(gross profit / sales) x 100%*.

Net profit as a percentage of sales is used to calculate what percentage of their sales they have turned into net profit. Where a low figure is calculated, this shows that the company's expenses may be high and should be further investigated. This ratio is often used to highlight efficiency and control of costs.

The formula used is *(net profit / sales)* $\times$ *100%*.

Profitability ratios   Go online

Q1: For both years, work out the gross profit as a percentage of sales and net profit as a percentage of sales, based on the information given:

- Gross profit - £250,000 in Year 1 and £300,000 in Year 2;
- Net profit - £100,000 in Year 1 and £110,000 in Year 2;
- Sales - £450,000 in Year 1 and £500,000 in Year 2.

3.1.3 Liquidity ratios

Liquidity ratios analyse how the business has performed over the time period in the use of its assets and the control of its debts. The two ratios used are **current ratios** and **acid test ratios**.

The **current ratio** is used to show the business's ability to meet its short-term debts. There is no ideal figure for this ratio although it should normally fall within the region of 1:1 and 3:1.

Where the ratio is very low, this indicates that the business may have liquidity problems. Where the ratio is high this indicates that there is more than enough money to cover short-term business debts, however, it can also indicate that there is too much cash in the business not being used to best advantage. Spare cash can be invested, even in the short-term, and earn additional income for the business.

The formula used is *current ratio = current assets:current liabilities*.

The **acid test ratio** is similar to the current ratio although it takes into account the fact that stocks of raw materials and goods for resale can often take some time to be turned into cash. The business's ability to pay its short-term debts is therefore looked at without including stock.

The average figure of 1:1 should be used as a guideline although anything less than this would show that the business may not be able to meet its short-term debts without selling stock or borrowing money. However, some types of businesses can operate with an acid test ratio of less than 1:1 so the typical ratio will depend on the type of business.

The formula used is *acid test ratio = (current assets - stock):current liabilities*.

Liquidity ratios Go online

Q2: For both years, work out the current ratio and acid test ratio, based on the information given:

- Current assets - £1,500,000 in Year 1 and £1,700,000 in Year 2;
- Current liabilities - £800,000 in Year 1 and £750,000 in Year 2;
- Stock at end - 600,000 in Year 1 and 800,000 in Year 2.

3.1.4 Efficiency ratios

Efficiency ratios analyse how easily a business can meet its debts. The current assets and current liabilities are analysed here.

Return on capital employed (ROCE) is a ratio which is expressed as a percentage. ROCE measures how well, or how badly, a business has utilised the capital (money invested by the owner) that has been invested in it. This gives a more useful interpretation of performance than merely looking at the profit figure.

When you invest money in a bank, you will probably pick the one with the best interest rates. The concept is similar here. The owner(s) want to know how much their investment will earn in percentage terms.

One business might return a profit of £50,000 based on capital employed of £100,000, while another may have a profit of £100,000 on an investment of £500,000. Although the second business has a higher profit figure, the first business provides a much better return for each £1 invested.

The formula used is *return on capital employed = (net profit / capital employed) $\times$ 100%*.

Efficiency ratios Go online

Q3: For both years, work out the return on capital employed (ROCE), based on the information given:

- Gross profit - £250,000 in Year 1 and £300,000 in Year 2;
- Capital employed - £1,000,000 in Year 1 and £1,110,000 in Year 2.

TOPIC 3. EVALUATING FINANCIAL INFORMATION 253

3.1.5 Ratio analysis - a worked example

Ratio analysis - a worked example   Go online

The table below shows statistics from a company's annual report.

	Year 2 (in £)	Year 1 (in £)
Revenue (sales)	7,000m	6,300m
Net profit	700m	970m
Current assets	10,000m	12,000m
Current liabilities	14,300m	10,900m
Capital employed	5,500m	6,000m
Share price	1.75	2.03

Q4: Using these statistics, complete the table below.

	Year 2	Year 1
Net profit as a percentage of sales		
Current ratio		
Return on capital employed		
Share price (in £)	1.75	2.03

....

Q5: Give your analysis of the business based on the above statistics and your answer to the previous question.

3.1.6 Limitations of ratio analysis

Ratio analysis can highlight potential issues, but it does not provide detail or answers. The limitations of ratio analysis are:

- the information is historical and becomes out of date quickly which means borrowing decisions may not be based on current need;
- comparison has to be made with previous years' performance or predicted performance - ratios are meaningless on their own;
- comparison must also be made with similar businesses of the same size in the same industry - this can be difficult to predicate as you will not be aware of the unreported reasons for a competitors increase or decrease in fortune;

© HERIOT-WATT UNIVERSITY

- different businesses may not calculate ratios in the same way, making comparison difficult;
- if used for comparison purposes it is imperative that businesses prepare their final accounts in the same way following Financial Reporting Standards and Companies Acts;
- the external environment of the business changes from year to year, and these changes do not need to be reported; changes in staff, initiatives, product development, production processes... there are many reasons why a business may show a greater or reduced profit one year to the next.

To summarise, a ratio calculated on it's own is meaningless unless it is compared to a yardstick - previous year's performance, budgeted performance or the performance of a competitor.

Ratio analysis does not take account of other changes within the business such non- financial performance indicators such as staff changes, changes in methods of production, or any new product developments or launches.

3.2 Annual reports

Annual reports are produced to coincide with the publication of the annual accounts. They set out to show the business's successes over the past trading period as well as highlighting the business's programme for change in the coming year.

They audience for annual reports is both internal and external to the business. The report is aimed at existing investors who they will be keen to show growth and sound decision making. It will also be aimed at potential future investors who will be looking for a history of improvement and financial stability. The report will also be aimed at employees as it will contain key messages pointing towards the organisations future strategies.

Annual reports also contain messages from the business's senior management team. The report is usually introduced by the Chief Executive Officer (CEO) who will outline the key strengths of the past year and the action that the business is prepared to take in the coming year. As well as containing the business's financial statements, it may also include reports on key initiatives such as sustainable development and new growth opportunities.

Whilst financial information must be 100% accurate, the wording and tone of the written reports will be blushed with a certain degree of bias. This is the business's opportunity to sell itself to the market.

In the past, annual reports would be written documents, downloadable from the organisations website in pdf format. Whilst this is still the case, many businesses are now taking advantage of web based technology and are including video and interactive timeline content to their reports. The 2015 Marks and Spencer annual report, for example, begins with a video highlighting the key strengths, as they see it, of the business over the past year.

Annual report analysis

Find the latest Marks and Spencer annual report online. Spend about 20 minutes reading it, noting anything interesting that you find.

Look out for financial data, key messages, new initiatives and interesting performance stats.

3.3 Other information

You will also need to look outside of the business to glean information concerning the external factors and trends of the market the business operates in. There are a number of sources of information, such as government departments which are funded by tax payers and are required to document and make available everything that they find.

This means there is a wealth of information available online. When you are deciding on a topic for your Advanced Higher report, you should take some time to search through the following websites:

- UK Government statistics (http://bit.ly/1OfAosd) ;
- Office for National Statistics (http://bit.ly/1JOyTLu) ;
- Scottish Government statistics (http://bit.ly/1OhKVoD) .

Government statistics can be used to investigate trends in a market or sector. These trends can then be compared to the business in question. How does the growth match up? Is the wider economy growing or contracting in the same way? Has the population changed or does changes in the age of the population confirm why a business may be seeing a rise or decline of sales over time?

Of course, government statistics are only helpful to decision making if the information exists. To ensure current and relevant information a business may be required to carry out the research for themselves.

You studied market research at both National 5 and Higher level and may have conducted your own as part of your reports. You may choose to do the same for you Advanced Higher report. You should be aware that market research companies exist - businesses do not always complete the market research activities for themselves. Although you cannot influence the questioning or topics, they often publish reports that you may find useful.

Two of the leading market research companies are:

- Ipsos MORI (http://bit.ly/1Ltejrp);
- http://www.mintel.com/.

3.4 Summary

Summary

After studying this topic, you should now be able to reach conclusions from:

- reported financial information;
- annual reports;
- government statistics;
- market data;
- customers surveys.

3.5 End of topic test

End of Topic 3 test — Go online

Q6: Ratio analysis is used to:

a) predict the future.
b) compare a business's performance over two time periods.
c) explain why a performance has increased.
d) justify an operations decision.

....

Q7: Net profit as a percentage of sales is an example of a:

a) profitability ratio.
b) liquidity ratio.
c) efficiency ratio.

....

Q8: Gross profit as a percentage of sales is interested in a business's efficiency.

a) True
b) False

....

Q9: Ratio analysis can only be used to compare a business's performance with previous years.

a) True
b) False

....

Q10: An increase in net profit as a percentage of sales could indicate a business is using cheaper suppliers.

a) True
b) False

....

Q11: Return on capital employed ratios require a business to know its opening capital.

a) True
b) False

....

Q12: Ratio analysis can also highlight issues with staff morale and turnover.

a) True
b) False

Q13: The table below gives figures from year 1 and year 2 for a business.

	Year 2 (in £)	Year 1 (in £)
Revenue (Sales)	24,000 million	10,500 million
Profit/(Loss) for the year (Net profit/(Loss))	2,250 million	550 million
Current assets	18,000 million	12,000 million
Current liabilities	8,000 million	10,900 million
Capital employed	12,500 million	6,000 million
Share price	5.60	3.20

Using the figures provided in the table above, complete the following table and provide an analysis of your findings.

	Year 2	Year 1
Net profit as a percentage of sales		
Current ratio		
Return on capital employed		
Share price (in £)	5.60	3.20

(6 marks - 3 marks for correct figures plus 3 marks for analysis)

Glossary

Acid test ratio
    shows a business's ability to pay its short term debts but with stock removed from the calculation

Acquisition
    when one company buys a controlling interest in another usually against its wishes. This is sometimes referred to as a takeover

Adam Smith
    Scottish economist from the 18th Century - the "father" of modern economics

Assets for change
    things the organisation already has that enable change to take place

B2B
    companies order direct from their suppliers

B2C
    consumers order direct from the business and the goods

B2G
    government orders direct from the business

Balance of payments
    a statement showing a country's trade and financial transactions with the rest of the world over a specific time period - usually one year

Bureaucracy
    a hierarchy with strict rules and procedures

Business ethics
    the moral principle that underline decisions made by businesses

Carbon neutral
    when an organisation calculates its total carbon emissions, reduces them and offsets the remainder, e.g. by paying towards reforestation or investing in wind farms

Centralised
    decisions are made from the one central location

Citing
    providing a list of sources used

Computer-aided design
    the use of sophisticated computer software to design three-dimensional images of products quickly and relatively cheaply

Computer-aided manufacture
: the use of computers and software for a wide variety of production tasks, including automated production lines where software controls the machinery used and stock control systems such as bar codes and laser scanners

Contingency theory
: the view that the best approach to management varies according to the situation

Corporate culture
: refers to a company's values, beliefs, business principles, traditions and ways of operating

Corporate social responsibility
: taking account of the needs of all stakeholders, both internal and external, ensuring the business contributes to society

Critical path
: a tool used to show the shortest number of activities a business must go through to complete a project

Current ratio
: shows a business's ability to pay its short term debts

Deindustrialisation
: the removal of heavy industry or large scale manufacturing from a country or region

Direct quotes
: taking a quote from a published works and including it word for word and citing the original

Disposable income
: the income left available to an individual, for spending and/or saving, after taxes have been paid

Diversification
: when a business expands by moving into a new market

Driver
: a force that makes change happen

E-commerce
: refers to business transacted using electronic media, primarily the internet

Economic factors
: relate to changes in the wider economy, such as inflation, unemployment, taxation, interest rates, exchange rates and business cycles

Economies of scale
: a reduction in average business costs which arise from increased size or production

Efficiency
: ratios used to show how a business is performing and the returns it is generating

GLOSSARY

Exchange rate
the price of one currency in terms of another, e.g. £1 = €1.3 or £1 = €1.5

Fiscal policy
government policy regarding taxation and spending in the economy

Force field analysis
a management tool deigned to assess whether change should take place

Force-field diagram
a tool used to show the drivers for, and resistors against, change including assets for change that an organisation already has that enable change to happen

Foreign direct investment
overseas investment into a country by a multinational company

Franchise
contractual agreement whereby the rights are given by one business to another in the use of its business idea, products or name

Gantt chart
a method of scheduling a project by plotting time and tasks on a bar chart

GDP per capita
GDP of a country divided by its total population

Globalisation
the increased interconnectedness of the world due to advancements in technology and reductions in trade barriers

Glocalisation
when a global business attempts to act locally

Gross Domestic Product
the value of all goods and services produced within a nation in a given year

Gross National Product (GNP)
total value of goods and services produced by a country over the course of a year

Gross profit percentage
the percentage of sales that a business has turned into gross profit

Harvard Reference style
a reference style, first used at the university of the same name, where sources are listed alphabetically by surname of the author

Hawthorne effect
the idea that workers are motivated by being recognised by management

Home country
the country of origin where the MNC is based

Host country
> the country into which a foreign direct investment is made

Industrial Revolution
> the introduction of mechanised manufacturing in the production process

Inflation
> the change in value of goods and services, measured by a percentage rise

Infrastructure
> the network of transport, communications and public services supporting an economic environment

Internet banking
> banking transactions such as payments, transfers and account balances are made via the internet

Joint ventures
> when two or more businesses undertake a project together sharing revenues, costs and risks

Liquidity
> ratios used to show how easily a business can meet its debts

Management by objectives
> a process of agreeing individual targets throughout an organisation and holding each worker accountable for achieving them

Mechanistic
> theory that says workers are physical - like a machine

Merger
> when two businesses jointly agree to combine together

Micro-multinationals
> smaller businesses who operate in several countries enabled by internet communications

Monetary policy
> measures which control spending in the economy through the use of interest rates and changes in the money supply to achieve economic stability

Multinational
> a type of business that operates in at least two countries with a clear home base

Net profit percentage
> the percentage of sales that a business has turned into net profit

Organic growth
> when a business increases in size naturally, without taking over another business

Organisational objectives
> the combined aim or vision of an organisation

Outsourcing
   paying an external provider to deliver/operate what once were internal company functions

Paraphrasing
   taking information from a published works but changing it into your own words and citing the original

Plagiarism
   using someone else's published work and passing it off as your own

Political factors
   relates to the way in which changes in government policy can influence business, e.g. fiscal and monetary policies, competition policy, laws and regulations

Profitability
   ratios used to show how profitable a business is compared to previous or competitor performance

Referencing
   providing a quote or acknowledgment of a source from a published author

Regional policy
   measures taken by government to redress the balance in terms of employment, income and wealth between areas of the UK

Resistor
   a force that would dissuade managers from change taking place

Return on capital employed
   measures the expected return to be paid on an investment into the business

Social responsibility
   taking account of the needs of external stakeholders, ensuring the business contributes to society

Socio-psychological
   people's feelings, thoughts and behaviours

Summarising
   taking information from a published works but summarising it to reduce the content and citing the original

SWOT analysis
   a tool used to show the internal strengths and weaknesses and the external opportunities and threats a business faces

Systems theory
   an approach to management that takes into account the interactions between different systems within and outside an organisation

Takeover

when one business buys over another

Taxation

money collected by government through employee pay and the purchase of goods and services

Technology transfer

the introduction of better production and management techniques learned from other countries when a business locates abroad or when other business locate in your country, e.g. JIT and Quality Circles

Transfer pricing

when a business sells component parts to another part of the same business at a greater/lower price to manipulate taxation

Transnational

a company that operates in a least two countries but without a clear home base

Uniformity

everything or everyone being equal, the same

Video conferencing

communication in real time with two or more people at different locations possibly in different countries via video

Answers to questions and activities for The external business environment

Topic 1: Globalisation and its effects on business

Globalisation issues (page 5)

Q1: a) True

Q2: b) False

Q3: a) True

Q4: b) False

Q5: a) True

Q6: a) True

Effects of globalisation on UK businesses (page 7)

Q7: a) Positive effect

Q8: a) Positive effect

Q9: a) Positive effect

Q10: a) Positive effect

Q11: a) Positive effect

Q12: a) Positive effect

Q13: b) Negative effect

Q14: b) Negative effect

Q15: a) Positive effect

Q16: b) Negative effect

Q17: b) Negative effect

Q18: a) Positive effect

Q19: b) Negative effect

Q20: a) Positive effect

Q21: a) Positive effect

HSBC (page 9)

Q22: Increased advances in technology, particularly in e-commerce.

Q23: It can gain purchasing and marketing economies of scale in the development of its products and services.

Q24: To gain a competitive edge by differentiating its brand by giving it a unique selling point.

Q25:

- It will enable HSBC to respond quicker to customers needs in the local area as "one size cannot fit all".
- It may increase costs of its operation to do so but these should be offset by the additional customers it receives.
- Local cultures are taken into consideration re investment decisions that will encourage more customers to use the bank's products and services.
- Its reputation in the local community will be enhanced as it is choosing its CSR projects based on local needs rather than what it decides is best.
- As a global company new technological advances are spread throughout the whole company helping to keep its competitive edge and therefore its ability to keep supporting local needs.

End of Topic 1 test (page 11)

Q26: a) The increasing universal nature of the business environment.

Q27: c) Freezing up of financial markets.

Q28: c) New opportunities in home markets.

Q29: d) support local cultures and issues.

Q30: b) Increasing awareness from consumers.

Q31: a) True

Q32: a) True

Q33: b) False

ANSWERS: UNIT 1 TOPIC 1

Q34: ***Positive effects*** include:

- larger market - allows for increased sales, economies of scale;
- access to cheaper raw materials; closer to source of raw materials cutting down transport costs; exploitation of local resources, e.g. lower labour costs;
- transfer pricing can reduce tax bills;
- increased internet shopping - websites necessary;
- can serve a missing market;
- can learn new techniques (production and management) from other countries;
- can allow expansion where monopoly legislation in home country prevents it;
- allows organisation to control production from start to finish, e.g. oil industry;
- low cost transportation allows organisations to ship products all over world;
- increased demand for Western products in newly industrialised countries;
- large organisations may be able to influence government policy in their favour.
- allows standardisation of products.

Negative effects include:

- cultural difficulties may lead to conflicts and misunderstandings;
- organisations which are not decentralised may find it difficult to react to changes in the local market;
- preferences are not universal so standardised products may not be feasible;
- increased travel for senior managers of organisations - time away from office;
- increased competition;
- may have employees working in politically unstable countries - at risk.

Topic 2: Multinationals

Head office locations (page 14)

Q1:

Country	Number of head offices
Canada	10
China	95
France	31
India	8
Japan	57
Netherlands	13
South Korea	17
Sweden	3
UK	28
USA	128

Q2: Reasons include:

- rise in dominance of China and other Asian nation due to high tech investment and relatively low wage structures;
- America continues to dominate, with Walmart again number 1, but they are rising at a slower rate than Asia;
- some countries have been better at taking advantage of industrialisation;
- some countries have lost out to others who charge less taxation to floating MNCs.

Multinational companies (MNCs) (page 15)

Q3: a) True

Q4: b) False

Q5: b) False

Q6: a) True

Reasons for growth of MNCs (page 17)

Q7:

Reason for growth of MNCs	Example
Increased market share	Apple dominated the computer tablet market for years
Closeness to local market	Cadbury established production plants in Australia and New Zealand where the cocoa is harvested
Can avoid import tariffs	Japanese car producers setting up in the UK
Can benefit from government incentives	Scottish Government offered Clough a £1.5m grant

Vodafone (page 18)

Q8: It has 66,000 employees in its worldwide operations. Its investments in emerging markets shows it owns operations outside of its home base.

Q9: The main reason may have been to increase its profits and market share. It will also benefit from economies of scale from its increased size which will reduce its average costs. Furthermore by becoming a multinational business it has the back up of the financial resources that allow expansion into emerging markets that smaller businesses may not have access to. Promoting its products through a worldwide network allows the business to gain brand recognition on a global scale.

Santander UK call centre (page 18)

Q10: d) Responding to customer need

Advantages of each method of FDI (page 20)

Q11:

Creating new facilities in host country	Buying over an existing company in host country
Can gain competitive advantage in emerging markets	Able to reduce competition
Custom built to suit the organisations requirements	Allows a large market presence to be built up quickly
Enables the company to establish its own business philosophy and corporate culture	Enables moves into markets where you can attract a different segment
Ensures uniform global facilities	Gain access to management and their experience of local conditions reducing risk of failure
Only option as no suitable facilities are available	May be able to acquire a loss making business cheaply
Problems of integration into the existing business structure are minimised	Start earning revenue and profits straight away

What benefits does FDI bring to the UK? (page 21)

Q12: Foreign investment is essential for the long-term health of the UK economy because of *its contribution to creating and underpinning British jobs*, as well as *boosting local and regional economies*. International investors are some of our biggest and most innovative manufacturers, and service providers, bringing enormous benefits to the UK. These include not only job and wealth creation, but also an *injection of innovation to process and produce* which *add to UK capacity in output, R&D and exports*.

International investment allows companies to *achieve growth and economies of scale that domestic markets alone would not allow*. This makes them *more productive and profitable with greater capacity for job and wealth creation*. The expansion of high productivity businesses *helps strengthen competition within the economy as companies are exposed to new ideas and practices*.

ANSWERS: UNIT 1 TOPIC 2

Stagecoach (page 21)

Q13: *Benefits*

- Purchasing already existing bus companies meant that Stagecoach could begin operations immediately without having to acquire new buses, build depots etc from scratch;
- Stagecoach could tap into the market of existing customers;
- Stagecoach could use the expertise and local knowledge of indigenous staff;
- Stagecoach could benefit from reputations already established;
- Stagecoach already has enormous experience in the bus market and as one of the market leaders in the UK is well placed to develop its own superior facilities from scratch;
- Diversifying into other areas of transport could mean that Stagecoach quickly gets a foothold in new markets with which it was unfamiliar;
- It could build on the experience the firms taken over had built up.

Costs

- Stagecoach could be disadvantaged if the firms bought were previously struggling to maintain custom and reputation;
- It may take a long time to build up confidence again, especially if Stagecoach is seen as operating the same organisation under a different name;
- Rebranding and updating (buses, systems, etc.) may be costly.

Reasons for forming joint ventures (page 22)

Q14: The table below outlines the main reasons for forming joint ventures.

Internal reasons	Competitive goals
Access to new customers	Creation of stronger competitive units
Access to new technologies	Defensive response to market conditions
Build on company's strengths	Improved responsiveness to customer needs
Gain advantages of economies of scale	Pre-empting competition
Improving access to financial resources	Speed to market
Specialist knowledge shared	
Spreading costs and risks	

Edrington (page 22)

Q15: The maker of whiskies including Famous Grouse, Highland Park and The Macallan yesterday unveiled a new joint venture to sell its Scotch in the Americas alongside brands including Disaronno, Tennent's lager and Tia Maria.

Edrington has teamed up with World Equity Brand Builders (Webb) to launch Edrington Webb Travel Retail Americas.

The new entity will market drinks in the duty-free sections of airports, cruise liners and other travel retail locations in the Americas, including Canada and the Caribbean. This new partnership will allow both businesses to **spread their costs and risks**.

More than five million cases of spirits are sold through travel retail in the Americas each year, accounting for nearly one quarter of global duty free volumes and worth a total of more than £660 million. Glasgow-based Edrington - which also makes Brugal rum, Cutty Sark blended whisky and Snow Leopard vodka - announced in August that it was in exclusive talks with Webb, which has been marketing and distributing the Scottish group's brands in the Caribbean for the past four years.

The switch is in-keeping with Edrington's recent strategy of **taking closer control of its brands in key markets**, using joint ventures or setting up dedicated companies rather than employing third party distributors, as **a longer term relationship can be developed under this model**.

Other brands marketed by Webb in the Americas include Armand de Brignac Champagne, Cape Classics wines, Magners cider and Tito's Handmade Vodka.

Juan Gentile, Edrington's area director for the Americas, said: "**The creation of Edrington Webb expands our reach** and **bring us closer to customers and consumers** in this valuable and dynamic market.

"Edrington and Webb have worked together in the Caribbean since 2010 and I am delighted at this opportunity to extend such a successful relationship."

Mergers and acquisitions (page 24)

Q16: b) False

Q17: a) True

Q18: a) True

Q19: a) True

Q20: a) True

Franchisor and franchisee - advantages and disadvantages (page 26)

Q21:

Advantages for franchisor	Advantages for franchisee	Disadvantages for franchisor	Disadvantages for franchisee
Market share increased with little investment	Additional brands can be added to existing portfolio very cheaply	Only receives a small share of profits	Can be costly to buy a successful franchise
Receives a percentage or turnover or set royalty payments	Recognised brand therefore minimal advertising needs	Reputation can be tarnished by franchisee	Franchise contract may not be renewed
	Risk of failure is reduced		Has less control over products, selling prices and store layout
	Training and support offered by franchisor		Royalty payments of a percentage of profits are paid to franchisor

AG Barr (page 26)

Q22: Your answer should contain the following points.

Advantages:

- Barr's gain additional brands for its product portfolio - in this case internationally known brands so Barr's can perhaps exploit this;
- less risky and costly than trying to develop new brands, very important to a smallish multinational firm like Barr's;
- it allows Barr's to target other market segments - older ages group than IRN-BRU and Tizer;
- it fits in with Barr's marketing strategy of focussing on brands;
- it can reach markets in Russia and Spain with little effort on its part increasing the brand's awareness more globally;
- all contracts help to maintain or increase its income, profit, overall market share.

Disadvantages:

- Barr's produces a similar product to Orangina, Simply Citrus, which may be adversely affected;
- it is bound by its terms of agreement with Pernod Ricard and Unilever (e.g. in packaging) and may have less control over the way the products are promoted;
- what happens if the contracts are not renewed? This could lead to a waste of time and money for Barr's in developing the brand further;
- IRN-BRU's reputation as a global brand may be tainted if the franchisee's operating it do not conform to AG Barr's quality standards.

Transfer pricing (page 29)

Q23: Transfer pricing refers to the price charged between one international subsidiary of a multinational company and another for the goods and services supplied between them.

Q24: b) False

Q25: a) True

Q26: a) True

Q27: b) False

Q28: b) False

Q29: a) True

Q30: b) False

Impact of using transfer pricing (page 30)

Q31: Transfer price is the price at which goods and services are transferred between branches of MNCs in different countries, e.g. from Thailand to Scotland, and it is used to reduce the company's overall tax liabilities.

Transfer price is determined by the company and is not influenced by market forces as it relates to internal transfer of goods.

The company will want set a high transfer price on goods and services going to a high tax countries because by doing so the costs of production in the high tax countries will be increased narrowing their profit margins and reducing the final tax bill in that country. On the other hand a MNC will set a low transfer price for goods and services going to a low tax country because this will reduce their costs of production.

This will increase profits in that country and they will be liable for more tax. However, as the increase the amount of tax liability in low tax countries is relatively small, the overall tax liability is minimised.

The net effect is an increase in overall profits which can be used to increase investment, spend more on research and development or pay bigger dividends to shareholders.

Transfer pricing strategy may impact negatively on the company through adverse publicity if it is seen to be evading taxation in a country. This may foster poor relations with the government of the country that is losing out on tax revenue.

Transfer pricing strategy may impact on the behaviour of managers within each subsidiary, e.g. managers in one subsidiary may be unwilling to use transfer pricing if it reduces the reported profit in their subsidiary as it makes them seem inefficient. The company may have to give them incentives for buying in at a high transfer price.

Starbucks (page 30)

Q32: It can reduce the overall tax liability of the MNC when a high transfer price is used when transferring goods or services from a low tax country to a high tax country and vice versa.

Q33: UK citizens are aware of how successful Starbucks are in the UK and did not feel it was fair that the company were not paying any money to the UK exchequer. They started voting with their feet and the loss of custom was becoming news worthy. Starbucks now pay tax in the UK to stop this decline in sales.

Is Britain up for sale? (page 31)

Q34:

UK is home country	UK is host country
29% of grocery brands operating in the UK	Branston pickle
Aston Martin	Cadbury
BP	HP sauce
Diageo	Jaguar
HSBC	Land Rover
Standard Chartered	Rolls Royce and Bentley
Tesco	Santander
Vodafone	Unilever

Q35: a) 13.5%

End of topic 2 test (page 33)

Q36: b) they can create wealth in an area by providing local jobs.

Q37: c) New management skills can be learned from the host country.

Q38: a) it enables the company to establish its own culture and philosophy.

Q39: c) enables you to move into markets where you have limited expertise.

Q40: c) Both companies have head offices in the same country.

Q41: b) franchise contract may not be renewed.

Q42: d) It is more advantageous for the MNC to use a low transfer price when transferring goods from a high tax country.

Q43: c) aggravating relationships with governments.

Q44: b) Working conditions of employees in subsidiary countries compare favourably to those in the home country.

Q45: Transfer pricing is the price at which goods and services are transferred between branches of multinational companies in different countries.

The goods and services do not go outside the company and so no actual buying and selling of them takes place. This means that the multinational company itself decides what the transfer price will be so it can set prices in a way that suits the company.

Transfer pricing can be used to position funds within an international business to the benefit of the organisation - tax liabilities can be reduced by using transfer pricing to shift earnings from a high tax country to a low tax one.

Their goal is to declare low profits in high tax countries and high profits in low tax countries to minimise global tax liabilities. In a high tax country they would sell their goods to a foreign subsidiary at a low price to ensure low profits and vice versa in low tax countries.

Import duties can be reduced where the tariff to be paid is calculated as a percentage of the value of the goods (which is shown by the price).

Where a large currency devaluation is expected in a country, transfer pricing can be used to reduce exposure to foreign exchange risk.

Use of transfer pricing strategies by large US multinationals, such as Starbucks and Google, to minimise UK tax has put UK firms at a competitive disadvantage.

Q46: Any four from:

- Vertical integration - organisations at a different stage in the same industry combine together.
- Horizontal integration - organisations at the same stage of production combine together.
- Backward vertical integration - when a business takes over a supplier.
- Forward vertical integration - when a business takes over a customer.
- Conglomerate/diversification - organisations in completely different industries combine together.
- De-integration/demerger - organisations cut back and concentrate on only their core activities.
- Divestment - when a business sells off assets or subsidiary companies to raise finance for growth.
- Organic growth - organisations increase the number of products sold or number of outlets.
- Foreign direct investment - when a business sets up abroad by buying out an existing business in that country.

Q47: Advantages of investing directly in facilities to produce a product in a foreign/host country:

- constructing your own facilities means you can choose any locations and purpose build facilities;
- a company operating this policy can be sure that it can effectively replicate facilities across the world, manage them on a common footing;
- more easily instil new company culture in a foreign land.

Disadvantages:

- time to find a suitable location and construct the building;
- effort and negotiation with national or local authorities in host country;
- possible need to develop new infrastructure;
- cost of new building and up to date technology may be high;
- time taken to hire and train employees.

Advantages of buying an existing enterprise in a foreign/host country:

- this has the added advantage of having knowledge and experience of local market conditions available from the initial stages;
- suitably skilled staff knowledgeable about the language and culture of the country may already be in place;
- the company could trade on the other firm's reputation - customer base may be there;
- it allows firms to enter new markets where they have little or no experience;
- firms can buy up loss-making companies abroad very cheaply;
- less investment in management and technology is needed;
- can turn around the company much more quickly than setting up a business from scratch.

Disadvantage:

- it may be difficult to find a firm with the facilities it needs.

Topic 3: Effects on host country and home countries

Investing in a host country (page 38)

Q1: b) False

Q2: a) True

Q3: a) True

Q4: a) True

Q5: b) False

Q6: a) True

Q7: b) False

Q8: a) True

Q9: b) False

Q10: b) False

GlaxoSmithKline (page 39)

Q11: When companies like GSK expand overseas they bring both advantages and disadvantages to the host country. Quite often they will bring in new production and management techniques and other expertise known as technology transfer which can then be shared with other companies within the host country to increase their productivity and efficiency. This will ultimately boost the GNP of the host country increasing the overall standard of living.

Local workers can benefit from greater employment opportunities and it is more likely they will receive higher wages from GSK than they would from a domestic company. There is also the possibility that local firms will be used as suppliers giving them a greater market than they had before. More tax revenue will be gained by the host country from the profits of GSK and the country's balance of payments will improve from the initial capital inflow of the investment. The balance of payments may also improve due to increased exports as any manufactured drugs are shipped and sold abroad to the many other countries that GSK operate in. However very often these large companies can be socially irresponsible by exploiting natural resources and causing pollution in the host country, although it seems unlikely that GSK could be accused of this.

Another major disadvantage for the host country is that these large companies have no loyalty to the host country and will without conscience switch production to lower cost countries, which will have adverse affects on employment and economic growth of the host country. Big companies often employ their own managers in key positions leaving only the lower unskilled jobs available to local labour. This may be particularly true of GSK as their company's reputation is steeped in science and research and therefore they need to ensure the quality of their employees in terms of educational standards.

Another major problem for the host country's government could be in controlling these larger organisations purely because of their size and financial power as they can exert their influence on governments to gain preferential tax concessions, subsidies and grants.

ANSWERS: UNIT 1 TOPIC 3

Expanding abroad (page 40)

Q12: a) True

Q13: b) False

Q14: b) False

Q15: a) True

Q16: a) True

End of Topic 3 test (page 42)

Q17: a) Advantage

Q18: b) Disadvantage

Q19: a) Advantage

Q20: a) Advantage

Q21: a) Advantage

Q22: b) Disadvantage

Q23: a) Advantage

Q24: b) Disadvantage

Q25: c) Host governments find multinationals easy to control.

Q26: b) Balance of payments is improved due to the capital injection from multinational.

Q27: b) Other businesses in the home country may become more efficient because of technology transfer.

Q28: d) The introduction of scientific and technological developments to businesses who can develop them into new processes and products.

Q29: *Positive effects*

Employment prospects for British citizens may be enhanced as firms setting up plants overseas may recruit from UK universities for jobs all over the world. This may lead to spin-off benefits for the universities themselves who may be able to recruit a higher calibre of student and may help to keep academic expertise in UK.

UK multinationals may pass on expertise to others in the UK. This may include firms who deal with the company but also covers employees who may move on to work for other UK firms and the wider business community e.g. through Business Gateway.

UK may benefit from the repatriation of profits and its national income may rise. This may help the UK balance of payments.

Additional jobs may be created in Scotland, e.g. in company HQ if it remains in Scotland. These are likely to be high quality technical and managerial posts which could encourage local people to pursue education and training to access these jobs.

UK financial institutions and others may gain opportunities which they can exploit, e.g. providing investment advice.

Negative effects

Employment opportunities in UK may be reduced, especially if expansion overseas means that jobs are transferred to countries where wages are lower. There will be a need for additional training and skills development to enable workers to find jobs. This may involve changes in provisions within education system to produce higher level of skills amongst UK citizens.

Investments being made abroad rather than here in the UK will lead to short term capital outflows which will negatively affect the balance of payments in the short run.

UK firms may choose to relocate completely to more cost efficient location leading to job losses, negative impact on local suppliers, reduced spending in the area affected, increased government spending and reduced government income through taxation.

Topic 4: Current developments in the EU and their effect on UK organisations

EU institutions (page 48)

Q1: a) The Council of EU

Q2: b) The European Commission

Q3: c) The Court of Justice

Q4: b) The European Commission

Q5: d) The European Parliament

Q6: b) The European Commission

Q7: c) The Court of Justice

Q8: a) The Council of EU

Costs and benefits of a single market (page 50)

Q9: a) Cost

Q10: a) Cost

Q11: b) Benefit

Q12: b) Benefit

Q13: b) Benefit

Q14: a) Cost

Q15: b) Benefit

Q16: b) Benefit

Q17: b) Benefit

Q18: Face fierce competition from European businesses. May have to alter specification of product to suit European laws/regulations. Possibility of a takeover bids from European rival. Differences in cultures may make it difficult to produce a single good to satisfy all tastes

Social Chapter impact (page 52)

Q19: The social chapter consists of a number of measures designed to harmonise social legislation within the EU. Its effects on business may be general or specific depending on the issue concerned, e.g. the fear it may lead to increased costs because of minimum wage and paid holidays. Businesses may have to charge higher prices in an effort to maintain profit margins which may reduce their competitiveness compared to countries operating outwith the EU, e.g. China and India. There is also the fear that the 48-hour maximum working week may inhibit labour market flexibility. However, it could lead to increased productivity as workers will be more motivated due to their protected rights.

© HERIOT-WATT UNIVERSITY

End of Topic 4 test (page 53)

Q20: c) goods, services, capital and people between EU members.

Q21: b) National differences in cultures and tastes can be a barrier to market entry.

Q22: d) social legislation within the EU.

Q23: b) It can increase workers' productivity due to the motivational effect.

Topic 5: Asian nations and their effect on UK businesses

Answers from page 58.

Q1: China represents a huge market with lots of potential.

Q2: They misjudged the Chinese people, they failed to stock suitable sizes of garments, they thought they could replicate their knowledge of Hong Kong, and they suffered from an unfortunate fatal accident.

Q3: They do not have the capital or experience required.

End of Topic 5 test (page 59)

Q4: a) True

Q5: b) False

Q6: b) False

Q7: a) True

Q8: a) True

Q9: Inward investment opportunities exists as Chinese organisations attempt to enter the UK market.

Cheaper materials can be purchased from ASEAN/China due to their lower wage rate and production costs.

ASEAN/China have access to newer technologies, allowing for better quality products to be introduced into UK production processes.

ASEAN/China have a combined population of 1.8 billion people meaning UK businesses have a larger market in which to export their luxury goods.

Cultural differences could make trading with China and ASEAN nations problematic as UK businesses may be unfamiliar with local customs and cultures.

UK businesses may have to lower their prices to compete with Chinese and ASEAN businesses.

The buying power of Chinese and ASEAN businesses may leave UK businesses vulnerable to a takeover.

Exporting to ASEAN/China can take a long time and is expensive due to the large distances involved.

Topic 6: Business ethics and corporate social responsibility

Business ethics (page 62)

Q1: Consumers and investors are now expecting it and their competitors may have just introduced one. Research evidence has shown that it brings positive outcomes for the business.

Q2: Yes, the business was willing to forgo profits and perhaps sought to encourage a change of practice in the company using child labour. Its refusal would help to improve its own public image as well.

Q3: No, the hospital was more concerned with its income and shareholders return than in the needs of the sick elderly patient.

Q4: Yes, because intensively reared chickens often suffer due to their high-density housing and regularly need treatment with antibiotics. Organically reared chickens are kept outside but have access to shelter and are not given antibiotics or genetically modified (GM) food. It may encourage more farmers to produce organically and then prices will drop as more companies enter the organic market.

Q5: Yes, because of the various concerns with non-GM flour, such as safety of GM crops due to inconsistent regulation of GM crops worldwide, economic concerns about intellectual property and doubts about the necessity of GM crops. A relevant but non-ethical consideration is that it may also give the baker a USP when branding his/her goods.

Q6: This is quite an emotive subject and it depends on your individual point of view of whether you agree or not to animal experimentation in any form. Bear in mind companies engaging in animal research are governed heavily by legislation and are subject to Home Office scrutiny and control. One question you might consider is whether bullying on any level can ever be ethical.

Waitrose and Fairtrade Foundation (page 63)

Q7: Ethics are moral principles, not guided by law but by the conscience of consumer and corporate behaviour. The art of doing good for others.

Q8: The brand will be strengthened due to its enhanced reputation for investing ethically. Customers will be more willing to stay loyal. It offers a USP as it is the only supermarket to make such a deal. Customers have proven in the past that they are more willing to pay extra for Fairtrade products.

Costs and benefits of pursuing a policy of CSR (page 66)

Q9: b) Benefit

Q10: b) Benefit

Q11: a) Cost

Q12: b) Benefit

Q13: a) Cost

Q14: a) Cost

Q15: b) Benefit

Effects of a CSR policy (page 67)

Q16: Corporate social responsibility refers to how an organisation meets its obligations to society as a whole, including both internal and external stakeholders. These actions can affect the profits of the organisation in many ways.

CSR provides benefits in terms of good publicity and research has suggested that this helps gain more customers which in turn will increase sales and therefore profits. If rival firms are also perceived as being socially responsible it may prevent losing sales to them because of customer loyalty thereby maintaining its profit level. Additionally firms with very good social reputations may not lose out on profits if some of their actions do not work out as expected as their previous good reputation may be remembered, again maintaining profit levels.

CSR policies attract or keep employees whose values are similar to the firms resulting in higher motivation and productivity which increases profits as well as reducing costs of recruitment and selection as employee turnover rates are reduced, again translating to higher profits. CSR can also enable a firm to gain a niche market for itself, increasing its profits, e.g. Co-operative Society with its Fair Trade stance.

However, CSR may not always lead to higher profits. It can lead to additional costs in terms of equipment and staff resources which may make it difficult for the firm to remain competitive and having to sacrifice profit margins to maintain sales. Also, lucrative investments may have to be turned down in favour of more ethical ones which reduce profits e.g. Co-operative Bank. It can sometimes backfire on firms and reduce their profitability, e.g. Walkers Crisps, attempt to offer educational material in return for volume purchases that encouraged unhealthy eating turned good publicity into bad.

Diageo (page 67)

Q17: Social responsibility refers to an organisation's obligations to all its external stakeholders in the widest sense whereas corporate social responsibility goes further to include obligations to both internal and external stakeholders.

Q18: Community involvement:

- helps Diageo get good publicity e.g. Its 'Water for Life' initiative and thereby maintains its good reputation particularly in the communities it helps.
- can help gain customers as they are aware that some of the companies profits help good causes.
- motivates staff since they can become directly involved in projects that they are passionate about leading to all the associated rewards that a motivated workforce brings ie better productivity, more job satisfaction.
- helps reduce staff turnover costs as staff are happier to work for an organisation whose corporate values are close to their own personal ones and therefore they do not seek employment elsewhere.

Q19: No right or wrong answer here as long as points made are backed up with reasoned arguments. Some points may include the following.

There is a huge concern over the UK nation's health record in terms of obesity and alcoholism. It could be argued that Diageo's products contribute to this therefore not truly socially responsible for its burden on National Health Service.

Diageo uses aggressive marketing to promote its products, particularly Guinness and Haagen-Dazs, thereby encouraging more people to an unhealthy lifestyle which is not very socially responsible. It could be argued that social problems of obesity and alcoholism lie in the way people choose to consume these products which cannot be blamed on the company - it has to follow strict labelling of its products as to their content.

There is lots of evidence to illustrate all the company does to give back to society therefore it is socially responsible. It could be argued that 1% of pre-tax profits is too little and that perhaps 5% would be a more socially responsible figure.

End of Topic 6 test (page 69)

Q20: d) Businesses are unwilling to give up profits to increase shareholders' returns.

Q21: b) consumers and investors are now expecting it.

Q22: b) offering your staff's time and skills in developing and maintaining local projects.

Q23: c) Staff motivation and turnover rates decrease.

Q24: c) Having to turn down a lucrative contract.

Q25: b) the good publicity gained generates more customers for the business.

Q26: Management should be reminded that they lead by example, allowing them to provide a positive corporate culture incorporating CSR. A written policy of CSR can be used to attract quality employees; this encourages employees to remain with the firm. Staffing issues can occur as employees require time off to work with local community projects. Treating staff well increases their commitment to the business and results in increased motivation.

Effective marketing can be used in advertising campaigns to boost sales, e.g. Marks & Spencer's Plan A. Marketing may need to be changed to include the organisations work on CSR. Working with the local community could increase sales and custom. Firms can find a niche in the market by incorporating CSR, e.g. Scottish Nappy Company, recycling phones.

Operations can help organisations who might need to alter production methods to become environmentally friendly. If staff are involved in community projects then production/service could be reduced. Product/packaging may need to be altered to make it more socially acceptable, e.g. smaller engine car, hybrid car. Firms need to find environmentally friendly ways to dispose of waste; increased recycling can positively affect an organisation's costs but it can take time to organise waste disposal.

Finance will be involved in the purchase of new environmentally friendly production equipment which will increase costs. More efficient ways of production may reduce costs. A business may have to increase staff training to ensure all employees know how to act in responsible ways. Retaining staff reduces recruitment and selection costs.

Increase in R&D increases costs. Companies can increase profits by charging more for CSR products, e.g. Fair Trade.

Topic 7: Government influence / technological developments
Marks & Spencer (page 74)

Q1: M&S's decision has been prompted by:

- increasing concern for the environment highlighted by the Stern Review;
- increasing awareness and intent of consumers to use eco-friendly products and services;
- pressure on firms via UK and EU legislation;
- long-term cost-saving opportunities.

Q2: Examples include:

- running its stores on renewable power;
- offsetting its CO_2 emissions by investing in reforestation or windfarms;
- developing low carbon products and services;
- encouraging consumers to wash clothes at lower temperatures;
- any three taken from case study.

Q3: The impact of the plan is that:

- costs will increase in the short term - plan to cost £200m;
- new policies and procedures have to be introduces to meet its targets;
- more use of recycled materials encouraged, e.g. fleeces for staff made from recycled plastic bottles;
- increased spending on research and development;
- possible increase in customers who like to be associated with a "green" company;
- staff training to be more environmentally friendly - costs increase in the short term.

Research (page 75)

Expected answer

Tesco believes that by reducing their impact on the environment is not only essential as part of their commitment to be a responsible business, but it can also increase their chances of success, help secure the supply of their products and provide opportunities to save money on areas such as energy and waste reduction.

Over the last year they have been working with external experts and colleagues to update their environmental strategy, ensuring it remains credible in meeting their commitments to reduce their impact on the environment. From this consultation process they have identified five key environments that they have an impact on, either through their direct operations or through their sourcing activities:

- *Climate* - they continue to recognise climate change as the biggest environmental threat the world faces. As such, they have an ambitious target to be a zero carbon business by 2050 and have set medium-term 2020 targets to help them achieve this. Their work in this area is more advanced than the other environments however they recognised that they needed to be clear on their path to reaching their 2050 goal and therefore have asked The Carbon Trust to help them with this thinking. The 'F Plan' continues to be their strategy for reducing emissions from distribution and is based on four areas: fuller cages and pallets, fuller trucks and containers, fewer miles and fuel economy.

- *Forests* - they have pledged to help achieve zero net deforestation by 2020, starting with the four global drivers for deforestation that are relevant for their business: palm oil, cattle products, soy and timber. For each commodity they are mapping their supply chains to understand their exposure, and putting in place sustainable procurement policies.

- *Marine environment* - the Sustainable Fisheries Partnership have been helping them risk assess their fisheries for a number of years. They now want to go further and are working to improve the traceability and sustainability of fishmeal - the wild fish fed to farmed fish.

- *Farmlands* - sustainable agriculture covers a broad range of issues and raw materials - from livestock to non-food agricultural materials like cotton. They are working to define a set of priority raw materials and environmental issues where they think they can make a real impact. These will then start to form the basis of their new sustainable agriculture strategy.

- *Freshwater environments* - they know that the majority of fresh water globally is used in agriculture, including in countries and regions where there are issues with water scarcity and quality. They want to ensure that their supply chains are using water as efficiently as possible, and are addressing any water quality risks.

Government influence (page 76)

Q4: b) Monetary policy

Q5: c) Regional policy

Q6: b) Monetary policy

Q7: a) Fiscal policy

Q8: a) Fiscal policy

Q9: c) Regional policy

Government influence on business activity (page 79)

Q10: b) Health and Safety at Work Act 1974

Q11: a) labour law.

Q12: a) The Prince's Trust

Starbucks (page 80)

Q13: a) Political

Q14: b) Social

Q15: b) Transfer pricing

Q16: By declaring more profit in a country with a lower tax rate, and less profit in a country with a high tax rate, the overall rate of taxation paid by the company is reduced.

AG Barr (page 81)

Q17: External factors include:

- *legislation* - e.g. health and safety, environmental health inspectors, consumer protection laws. AG Barr must comply with all of these or run the risk of facing prosecution or being shut down. Employment protection laws such as minimum wage may add to Barr's costs and restrict employee numbers which can have a knock on effect for productivity, although this seems unlikely due to the fact that many employees stay with the company for a long time suggesting they have a loyal workforce.
- *social / changes in demand* - consumers are being made more aware of healthy eating and drinking and so sales of its famous brands like IRN-BRU might decline because of this. Also factors linked to hyperactivity in children are often blamed on soft fizzy drinks. Parents could stop buying Barr's products for their children if this is proved to be the case. This could have prompted AG Barr to enter the mineral water market as more and more people are drinking this instead of fizzy drinks.
- *actions of competitors* - Coke has over 30% share of the fizzy drinks market and can put pressure on Barr's marketing ability to compete because it has more resources available to promote its products.
- *technological changes* - more advanced production facilities at its four sites may be a drain on Barr's financial resources but failure to keep up to date with the latest production techniques could mean loss of competitiveness - hence it was the first to introduce the returnable glass bottle line.
- *environmental* - the introduction of its returnable bottle means that AG Barr is taking positive steps to reduce its carbon footprint and is taking heed of the changes in the world around them which can directly affect demand for their products.

Increased competitiveness through ICT (page 83)

Q18: Use of the internet can *improve communications between companies and their customers through continuous access*. This enhances customer services. It can *provide links so that customers can buy and pay online and have access on the status of their orders* whilst simultaneously *providing customer advice and support*. Having access to customers' personal details allows the company to *email information to them about new products and services that may be of benefit to them*, satisfying their needs more fully.

Online surveys and market research can be carried out to ensure current products and services meet customer expectations. Use of the internet will also *help companies scan their environment and keep up to date with developments within their own industry*.

Companies can *set up their own internal intranet to manage email and video conferencing which enables swift communication between all parts of the organisation*, wherever they are located. This *helps maintain an efficient communication system within the company* and can *co-ordinate projects or developments that are taking place in different locations within the company*.

Costs and benefits to businesses of technological change (page 83)

Q19: b) Benefit

Q20: a) Cost

Q21: b) Benefit

Q22: b) Benefit

Q23: b) Benefit

Q24: a) Cost

Q25: a) Cost

Q26: a) Cost

E-commerce advantages and disadvantages (page 87)

Q27:

Advantage	Disadvantage
Can find out if products are in or out of stock	Concerns about security when purchasing/banking online
Can increase global market share	Delivery problems
Customer data can be used for marketing	Fear that retail shops will be replaced by storage warehouses
Improved relationship with suppliers	Shopping is more impersonal and less of a social affair
Often reduces lead time	
Saves costs and improves efficiency	

Internet shopping (page 88)

Q28: Three reasons are:

- online shopping is convenient, saves times and costs and gives consumers more choice, customisation and control;
- consumers are becoming increasingly confident in shopping online;
- as broadband internet use is spreading, faster browser speeds enable consumers to compare more sites.

Q29: If they had not entered this market, it would have meant losing out to competitors which would have reduced their profit margins.

End of Topic 7 test (page 89)

Q30: c) Increase greenhouse gas emissions

Q31: c) reducing waste.

Q32: c) consumer, competition and employee laws.

Q33: c) consumers.

Q34: d) taxation and government spending in the economy.

Q35: c) To ensure employees get appropriate training.

Q36: a) It adds to business costs and can put constraints on business activity.

Q37: b) pest analysis.

Q38: b) new products for consumers can be developed relatively cheaply.

Q39: c) businesses buying from their suppliers using electronic media.

Q40: b) The financial costs of setting up a sophisticated ICT presence are relatively cheap.

Q41: d) Concerns about security when purchasing/banking online.

Q42: d) firms will have to develop new ways of offering customers a personal touch.

Q43: c) Customers are now more confident in placing orders online.

Q44: *Economic policy / Monetary policy*

Increases in interest rates put up cost of borrowing, negatively affecting cash flow and profits; firms may react by reducing gearing, trying to reduce dependency on borrowed funds, e.g. by selling more shares or retaining more profit to finance capital expenditure.

Reductions in interest rates make borrowing cheaper and may encourage firms to borrow to expand.

Fiscal policy

Income tax increases reduce disposable income and hence demand; firms may devise ways to attract customers, e.g. advertising campaign, sales promotion.

Increases in VAT and excise duties add to the price the consumer pays; firms may decide to bear part or all of the cost of increases themselves, reducing their profit margins.

Increases in corporation tax reduce firms' net profit after tax and could cause them to put expansion plans on hold.

A fall in any of these taxes would have a beneficial effect, reduced income tax allows consumers to spend more, reduced VAT stimulates demand by making prices lower and reduced corporation tax allowing the firm to keep a bigger share of its profit to finance its future plans.

Topic 8: The external business environment test
The external business environment test (page 94)

Q1: a) True

Q2: b) False

Q3: a) True

Q4: a) True

Q5: a) True

Q6: a) True

Q7: b) False

Q8: b) False

Q9: b) False

Q10: b) False

Q11: a) True

Q12: a) True

Q13: a) True

Q14: a) True

Q15: a) True

Q16: a) True

Q17: b) False

Q18: a) True

Q19: b) False

Q20: a) True

Q21: b) False

Q22: b) False

Q23: c) world trade.

Q24: d) their facilities abroad.

Q25: c) costs and risks.

Q26: a) transferred between one international subsidiary and another.

Q27: d) Accelerating use of transfer pricing in business.

Q28: b) tax on the MNC's profits can be used as a source of revenue for the host country.

Q29: c) It increases staff turnover as staff prefer to work for companies involved in community projects.

Q30: d) Businesses can respond quicker to customers' needs in the local area, ensuring loyalty.

Q31: b) Consumers find online shopping to be secure at all times.

Q32: Aegon became a multinational company to seek out new markets, e.g. China, as markets became saturated at home, to increase market share and dominance worldwide.

The emergence of worldwide financial markets eased access to external finance and it meant Aegon also gained economies of scale.

Q33: One reason is that buying over existing companies allows a presence to be built up quickly.

Another reason is that setting up its own companies enables Aegon to establish its own culture and philosophy.

Q34: Tax gained from Aegon is a source of revenue for UK government.

Direct and indirect employment opportunities increase thereby reducing unemployment in the UK.

Balance of payments in the UK increase from the initial flow of investment capital into the UK.

Q35: Employees of Aegon in other parts of the world, e.g. China and Taiwan, may expect the same guaranteed working conditions as those in the EU. This could impact into even greater costs for Aegon, e.g. in providing a minimum wage, parental leave, at least four weeks' paid annual leave.

Q36: Becoming involved in local community projects and ethical investments will give Aegon good PR and strengthen its image and brand locally. It can help gain customers and this increases revenue. It attracts and keeps good employees, reducing staff turnover costs.

Q37: Products tailor-made to suit local needs - not "one size fits all".

Economies of being global means Aegon can pass on cost saving to customers by way of cheaper products.

Global expertise means it can utilise its resources more effectively to suit local needs.

Q38: Aegon might offer customers online quote facilities and discounts for buying its products online.

It might offer customers quizzes, the answers which illustrate how much needs to be invested in a pension each month to secure a reasonable income on retirement.

Q39: The FCA can introduce more stringent rules governing life insurance and pensions which may limit Aegon's potential to maximise profits.

They can enforce financial organisations to comply with the rules or run the risk of being closed down.

They can investigate on behalf of consumers, e.g. misselling of products, which can lead to bad publicity.

Q40: Aggreko has many worldwide locations all offering continuous support for customers. It offers improvements and solutions to a diverse range of industries, from construction to contracting, to help them enhance their operations. Aggreko has highly-trained, expert staff who are committed to delivering outstanding service. It introduced a new 'green area' at Glastonbury Festival in response to customers' demands.

Q41: Aggreko may operate in some countries where there is no suitable local company therefore setting up on its own is the only option. Mixing the two methods means that Aggreko can grow quickly in some places but can move into others where things can be taken at Aggreko's own pace. Acquisitions allow markets and profits to be taken advantage of straight away as well as bringing in local expertise from management with local knowledge. This reduces the risk of failure.

Acquisitions can bring complementary businesses into Aggreko's portfolio, e.g. GE Energy Rental adding further geographic reach for Aggreko. Growing organically can give you the competitive advantage in emerging markets. By growing organically, Aggreko can establish its own philosophy and culture, e.g. its customer-focussed mission statement, and does not have to instil them in new acquired companies. By using the two methods the speed of growth can be tailored to the needs of the local market.

Q42: The nature of Aggreko's line of business means that it could get a lot of bad publicity if it did not act in the interests of people or the environment - this could reduce its turnover and status in the global market. There is increasing concern for the environment as highlighted by the Stern Report. Therefore, it is vital that Aggreko do all they can to reduce the carbon footprint of their business at the earliest opportunity, e.g. by working in cooperation with the manufacturers of diesel engines in order to meet new emission requirements.

Firms with very good social reputations may not lose out on profits if some of their actions do not work out as expected, as their previous good reputation may be remembered. CSR policies attract or keep employees whose values are similar to the firms resulting in higher motivation and productivity which increases profits. This can also lead to reducing costs of recruitment and selection as employee turnover rates are reduced - this is important as Aggreko rely on its employees to maintain its reputation for good customer service. Good CSR can also enable a firm to gain a niche market for itself.

Q43: Joint ventures enable organisations to reduce the risks when entering markets where they have little expertise, e.g. the Olympic Games can benefit from Aggreko's expertise in providing energy for other major sporting events. The Olympic Games joint ventures gave Aggreko a very lucrative contract, estimated to be worth 35 million US dollars as the sole supplier of energy.

Joint ventures can give you a foothold in an untried market and, because they are often time limited, it does not need a long term commitment. Firms have the option of pulling out if necessary.

Q44: Features of globalisation include:

- reduction in barriers to trade through agreements such as WTO and GATT;
- instant worldwide communications through internet, email, etc.;
- improved technological advances;
- greater international cultural exchanges leading to consumers' tastes being similar.

Ways in which globalisation can affect how a business operates include:

- opening up opportunities for Aggreko to reach more customers more quickly through technological advances;
- opening up better opportunities for Aggreko to pursue its growth strategy through the emergence of worldwide financial markets;
- possibility of increased competition from other companies elsewhere in the world who are also now able to access wider markets;
- companies have to take account of international factors when making decisions - this is important in Aggreko's line of work.

Answers to questions and activities for The internal business environment

Topic 1: Management theory

Fayol's management functions (page 107)

Q1: c) Commanding

Q2: b) Organising

Q3: a) Planning

Q4: e) Controlling

Q5: d) Coordinating

Fayol's functions in action (page 108)

Q6: A marketing manager of a large manufacturing company

- Planning: deciding on the best methods of promoting a new product
- Organising: setting up a team to create the advertisement, employing graphic designers, copywriters
- Commanding: giving the team their brief, issuing instructions to designers and copywriters
- Co-ordinating: liaising with the finance department to ensure enough money is available, and with the production department to ensure enough goods are available if the advertisement increases demand
- Controlling: checking the work is proceeding on schedule - e.g. that it is not going over budget by holding progress meetings, checking that target dates are met etc. Taking corrective action e.g. cutting spending on another part of the project if necessary.

A football club manager

- Planning: devising a strategy to achieve promotion to a higher league
- Organising: acquiring players, assigning positions to players
- Commanding: telling players to use a certain formation, attend training sessions at set times
- Co-ordinating: maintaining the team's effectiveness by altering the formation e.g. changing from 433 to 442
- Control: checking the team's position in the league, taking corrective action e.g. selling ineffective players, devising new fitness regimes

A human resources manager

- Planning: developing a plan of action to ensure sufficient numbers of appropriately qualified staff will be in position in five years' time
- Organising: allocating people to create job analyses, job and person specifications, advertisements, and to interview applicants; arranging other tests of suitability
- Commanding: issuing instructions about the budget available for the advertisement, deadlines for applications

- Co-ordinating: ensuring that the stages flow smoothly e.g. interviews are arranged on days when departmental and HRM managers are both available
- Controlling: checking that the best people have been selected - how productive are the new employees?; analysing the recruitment and selection process with a view to improving its effectiveness; arranging post-induction training to deal with problems.

The head teacher of your school

- Planning: setting overall objectives for the school e.g. for academic progress, sporting success, staff development
- Organising: appointing new members of staff; allocating staff and resources to departments
- Commanding: issuing instructions at school assemblies and staff meetings
- Co-ordinating: chairing staff meetings to ensure staff support for new initiatives, settle any areas of disharmony
- Controlling: examining results in SQA exams, checking pupil progress against targets, holding appraisal interviews with teachers

Management by objectives (MBO) (page 109)

Q7:

Advantages	Disadvantages
Basing rewards and promotion on the achievement of targets rather than the subjective view of managers is likely to be seen as fairer by the workforce.	Areas where specific objectives have not been set may be seen as less important and ignored.
Everyone's focus is on the main objectives of the organisation.	Employees may be tempted to take excessive risks in order to ensure they meet targets.
Individual targets act as motivators.	Employees may cheat and cut corners e.g. leading to quality problems in order to achieve their targets.
MBO helps to identify training needs.	Failure may undermine confidence and demotivate employees.
MBO increases each employee's awareness of responsibility for their own work.	Striving to reach targets may put stress on employees, leading to absenteeism and illness.

Q8: First of all, managers would look at the objectives of an organisation. They would then set the objectives of their department which would fit in with the organisation's objectives. They would then set targets in individual's appraisals to enable the department to achieve their objectives.

Mintzberg's roles (page 110)

Q9:

Description	Role
Describes the organisation to those outside	Spokesperson
Represents the organisation	Figurehead
Passes data on to other people in the organisation	Disseminator
Chooses how to use resources such as money and people	Resource allocator
Deals with unusual situations and unforeseen problems	Disturbance handler
Keeps track of what is going on inside and outside the organisation	Monitor
Acts as a link between the organisation and external organisations	Liaison
Mediates in, and helps to resolve, internal and external conflicts	Negotiator
Harmonises the needs of the individuals with the needs of the organisation	Leader
Initiates and plans how to exploit opportunities and solve problems	Entrepreneur

Demands, constraints and choices (page 112)

Q10:

Demand	Constraint	Choice
Managing Director needs budget projections by Monday	Buying a new machine will go over budget	Deciding which workers should be given overtime
Senior management need workers to increase output	Working Time Directive limits workers to a 48-hour week	Negotiating a further discount from a supplier
	The cheapest supplier has closed down	Scheduling double shifts

Classroom manager (page 113)

Q11: ***Constraints*** - teacher's knowledge and experience, pupils' ability and attitude, availability of equipment and textbooks, legislation (e.g. data protection, human rights), time available;

Choices - about how to deliver the lesson, activities, assessment dates, homework, punishments;

Demands - expectations of senior management, parents, pupils, local authority, school inspectors, Scottish Qualifications Authority.

Management thought - revision (page 113)

Q12: a) True

Q13: b) False

Q14: a) True

Q15: b) False

Taylor's five principles (page 114)

Q16: thinking

Q17: efficient

Q18: scientifically

Q19: trained and efficiency

Q20: monitored and procedures

Scientific management (page 115)

Q21: Scientific management is based on observations of *manufacturing* workers. Each worker *specialises* in doing one small task. This makes them more efficient as practice makes perfect. *Time and motion studies* can be carried out. This involves timing workers and observing their movements in order to find out the best way to do the task. A standard rate of pay called *piece rate* can then be set per item produced. This gives workers a financial *incentive* to be more productive. Giving workers *training* for their particular part of the process also improves efficiency. Workers have to follow the *procedures* laid down by management exactly and are closely *supervised*, ensuring a standardised product.

Results of scientific management (page 116)

Q22: a

Q23: e

Q24: b

Q25: c and d

Q26: a, c, d and e

Classical school theorists (page 117)

Q27:

Management thought	Theorist
Believed managers have five roles	Henri Fayol
Introduced the term 'bureaucracy'	Max Weber
Pioneered motion study using 'therbligs'	Frank and Lillian Gilbreth
Raised the importance of organisational objectives	Mary Parker Follett
The 'father' of scientific management	Frederick Taylor

Fayol's 14 principles of management (page 118)

Q28: b) Division of work

Q29: c) Discipline

Q30: d) Unity of command

Q31: a) Scalar chain

Q32: e) Subordination of individual interest to general interest

Bureaucracy (page 119)

Q33: a, b, e and f. These were the features Weber said a bureaucracy should have.

We often think of bureaucracy as a bad word involving lots of rules and regulations and delays, but Weber said a bureaucracy was a good word which described the ideal organisation.

Criticisms of the classical school (page 120)

Q34: Classical writers shared a *mechanistic* view of human nature, with people motivated only by *self-interest*. The classical school *ignored* social and psychological factors. Nowadays, the word *bureaucracy* often has negative connotations of initiative being *stifled* and an organisation being *unresponsive* to people's needs.

Classical theory is less relevant to modern organisations due to *deindustrialisation*. Classical structures are *rigid* and *unchanging* when compared with the modern flexible workplace and management techniques. Division of labour arguably led to *boring*, repetitive jobs and a feeling among workers that they were *unimportant*.

What motivated the workers? (page 121)

Q35: b and c

The human relations school (page 122)

Expected answer

Some changes include:

- Changing attitudes to woman - a gradual shift over recent decades has improved the perception of woman in the workplace;
- Woman are rightly treated as equals;
- More woman are in positions of authority in the workforce;
- Women are more likely to move out of the family home at a younger age;
- Equality Act 2010 - legislation ensures that woman are treated the same as men.

Relevance of the human relations school (page 122)

Q36: b) False

Q37: a) True

Q38: b) False

Q39: b) False

Q40: a) True

Maslow's hierarchy (page 123)

Q41: The order in the pyramid (in descending order) is as follows:

- Self-actualisation;
- Self-esteem;
- Social;
- Safety;
- Physiological.

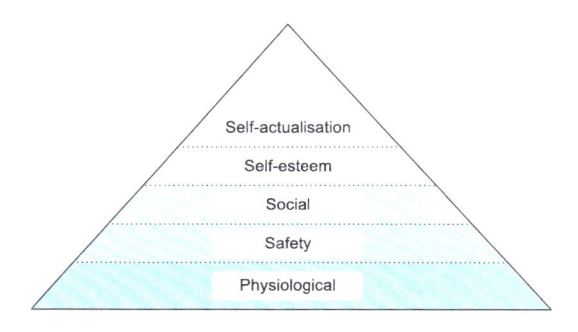

Hunger (page 124)

Q42: Hunger is a physiological need which is lower than the social need of wanting to work in a group so the offer of group working will not motivate; the need for food has to be fulfilled first.

Herzberg's motivator-hygiene factors (page 125)

Q43:

Motivators	Hygiene factors
Challenging work	Machines that work
Empowerment	Supervision
Profit sharing schemes	Working conditions
Promotion	Job security
Target setting	Fair pay

Theory X and Theory Y (page 126)

Q44: The theory you tend to believe in depends on your own experience. In terms of believing in both, you might take a Theory X view if workers were doing a boring, routine task where motivation was not high. You might take a Theory Y view where workers were involved in something creative, e.g. making a dance video.

Q45: a) Classical approach

Q46: b) Human relations approach

A business system (page 127)

Q47:

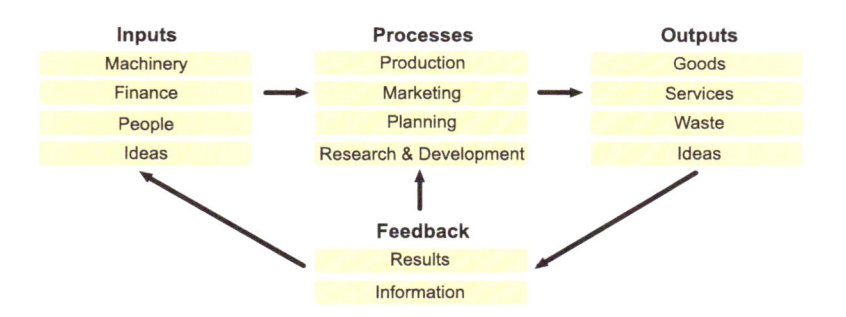

Inputs	Processes	Outputs
Machinery	Production	Goods
Finance	Marketing	Services
People	Planning	Waste
Ideas	Research & Development	Ideas

Feedback

Results
Information

Systems theory today (page 128)

Q48: This sees organisations as systems made up of several **subsystems** (individual parts) which are all connected to each other.

In a system, **resources** and **information** flow through and are **processed** into goods and services. The success of the system is monitored through the process of **feedback**. Businesses are **open** systems because they interact with their environment. They affect and are affected by happenings in the outside world (**PEST** factors).

The idea that departments and units in a business are more productive when they work together than when they operate separately is termed **synergy**. This approach calls for a lot of **interaction** between departments.

Tavistock institute research results (page 129)

Q49: b) False

Q50: a) True

Q51: a) True

Q52: b) False

Q53: b) False

Q54: a) True

Different ideas (page 130)

Expected answer

You probably found that the person who was managing the assembly line took a more classical approach than the boutique owner. Why was this? It was because the situations (contingencies) are different. The assembly line manager has a huge span of control, the work is likely to be routine and deviations from procedures seen as undesirable. On the other hand, the boutique owner will want to motivate and empower his/her assistant to deal effectively with customers when he/she is not present.

Different management approaches (page 131)

Q55:

Routine and unchanging	Non routine, constantly changing
Complete obedience and loyalty of subordinates to management are stressed.	The manager encourages lateral communication
Decisions are made by managers and communicated down the hierarchy.	The manager encourages subordinates to use their initiative.
The manager supervises employees closely to ensure they follow procedures.	The manager mainly offers advice and information

End of Topic 1 test (page 133)

Q56: b) piece rate.

Q57: b) managers need to vary their approach according to the situation.

Q58: c) sets out exactly how work should be done.

Q59: b) inputs, processes, output, feedback.

Q60: d) tends to cause a "carrot and stick" approach to motivation.

Q61: a) Systems theory

Q62: d) The classical school

Q63: c) The human relations school

Q64: a) Structure based on hierarchy

Q65: c) naturally avoid having to work.

Q66: c) unity of command.

Q67: b) technological subsystem without anticipating the knock-on effects on the social subsystem.

Q68: d) self-esteem and self-actualisation needs.

Q69: d) interacts with its external environment.

ANSWERS: UNIT 2 TOPIC 1

Q70: *Planning:* new production system.

Organising: grouping employees for training, arranging machine repair, recruiting workers.

Commanding: telling Joe to sort out health and safety issues.

Coordinating: harmonising production schedules with marketing plans, switching Rosie to Dan's team.

Controlling: checking production line is flowing, checking production figures, discussing improvements with Dan.

Q71: Interpersonal roles:

- *Figurehead* - representing the firm at the Gala;
- *Liaison* - liaising with Marketing;
- *Leader* - telling Joe to sort out health and safety issues.

Informational roles:

- *Spokesperson* - speaking to Marketing on behalf of Operations;
- *Disseminator* - giving Joe the health and safety report;
- *Monitor* - checking production figures.

Decisional roles:

- *Resource allocator* - moving Rosie to Dan's team;
- *Disturbance handler* - sorting out the dispute between Joe and Lucy;
- *Entrepreneur* - deciding to employ two new workers;
- *Negotiator* - negotiating the level of increase in production with Marketing.

Q72: Human skills:

- *Understanding* - Joe;
- *Persuasiveness* - Arnold;
- *Diplomacy* - Lucy, Marketing department.

Technical skills:

- Knowledge of the production system.

Conceptual skills:

- Devising the new production system;
- Assessing the relationship with Marketing.

Q73: Demands: Marketing department's demands, production targets.

Choices: how to deal with Lucy and Joe, whether to attend the Gala, how to respond to Marketing's demands, how to fix the labour shortage in Dan's department.

Constraints: machine not working, shortage of staff.

Q74: *Maximum 7 marks for description. Maximum 6 marks per school.*

The classical school is based on scientific management which emphasised efficiency above all things. Extensive division of labour was used; researchers such as Taylor carried out time and motion studies to find out the best way of doing a task, reflecting their mechanistic view of workers, and then set a standard rate of pay as they believed that employees were only interested in money.

The classical school established the principle of paying people by results which came to be known as the piece rate. Classical writers said the ideal organisation was a hierarchy (bureaucracy) with clearly defined rules and procedures. Initiative was discouraged - managers were responsible for thinking, workers for obeying instructions. Workers were closely supervised to ensure that instructions were obeyed and procedures followed.

The contingency school holds that no single ideal method of management exists; the best approach will depend on the variables (contingencies) of the particular situation faced. It builds on the ideas of the systems school, which focused on interrelationships between structure and behaviour in an attempt to reconcile the ideas of the classical (accused of focusing on the organisation structure but ignoring human needs) and human relations (accused of ignoring structure by focusing on human needs) schools. The contingency approach recognises that each situation is unique and the method of organisation needs to be tailored accordingly. Variable factors may include the size, type and history of a particular organisation, the nature of the work, the skills and experience of its workforce, the nature of the managers and the market environment - all of which can affect the approach to management chosen.

The ideas of the classical school are still relevant in manufacturing industries which have routine processes and require a standardised output. Many modern techniques like lean production and business process re-engineering are based on the principles of scientific management, e.g. attempts to measure the time it takes to get an order to a customer and to reduce the time spent on each of the steps in the processes involved. Elements of scientific management can also apply to service sector industries such as fast food outlets, so that a uniform service is provided throughout all branches, e.g. supermarket checkout operators may be trained in the precise way they have to deal with customers.

The classical approach has been criticised for demotivating workers by treating them like machines. Division of labour can lead to boring, repetitive work and worker alienation as workers feel themselves to be small cogs in a large machine where they never see the end product.

Measuring performance has become increasingly important because of greater expectations of employees in meeting targets. This may be more difficult to measure in some industries, e.g. the service sector.

The contingency school is relevant to current management because it suggests that no one approach will always work, so that management should be flexible and decide what is best in any set of circumstances. The contingency school helps managers adjust to changes in social and economic circumstances, e.g. by making changes to accommodate flexible working practices. This approach may lead to methods which have become out of date being replaced; in a rapidly changing global environment this may be important.

Topic 2: Leadership

Differences between managers and leaders (page 138)

Q1: b) Leader

Q2: b) Leader

Q3: a) Manager

Q4: b) Leader

Q5: a) Manager

Q6: a) Manager

Q7: b) Leader

Q8: a) Manager

Q9: b) Leader

Q10: b) Leader

Leadership styles (1) (page 140)

Q11:

Management phrase	Style of leadership
"I know best. I'll make you do as I decide."	Autocratic
"I know best. I'll persuade you that what I decide is right."	Persuasive
"I'll ask you what you think before I decide."	Consultative
"I'll take your views into account and let you help me decide."	Participative
"I'll let you decide within certain limits."	Democratic
"You know best - you can decide."	Laissez-faire

Leadership styles (2) (page 140)

Q12:
1. Autocratic;
2. Persuasive;
3. Consultative;
4. Participative;
5. Democratic;
6. Laissez-faire.

Advantages and disadvantages of autocratic and democratic styles (page 140)

Q13:

	Autocratic	Democratic
Advantages	Employees know exactly what they are required to do.	More responsibility motivates employees.
	Decisions are made by managers without discussion with employees so time is saved.	Managers will have a better view than employees of the needs of the organisation as a whole.
Disadvantages	Supervision can be expensive and time-consuming.	Better decisions can be made with input from those actually carrying out the work.
	The initiative and knowledge of employees is not fully used.	In an urgent situation there may not be time to allow employees to discuss options.

Leadership traits (page 141)

Expected answer

Possible leadership traits that you may find in an effective leader are: assertiveness, discipline, humour, ability to motivate, compassion, empathy, trustworthiness, charisma, an open nature, ambition, intelligence, ability to adapt and confidence.

Assessment of trait theory (page 142)

Q14:

First half	Second half
A long list of traits that leaders are born with has been developed	such as self-confidence, initiative, intelligence and self-belief.
Different people have different ideas about what makes a good leader	it is impossible to identify a common pattern of traits.
Even if leaders are born with certain traits	objective assessment of the traits needed is impossible.
Most leaders do seem to share certain general characteristics	but there is no general agreement about which are most important.
Part of the success of being a good leader seems to come from being unique	it may still be possible to train them to improve their effectiveness.

ANSWERS: UNIT 2 TOPIC 2

Different leadership styles (page 143)

Q15: a) Autocratic

Q16: b) Democratic

Q17: a) Autocratic

Q18: b) Democratic

Q19: a) Autocratic

Q20: b) Democratic

Contingency theory (page 144)

Q21: A 'contingency' is a particular *situation* faced by a manager. Each contingency has different *variables*. These include different *technological*, *external* and *human* factors. For example, when a job is routine and *unchanging*, the management style is likely to be more *autocratic* than in a job which presents workers with constantly changing demands.

Task or relationship orientation (page 144)

Q22: b) Task-oriented manager

Q23: a) Relationship-oriented manager

Situational leadership (page 145)

Q24: b) Participating

Q25: c) Selling

Q26: d) Telling

Q27: a) Delegating

Q28: b) Participating

Q29: d) Telling

Q30: c) Selling

Q31: a) Delegating

Action centred leadership (page 147)

Q32: c) Individual

Q33: b) Team

Q34: a) Task

Q35: b) Team

Q36: c) Individual

Q37: a) Task

Path goal theory (page 149)

Q38:

Description	Leadership style
Developing friendly relationships with followers	Supportive
Fitting in with subordinates' characteristics or with environmental factors	Situational
Setting challenging goals and helping followers to achieve them	Achievement-oriented
Telling people what to do	Directive

End of Topic 2 test (page 150)

Q39: a) manager

Q40: a) manager

Q41: b) leader

Q42: b) leader

Q43: b) leader

Q44: a) manager

Q45: a) True

Q46: c) measuring traits objectively is impossible.

Q47: d) persuasive.

Q48: b) False

Q49: b) False

Q50: a) True

Q51: a) directive.

Q52: Trudi is task oriented and autocratic. Greg is relationship oriented and democratic.

Q53: When time is short or where employees are inexperienced or new.

Q54: Creative tasks or where employees are experienced.

Q55: Employees do not feel appreciated, e.g. Helen was rebuked for low increase in sales, Sean's mood was ignored. Employees are not motivated to do their best only to do enough, e.g. Helen, unlike Joseph, does not volunteer to work extra hours.

Q56: Chatting to employees about their personal needs, e.g. Joseph takes up time which could be spent on work. Employees might take advantage of Greg, e.g. Anil may play on his wife's illness, Joseph may play on his own illness.

Q57: *Candidates can be given up to 4 marks for a description of each of two theories. Maximum 6 marks for answers that make no reference to UK managers, or those that examine only one theory.*

Leadership theories

- Trait theory - states that the ability to lead people is something you are born with, not something you learn; believes that people should be selected as leaders not trained; traits are personal characteristics; traits needed are initiative, decisiveness, self-assurance, assertiveness, intelligence, desire for work, achievement and desire for financial reward; people's physical appearance, dress code and stature can affect their ability to lead.
- Style theory - highlights what successful leaders do rather than what they are; the underlying principle behind this approach is that if leaders behave in a certain way they will be successful; most style theories argue that leaders have two main issues to tackle - achieving the task and maintaining good working relationships; there are many possible leadership styles, e.g. autocratic, democratic.
- Contingency theory - various examples of contingency theory, such as Fiedler's contingency model, Hersey and Blanchard's situation approach, the "best fit" approach. It suggests that the most suitable style of leadership will depend upon a wide range of variables; it assumes that just because one style of leadership works in one set of circumstances it will not necessarily work in another; the best leader is one who is able to adopt different styles in different situations.

Relevance

- Trait theory - criticised as it is felt that measuring traits objectively is impossible; deciding which traits are needed for particular leadership positions is impossible; there are too many traits that are said to affect the ability to lead; too many exceptions in real life to accept that these traits are needed for leader to be successful; difficult to train people to be leaders.
- Style theory - often leaders will use a combination of styles depending on a number of variables, e.g. task to be undertaken, environment in which the business operates and the people the manager is dealing with; employees will respond differently to being led by people with different styles of leadership, also implies there is one best style.
- Contingency theory - UK business finds itself in changing environments so managers should be able to adapt to all circumstances; some situations will call for a more authoritarian approach, e.g. in a crisis; however managers may not be flexible enough to adapt in the way the theory suggests.

Topic 3: Teams

Permanent, temporary or informal teams (page 156)

Q1: b) Temporary

Q2: a) Permanent

Q3: a) Permanent

Q4: c) Informal

Advantages and disadvantages of teams (page 157)

Q5: a) Advantage

Q6: b) Disadvantage

Q7: a) Advantage

Q8: b) Disadvantage

Q9: a) Advantage

Q10: b) Disadvantage

Q11: a) Advantage

Q12: b) Disadvantage

Q13: a) Advantage

Q14: a) Advantage

Q15: b) Disadvantage

ANSWERS: UNIT 2 TOPIC 3   313

What makes an effective team? (page 158)

Expected answer

All of the following make up an effective team:

- All the team members would share a common goal or goals.
- Each team member would understand the goals and know their role in helping to achieve them.
- Team members would trust and respect each other.
- Team members would accept each other's strengths and weaknesses.
- The team would consist of a variety of people with different gifts performing different roles.
- The team size would be appropriate to the task - e.g. fewer than 12 for problem solving, larger for tasks involving collecting or distributing a lot of information.
- The team would handle problems and conflict constructively.
- There would be effective communication between members.
- Leadership would be democratic/participative - teams might even rotate leadership among members.

Team roles (page 159)

Q16:

Team role	Description
Completer finisher	Checks details, makes sure the team meets deadlines
Monitor evaluator	Checks the value and feasibility of the team's ideas and proposals
Plant	Comes up with new ideas about how to achieve team goals
Implementer	Draws up schedules and plans to turn ideas into actual tasks
Teamworker	Ensures harmony in the team by getting along with and supporting everybody
Specialist	Expert in their field, others can go to them for advice on particular issues
Resource investigator	Finds new contacts and opportunities for the team
Coordinator	Natural leader who delegates appropriately
Shaper	Sparks life into the team, pushes other members into action

Influence of teams (page 160)

Q17:

Positive influences	Negative influences
By offering mutual support teams improve motivation and hence performance	Competition between teams could be divisive and lead to inter-group conflict, harming the achievement of organisational objectives
Healthy competition between teams can improve performance	Group decision-making is time consuming; time is money;
If a team member is absent the work still gets done if work is allocated to teams rather than individuals	'Groupthink' may develop where everyone in a team ends up thinking in the same way, so they are not open to new ideas that could generate more profit
Team members contribute many more ideas, leading to more efficient production and better quality products	'Parochial self-interest' - teams may become unable to see the viewpoint of other teams or management so that they are pursuing their own team goals rather than organisational ones
Teams combine the expertise of many people, allowing members to learn from each other and become more multi-skilled	'Risky shift' may occur, where people in teams may take ill-advised risks that they would not take if they were acting on their own
Teams increase the loyalty of employees as they develop relationships within the group; not wishing to let their fellow team members down will motivate them to work hard	Teams may operate as cliques against management and prevent the achievement of organisational goals

Place in group development (page 162)

Q18: *What the results mean*

The highest of your scores shows what stage your group is at. If you have equal highest scores for two adjacent stages you're probably in the middle of moving from one to the next. If your scores are all fairly equal then your team is probably still at the storming stage, i.e. not quite sure what it is supposed to be doing!

End of Topic 3 test (page 164)

Q19: b) False

Q20: a) True

Q21: b) False

Q22: b) it allows teams to share goals.

Q23: b) Conforming

ANSWERS: UNIT 2 TOPIC 3

Q24: *Maximum 3 marks per characteristic. Maximum 7 marks for points not linked to effectiveness.*

- Teams should be formed from employees with a variety of skills and knowledge so that all areas of expertise are available for the tasks. Meredith Belbin specified nine different roles that are necessary for a team to be effective.
- Problems can be shared so that each team can arrive at a decision which takes everyone's viewpoint into consideration - this increases the number of ideas available to the team, leading to a greater chance of success. This can also motivate team members to work more effectively together.
- Team size - if a team is too large this can make interaction more difficult and create changes in the decision-making process. The more members, the more complex a communication process is needed. However, a broader range of experience can be brought to the table. Having too small a team can limit the expertise available.
- Each team member must clearly understand the team's work, and the role of each individual, and have a high commitment to achieving targets in order to ensure the team stay on track working towards objectives.
- Team members should be empowered to control how they perform the tasks that have to be completed by the team - the fact that the teams are self-managing can raise productivity and increase the quality of the product.
- Members need to know why the team has been formed and the nature of the task - this enables them to focus on working towards the team goal.
- By working together on several projects, team members can build up expertise in decision-making, resulting in better quality decisions.
- Team members must build up trust among themselves and accept each other's strengths and weaknesses - this creates an atmosphere where members feel able to take bolder decisions.
- Good communication, as poor communication would lead to mistakes and delays.

Q25:

- Some teams are given responsibility for hiring and firing workers.
- Teams often elect their own leaders
- Teams are given responsibility for organising the flow of work - many American manufacturing firms are trying out cell manufacturing, where teams of workers make entire products.
- Teams can also devise ways to improve quality and efficiency.

Q26:

- Teams make workers happy by helping them to feel that they are shaping their own jobs.
- Managers no longer have to pass orders downwards which saves time.
- The firm can draw on the skills and imagination of everyone rather than rely on managers to spot mistakes and suggest improvements

Q27:

- Managers need to give teams clear objectives; otherwise they will be unclear about the tasks they should be undertaking.
- Managers need to ensure that employees receive training on matters such as self-management and how to handle conflict within the team.
- Managers need to adjust the appraisal and rewards systems in the organisation to ensure that they are based on group rather than individual performance.

Q28:

- Workers may see teams as an organisation's way of making them work harder, with peer pressure replacing pressure from managers.
- Some team members may not want responsibility, while others may come to dominate, stifling the creativity of quieter members.
- Employees are unlikely to support other team members if by doing so they risk sacrificing their own rewards, such as piece rate or commission.

Q29:

- Empowering teams of workers can result in lengthy team meetings about what to do which detract from time spent in carrying out tasks.
- Middle managers often see teams as a threat to their authority.
- Managers may also fear that their own jobs may be at risk.

Q30:

- One Swedish car manufacturer introduced team working to some of their factories in the 1990s to add interest to the work - the employees enjoyed working in teams, but the costs were so high that eventually the manufacturer disbanded the teams and rearranged workers on a traditional assembly line.

Topic 4: Time and task management

Roles of management (page 168)

Q1:

Fayol function roles	Mintzberg roles
commander	disseminator
controller	disturbance handler
coordinator	monitor
organiser	negotiator
planner	resource allocator

Time stealers (page 170)

Q2:

Scenario	Cause
Nobody remembers what happened at the last meeting so they discuss the same issues.	Poor meetings
People are confused about the purpose of a meeting so have not prepared for it.	Poor meetings
People call you about trivial matters when you are doing an important task.	Telephone time stealers
You put things in your pending tray and then forget to deal with them.	Too much paperwork
You are worried that people will take offence if you don't help them.	Inability to say "no"
You are worried you might make a mistake so dither about deciding.	Delays in making decisions
You find it difficult to get rid of people because you don't want to seem rude.	Interruptions
You like to be kind to people.	Inability to say "no"
You like to keep your door open to show you are available to your subordinates.	Interruptions
You realise that you forgot to mention something in a phone call and have to ring back.	Telephone time stealers
Your deadline is unrealistic and you need more time.	Delays in making decisions
Your filing system is disorganised.	Too much paperwork

Possible solutions to time stealers (page 171)

Q3: Draw up an agenda and circulate it before the meeting.

Q4: Take minutes at each meeting and give everyone a copy.

Q5: Plan phone calls in advance.

Q6: Switch the phone to take messages when you do not want to be disturbed; say you'll call back later.

Q7: Make the best decision on the evidence you have and accept that you may not always be right; adjustments can be made to most decisions later.

Q8: Leave time in your schedule for unforeseen events.

Q9: Learn to say "no" without offending, e.g. by suggesting something else the person could do.

Q10: Realise that if you always say "yes" people will take you for granted.

Q11: Tell them you will come and see them at a set time.

Q12: Establish a set time when you are not to be disturbed and close your door.

Q13: Ask your administrative assistant to organise your filing system.

Q14: Don't put anything in your pending tray without noting in your schedule when you will deal with it.

Good and bad time and task management (page 174)

Q15: a) Good

Q16: b) Bad

Q17: b) Bad

Q18: c) Not affected

Q19: c) Not affected

Q20: a) Good

End of Topic 4 test (page 176)

Q21: To ensure effective time and task management an organisation can create ***a to-do list*** to give each job a priority so important tasks are done first. Organisations can also make effective use of ***delegation*** by giving jobs to junior assistants - freeing up time to spend on more important tasks and developing the experience / skill set of the junior, known as ***empowerment***.

It is also important that managers do not allow meetings to overrun. To do this you can set an agenda and time for meetings - appoint a strong ***chairperson*** to manage the items / timing will also help.

Managers can also prepare ***an action plan*** to comment on the task needing done and by when. This provides accountability and allows for prioritising of tasks which is easier for senior management to track progress.

If managers are more visual they may prefer to use ***a Gantt chart*** to show the progress of a medium to long term project. This compares actual and projected time to help managers track progress to ensure deadlines are met.

Q22: Gerry could:

1. make a note in his diary of when he is going to deal with items he puts in his pending tray so that they are not forgotten, e.g. the invitation to the sales convention;
2. minimise interruptions by arranging set times to discuss matters with people, e.g. he could meet Alison after work to chat about her weekend;
3. plan phone calls to ensure he discusses all the necessary matters and doesn't forget anything, e.g. he will have to call Albert back;
4. use email as an alternative to phone calls to get specific information, e.g. Albert could email the attendance figures to Gerry as soon as they are ready, giving him a hard copy and removing the risk of figures being misheard over the phone;
5. avoid allowing social chit-chat to take up too much time during a phone call, e.g. pleasantries with Albert;
6. prioritise tasks on his to-do list - urgent ones first so that they are not overlooked;
7. allocate time according to urgency and importance - minimum time for urgent but not important, most time for important, e.g. the refreshment arrangements are urgent but not that important. Time was wasted on the trivial matter of the sausage rolls, more time needs to be allocated to the report which has long-term consequences for the department;
8. allocate a specific time when he is at his best to deal with important matters such as the conclusions to his report otherwise the quality of his work will suffer;
9. take breaks when he is not effective, e.g. when tired and hungry;
10. delegate less important work to subordinates, e.g. drawing up the staff rota.

Q23: One mark for each of the following:

- At the end of each day compile a to-do list for the next day, giving each job a priority, trying to note how long you expect to spend on each job to ensure that deadlines are met;
- Try to prioritise your tasks and develop your own code for prioritising tasks; if tasks prove too difficult seek help. This will ensure tasks are completed to a high standard and on time;
- At the end of each day try to clear your desk so that when you come in the next day you have a clear space to work in. This will allow other people access to any files you have been using and also eliminates a time stealer;
- Try to handle papers or tasks only once - read them, take any actions needed, and file them. If you deal with things promptly there is less chance of a backlog of work building up;
- Try to avoid being interrupted. Be firm with colleagues who just want to chat and learn to control time or protect time (phone or face to face). This will help the manager concentrate on the task in hand;
- Try not to take on too much work, delegate more tasks and learn to say no. This will ensure the important tasks are completed on time;
- Try to make sure that meetings take no longer than necessary - set time limits. This will avoid lengthy discussion on irrelevant topics;
- Use Gantt charts to make sure that projects are completed on time and within budget. This allows the team to see what tasks need to be completed in what order and by when.

Topic 5: Managing change

Internal and external factors (page 180)

Q1:

External	Internal
Changes in the economic framework	Resignations of managerial staff
Changes in the law or government policy	Research and development creating new products
Changes in the market	New objectives being set at the top of the organisation
Technological changes	Financial problems
Social and demographic changes	Changing staff skills and backgrounds
New management techniques being promoted in the media	Appointment of new managers

External pressures and change (page 181)

Q2:

External factor	Type of change
More firms entering a market for a product	competitive
A new law	political
A rise in the average age of the UK population	social
The development of e-commerce	technological
Increasing media pressure to recycle	environmental
Economic growth increasing	economic

Barriers to change (page 182)

Q3:

Barrier	Example
Communication problems	"... it's three months since the last staff meeting"
Fear of redundancy	"They're already talking about job losses"
Impact of other changes outside the firm's control	"... we've just heard our biggest customer is on the verge of going bust"
Lack of skills in the workforce	"... half of them can't work them"
Resistance from apathy to revolt	"... you're going to have a strike on your hands"
Resource limitations	"You don't have enough new machines"
Uncertainty causing anxiety	"Nobody knows what's going on"
Unrealistic time scales	"There's no way you can get them all trained up by the start of the year"

The five stages of change (page 184)

Q4:

Description	Stage of change
Bringing in the necessary alterations to the organisational structure, culture and processes	Changing
Checking that the change is happening as planned and whether further adjustments need to be made	Evaluation
Planning the change	Preparation
Reducing the forces maintaining the organisation's behaviour in its current state (resistors or restraining forces)	Unfreezing
Stabilising the organisation in its new equilibrium state with new structures, culture and processes	Refreezing

The manager's role in the change process (page 185)

Q5:

Preparation	Unfreezing	Changing	Refreezing	Evaluation
Decide on the objectives for change	Reassure employees that management will support them through the change	Ensure that all the resources needed are available	Remove opportunities to go back to the old way of doing things	Make sure those involved receive regular feedback on the results of the change
Identify driving and restraining forces	Involve employees in planning the change	Treat mistakes as learning opportunities	Offer positive affirmation for continuing to do things in the new way	Ensure feedback is quick and up to date
Identify the resources needed	Show the workforce how the change will benefit them	Be supportive, enthusiastic and positive	Give employees opportunity to practise the new working practices	Set a deadline for corrective action to be completed and subsequently assessed
Set timescales	Explain the reasons for change to the workforce	If possible, implement the change gradually		Make minor adjustments to plans if necessary
	Threaten redundancy if the change does not happen			Analyse the new situation and identify what further changes are needed
	Offer appropriate training			
	Offer incentives			

Forces for and against change (page 186)

Q6: The examples I thought of are listed in the table below (you may have included your own examples).

	Force for change	Force against change
Anti-discrimination laws	A new law, e.g. ending age discrimination, may force a firm to change its HR policies.	The cost of complying with legislation, e.g. creating disabled facilities, may prevent a firm from expanding.
Environmental protesters	A firm may change its production methods to prove itself environmentally friendly.	Protesters may stop a firm going ahead with a planned change if it involves testing on animals.
New competition	A firm may need to develop a new strategy to compete with a new competitor in the market.	A firm may be prevented from making the changes it wants because of a patent owned by the new firm.
Shortage of money	A firm may decide to change its production methods to cut costs.	A firm may not be able to afford to implement its new strategy.

Force field conclusions (page 188)

Expected answer

NB The marks for this answer are indicated in brackets. You may not have made all the points mentioned. What is important is that your conclusion selects some of the factors from your diagram and explains why they are drivers or resistors and/or how important they are compared to other drivers and resistors.

Analysis

Falling profits coupled with a saturated market mean that the firm must look abroad to capture new customers. *(1 mark)* Entering China will give faster and lower cost access to other world and European markets in which the firm already has customers. This is an important driver because the reduction in distribution cost will increase profit. *(1 mark)*

Easier access to other countries will also help the firm to increase its market share. *(1 mark)* Being able to lower costs of production is an important driver because it will increase profit margins. *(1 mark)*

The fact that the firm does not have the funds to finance the move is the most important resistor; it will need to borrow £3 million or increase equity. *(1 mark)* Such a large sum could be difficult and time consuming to arrange and the interest payable will increase costs. *(1 mark)* Bad publicity owing to the redundancies caused is likely to be short lived; many UK firms such as Dyson have moved production abroad in recent years with little long term effect on sales. *(1 mark)*

The firm might be able to lessen the effect of bad publicity by offering its UK workers generous redundancy packages and publicising this along with the reasons the move abroad will benefit UK consumers. *(1 mark)*

The fact that the drivers outweigh the resistors, backed up by the MD's expertise in the Chinese market, mean that the change is likely to go ahead. *(1 mark)*

Force field analysis (page 189)

Q7:

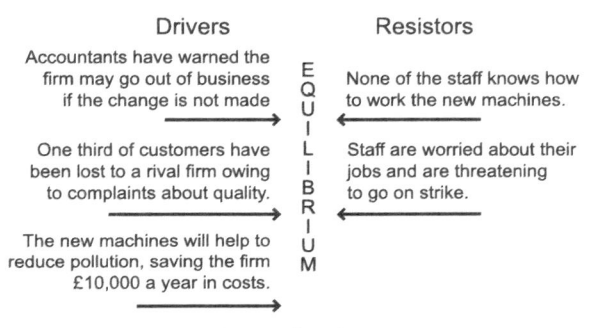

Drivers		Resistors
Accountants have warned the firm may go out of business if the change is not made →	E Q U I L I B R I U M	None of the staff knows how to work the new machines. ←
One third of customers have been lost to a rival firm owing to complaints about quality. →		Staff are worried about their jobs and are threatening to go on strike. ←
The new machines will help to reduce pollution, saving the firm £10,000 a year in costs. →		

Assets for change
The firm has a long history of good employee relations.
The firm has enough retained profit to finance the new machines without any borrowing.

Q8: This is subjective and there is no right answer so any reasons you put that are plausible are relevant.

Usefulness of force field analysis (page 189)

Q9: a) Advantage

Q10: a) Advantage

Q11: b) Disadvantage

Q12: b) Disadvantage

Q13: a) Advantage

Q14: b) Disadvantage

Q15: a) Advantage

Different approaches to managing change (page 192)

Q16:

Description	Approach to managing change
Change is brought in gradually through a series of small alterations.	Piecemeal
Change is made by running through a list of potential solutions to a problem until the best one is identified.	Action-centred
Changes are the result of a bargaining process between managers and employees, often represented by trade union representatives.	Negotiated
Employees are invited to contribute to decisions about change and the change incorporates their ideas.	Participative
Those at the top of the organisation make decisions about change and impose them.	Top-down

Benefits of the different approaches to managing change (page 194)

Q17:

Description	Approach to managing change
Changes can be implemented quickly as employees are not consulted.	Top-down
Employees can have an input into the pilot which improves motivation and confidence.	Action-centred
Involving all employees throughout the process leads to better decisions being made.	Participative
Mistakes can be rectified as they happen and everyone can learn from the process when changes are gradual.	Piecemeal
Negotiations empower employees to believe that their voice matters; this leads to an improved corporate culture.	Negotiated

Costs and benefits of the approaches to managing change (page 195)

Q18:

	Costs	Benefits
Action-centred	Some changes may conflict with others	Getting everyone accustomed to constant small changes makes it easier to introduce large changes later.
Negotiative	Employees may resist changes if they have not had an input.	Changes are carried out swiftly and exactly as management wants.
Participative	Negotiations can be time-consuming; some things may be non-negotiable e.g. redundancies.	Change will be quicker to implement as workers already know what they will get out of it.
Piecemeal	Workers may lack expertise to make good decisions about change.	Workers will "own" the change and be highly motivated to make it a success.
Top-down	Trying out a succession of different changes can be time-consuming.	This method avoids the cost of full scale implementation of a change that doesn't work.

Change agents (page 196)

Q19: b) False

Q20: a) True

Q21: a) True

Q22: b) False

Q23: a) True

Barriers to effective change (page 197)

Q24:

Internal	External
Availability of information	Bank agreeing further finance
Organisational culture	Changes to legislation
Staff resistance	Quality of specialist

Organisational culture definition (page 198)

Q25: The culture of an organisation is its customary way of *thinking* and *acting*: its shared *beliefs*, *attitudes* and *values*. It can take a long *time* to change an organisation's culture. Some of the factors that might influence the type of culture an organisation has include its *history*, *goals* and *size*.

Corporate culture and the change process (page 198)

Q26:

Easier to introduce change	Harder to introduce change
Adaptive cultures show trust in their workers and reassure them of their support.	An organisation may have several subcultures which may conflict with each other.
Cultures such as the net (matrix structure) stress teamwork based on expertise and empower workers to make their own decisions.	An organisation with a strong culture and past achievements may not see the need to do anything different.
Some cultures involve employees in decisions about change.	Many organisations with a strong culture have operated in much the same way over many years.
Some organisations encourage workers to take risks and treat mistakes as learning opportunities.	People in an organisation with a strong culture are sometimes blind to its failings.
Where a strong culture has developed, employees may be loyal to the organisation and eager to help it overcome problems.	Rigid cultures such as the temple have a hierarchical structure and strictly defined roles and procedures so that people always know what to expect in their jobs.

End of Topic 5 test (page 200)

Q27: b) Negotiated

Q28: f) Use of change agents

Q29:
1. Preparation
2. Unfreezing
3. Changing
4. Refreezing
5. Evaluation

Q30: b) Unfreezing

Q31: a) Preparation

Q32: e) Evaluation

ANSWERS: UNIT 2 TOPIC 5

Q33: d) Refreezing

Q34: c) Changing

Q35: *Force field diagram showing drivers and resistors with arrows of different lengths and assets for change pointing towards an equilibrium* (4 marks)

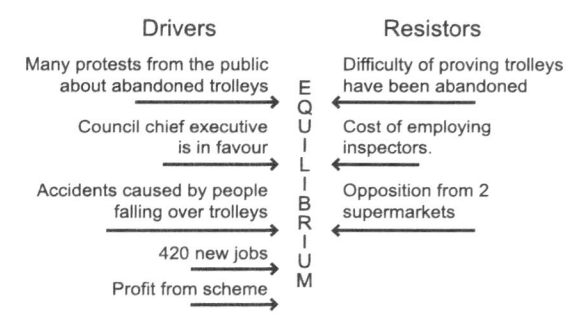

```
              Drivers                          Resistors
Many protests from the public           Difficulty of proving trolleys
  about abandoned trolleys        E     have been abandoned
  ─────────────────────────▶     Q     ◀─────────────────────
                                  U
     Council chief executive      I     Cost of employing
              is in favour        L     inspectors.
     ──────────────────────▶     I     ◀─────────────────
                                  B
 Accidents caused by people       R     Opposition from 2
     falling over trolleys        I     supermarkets
 ──────────────────────────▶     U     ◀───────────────
                                  M
              420 new jobs
     ──────────────▶
          Profit from scheme
     ──────────────────▶

                    Assets for change
         New chief executive's experience of handling change
```

Conclusions (6 marks)

The accidents caused by people falling over trolleys are an important driver because, as well as creating a bad reputation for the supermarkets and the council, they could lead to further expensive legal actions and compensation payments. *(1 mark)* Providing 20 new jobs would be important to the council as it would help to reduce unemployment - one of the aims of local government. *(1 mark)* The cost of employing 20 workers would be considerable but the council has plans in place to cover it from fines and charges on the supermarkets. *(1 mark)* This should mean council tax will not have to be raised. Further protests from local residents are therefore likely to be avoided. *(1 mark)*

The opposition of two supermarkets is a significant resistor as there are only four supermarkets altogether, so half are against the plan *(1 mark)*. The council could possibly reduce this resistor by increasing the charge to the supermarkets which owned the abandoned trolleys and lowering the levy on profits. *(1 mark)*

A particularly strong resistor is the cost of employing more workers as the company is short of cash. *(1 mark)* However, this is overcome by the projected profits from the new scheme. *(1 mark)*

Q36:

Drivers	Resistors	Assets for change
Marvel's investors had expressed approval of the deal at a recent meeting.	San Romano's Board of Directors had expressed opposition to the planned takeover.	Ms Blyth was responsible for the successful acquisition of three soft drinks companies in her previous job at Premier Beverages.
... more than half of San Romano's shareholders had written to say they were in favour of the deal.	Innes Black, the San Romano Chief Executive, says that Marvel's offer is too low.	
About 60-70% of Marvel's shareholders already hold stakes in San Romano and are keen to see the takeover go ahead.	The proposed takeover is likely to meet a series of regulatory challenges in the UK, where it has been referred to the Competition and Markets Authority (CMA).	
... combining the two groups would create a natural resources giant worth more than $500 billion.	San Romano is thought to be looking at potential 'white knight' deals with other mining companies.	
Marvel would become market leader in the iron ore, copper and coal mining.		
... the deal would create cost savings of $3.7 billion annually.		

Q37: Businesses could develop an adaptive culture which will allow it to cope with things that are new; this could also include a strong mission/vision which employees can relate to.

Continuous improvement through employee involvement in improvement or suggestion schemes; employees become used to change and accept it as the norm.

Becoming a 'learning organisation' taking opportunities for learning from past experience or tackling new problems so that change can be seen as something which is normal.

Development of regular communication systems, e.g. visits by senior management to discuss issues with staff. These can keep employees informed so that change does not come as a surprise, as well as allowing them the opportunity to suggest changes. If change is significant then it may need to be supplemented with other methods designed to tackle specific issues raised by the change, e.g. training staff in new technology.

Use of change agents who can act as intermediaries, co-ordinate aspects of change and communicate with those affected by it. However, internal agents tend to be more familiar with the organisation and may communicate with employees more effectively.

Offering education and training to those affected by the change so that they are fully informed and prepared to cope with the new situation; allaying fear and helping staff to recognise the benefits of change and cope with something new.

Empowerment of workers by giving employees responsibility for solving problems for themselves. This creates an environment which is responsive to change and provides workers with experience for tackling something new.

Offering financial or other rewards may ensure employees accept change more readily because they think they will benefit from it. Fringe benefits can encourage employees to be adaptable and to make personal changes. These rewards may not be successful on their own as they do not tackle fears of not coping with new things.

Topic 6: Equality and diversity

Protected characteristics (page 206)

Expected answer

Answer 1 - being able to move around an uneven construction site and climb ladders is intrinsic to this job and therefore not suitable for a wheelchair user. However, the applicant has the right to an interview to see if reasonable adjustments can be put in place to make the working environment suitable.

Answer 2 - being partially deaf is not a barrier to working in a music store.

Answer 3 - sexuality is not a barrier to working as a counsellor.

Answer 4 - sexuality is not a barrier to working as a counsellor but this is a case of occupational requirement. The organisation can lawfully only interview women as only women use the service and are unlikely to want to deal with a man.

Answer 5 - following a religion is not a barrier to working in a café.

Answer 6 - the law states that you need to be 18 years old to sell alcohol, therefore the Equality Act is not relevant in this case.

Q1: a) Yes

Q2: a) Yes

Q3: a) Yes

Q4: b) No

Q5: a) Yes

Q6: b) No

Discrimination (page 208)

Q7:

Example	Type of discrimination
A business hires 20 white males to work in an area populated by ethnic minorities. No job adverts were placed as all positions were filled by word of mouth.	Indirect discrimination
A business refuses to interview an internal candidate who has just returned from a career break.	Indirect discrimination
A manager makes an employee feel humiliated by telling jokes about their religion at a staff training session.	Harassment
A women is employed in a car garage as an engineer. Many of her male colleagues make lurid sexual remarks to her.	Harassment
An employer does not interview a candidate because they have heard the candidate may be pregnant.	Direct discrimination
You resigned your job despite winning an age discrimination case against your employer. You apply to a competitor but you do not receive an interview as they heard what happened.	Victimisation

Recruitment and selection (page 210)

Q8: Hairdresser required, **preferably with long hair**. **She** must be experienced with drive and passion. We are looking for a **young** and dynamic person with ambition. We are located on the first floor so **may not be suitable for a disabled person**. We pay above the minimum wage and have great holiday entitlements. Call in to apply.

Q9: Possible answer:

- Stating a preference for long hair indirectly discriminates against men who are more likely to have short hair;
- Using the word 'she' directly discriminates against men;
- The wording 'may not be suitable for a disabled person' directly discriminates against disabled people - not all disabled people will have an issue with stairs.

Equality training (page 211)

Q10: For workers to understand what equality law means for them, they will need to be informed. This is what is meant by 'equality **training** '.

Equality training can be an important part of showing that you are preventing discrimination, harassment and **victimisation** in your organisation. If an employee was to treat a colleague or customer unfairly by contravening one of the nine protected characteristics without receiving adequate training, the business would be held jointly liable for any action.

A business might choose to do this:

- as part of an **induction** process for new starts;
- during regular **team** meetings;
- by asking staff to attend specific whole or half day **courses**;
- by asking staff to complete an **online** training package at a time of their choosing.

Whatever the format the business chooses, they should also make sure that workers know about any **changes** and that anyone who joins the organisation (for example, any new employee who comes in after the training has taken place) knows what is expected of them. For this reason many businesses chose to make equality training an annual event.

Training should include:

- the law covering all the protected **characteristics** and what behaviour is and is not acceptable;
- the risk of ignoring or seeming to approve inappropriate behaviour and personal **liability**;
- how discrimination can affect the way an employer functions and the impact that generalisations, stereotypes, bias, inappropriate language in day-to-day operations can have on people's chances of obtaining work, **promotion**, recognition and respect;
- the business's equality **policy**, if they have one, why it has been introduced and how it will be put into practice.

End of Topic 6 test (page 213)

Q11: c) An employee is refused promotion as they are a carer for their wife.

Q12: c) Both the employer and the employee

Q13: a) True

Q14: a) True

Q15: b) False

Q16: The Equality Act 2010 simplifies the current discrimination laws and puts them all together in one piece of legislation making it easier for small businesses to follow.

The act makes it more difficult for disabled people to be unfairly screened out when applying for jobs, by restricting the circumstances in which employers can ask job applicants questions about disability or health. Employers must be aware of the wording of their recruitment documentation so that they are not hindering anyone from applying.

Employers must be aware of the nine protected characteristics.

Employers must be aware of the types of discrimination at work.

Employers need to be aware of the principles of the act when recruiting, promoting and making people redundant.

The act includes workplace victimisation, harassment and bullying which gives the employees more rights.

The act makes pay secrecy clauses illegal which has improved the gender imbalance between male and female employees.

Topic 7: The internal business environment test

The internal business environment test (page 216)

Q1: c) plan, organise, command, coordinate and control.

Q2: b) Drucker.

Q3: a) True

Q4: b) False

Q5: b) False

Q6: a) True

Q7: b) Physiological, safety, social, self-esteem and self-actualisation

Q8: d) Inspirer

Q9: c) forming, storming, norming and performing.

Q10: d) preparation, unfreezing, transforming, refreezing and evaluation.

Q11: a) True

Q12: b) False

Q13: resistors

Q14: b) False

Q15: a) True

Q16: *Autocratic style*

Autocratic leaders do not involve subordinates in decision making; they issue instructions and expect them to be obeyed, e.g. Greg tells Helen exactly how to groom Angus.

Advantages

An autocratic style may be appropriate in an emergency situation or where mistakes made by subordinates could lead to grave consequences, e.g in the Army, or in a factory where toxic chemicals are used. Greg had been a successful leader in the army, where his leadership style was a good match with the situation. If employees at the stable had been given less freedom prior to Greg's arrival, the Brimer's injury at the birthday party would have been avoided. Some employees may prefer to be told what to do; they may not want the responsibility that comes with delegation. An autocratic style may be better suited to new or inexperienced employees until they understand their role fully, e.g. Allan supervised Lewis closely until he had settled in. An autocratic style ensures that everyone stays on task and within the manager's control. For example, Ross was puzzled by the injury to Brimer's fetlock, but as Head Groom he should have been aware of such a potentially serious problem when it happened.

Disadvantages

An autocratic style can demotivate workers so that they do as they are told to avoid getting into trouble but do not volunteer for extra duties, e.g. Helen's change in attitude towards Cameron now he has adopted an autocratic style as Greg's assistant. The negative effect on worker morale can reduce quality of work.

Democratic style

This style involves workers in decision making and is exemplified by Ross, e.g. he let Helen and the experienced grooms get on with things.

Advantages

Subordinates will be more enthusiastic about decisions they have helped to make. Employees are motivated by being given responsibility, e.g. Helen enjoyed grooming Brimer because she was allowed to decide how to go about it. The experience and talents of subordinates are used more effectively resulting in more ideas being available to an organisation, e.g. most of the employees at the stables had worked there for years and Greg could have used their combined experience rather than ignoring it. Delegating decision making power means managers can concentrate on the tasks that only they can do leading to greater effectiveness, e.g. better strategic decisions.

Disadvantages

Managers have an overview of their organisation or department and so are more likely to keep the objectives of the business in mind when making decisions. Workers may abuse management's trust, e.g. there seems to have been a problem with workers arriving on time under Ross's democratic regime such as Helen's flimsy excuse that her alarm had gone off late. Workers may lack the experience to make effective decisions. Consultation with the workers can be time consuming.

Q17: *Classical approach*

The classical school is based on scientific management, which in turn was based on division of labour.

It stresses efficiency and the use of time and motion studies to identify the one right way to do a job and set a standard time for completing it, e.g. Greg's 30-minute time limit on grooming horses.

It had a mechanistic view of workers, believing that all they were interested in was a fair day's pay for a fair day's work.

The classical organisation is a hierarchy with clearly defined roles, e.g. Greg appointed an Assistant Head Groom and gave him responsibility for clocking the other grooms in.

Classical writers such as Fayol stressed obedience to authority, rules and procedure, e.g. Helen complains that things have to be done exactly the way Greg says or else.

Q18: Advantages

The classical approach works well in a traditional organisation where work is routine and follows a predictable pattern so that all workers are required to do is follow the rules and procedures laid down. The classical approach is important in manufacturing industries where work measurement and specialisation are key to increasing efficiency.

Disadvantages

The classical approach may not be appropriate in all situations. The contingency school is based on the view that there is no one correct way to manage; different approaches to management are suitable for different situations. A human relations approach, which seeks to meet employees socio-psychological needs, is likely to suit organisations where work demands are constantly changing and workers need to be able to cope with constant change.

Q19: All the team members share a common goal or goals. In this case, the grooms are united in opposition to Greg's new regime and their goal is to be treated like human beings.

Each team member understands the goals and knows their role in helping to achieve them.

Team members trust and respect each other. In this case, the grooms have all worked together for a long time and already get on well.

Team members accept each other's strengths and weaknesses. In this case, nobody objects when Bill says he would rather gather resources than plan.

The team consists of a variety of people with different gifts performing different roles, e.g. Belbin's team roles. In this case, Raza is a plant (has the idea for the protest), Bill is a resource investigator (he offers to get hold of what is needed), and Sean is a shaper (instigates preparing the action plan).

The team size is appropriate to the task, e.g. fewer than twelve for problem solving and larger for tasks involving collecting or distributing a lot of information. In this case the team has seven members, a good number for the type of task.

The team handles problems and conflict constructively.

There is effective communication between members. In this case, the all-channel network seems to be used, with everyone chipping in their contribution; this is effective because there are only seven in the group and they are all at the same location.

Leadership is democratic / participative. In this case, Sean is recognised by the group as a whole as leader after he takes charge of getting everyone's thoughts down on paper.

Q20: Force field analysis for new staff regime

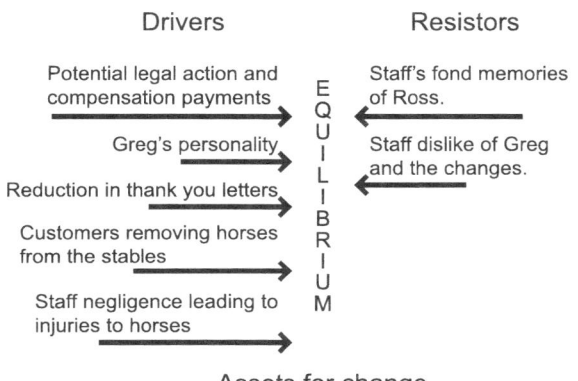

Drivers → ← **Resistors**

Drivers:
- Potential legal action and compensation payments →
- Greg's personality →
- Reduction in thank you letters →
- Customers removing horses from the stables →
- Staff negligence leading to injuries to horses →

Resistors:
- ← Staff's fond memories of Ross.
- ← Staff dislike of Greg and the changes.

(EQUILIBRIUM)

Assets for change
Staff loyalty built up over many years.

Conclusions

The drivers are more in number than the resistors, but the resistance of staff to the change is very strong. If this is not addressed the new regime may prove impossible to implement successfully; instead it may well worsen the quality of care given to horses and customers and result in many experienced grooms seeking jobs elsewhere. The fact that customers are actually removing horses from the stables is an important driver pushing the firm to keep a tighter control on staff, because it causes a loss of revenue for the firm and indicates serious dissatisfaction, since most of the customers have used the firm for at least ten years.

The reduction in thank you letters could be seen as fairly minor as it does not result in any loss of revenue for the firm and affects only a small number of customers; it does however reflect a fall in the standard of care and influences the firm to monitor staff more closely.

Exposing itself to being prosecuted for negligence could end up gaining the firm bad publicity as well as a court order to pay compensation; to avoid these the firm has to ensure that workers are carrying out their duties conscientiously.

While Greg's very autocratic style is driving the change of regime it has also led to increasing resistance from staff because it is too great a contrast to Ross's more laid back one; the loyalty built up over several years is in danger of being lost. It may well be that the change will fail unless a more participative approach is adopted.

Answers to questions and activities for Researching a business

Topic 1: Research

Asda (page 226)

Q1: "This last quarter has been unprecedented. We have seen deflation in the market and exponential shifts in the industry. Although I still believe that 18 months ago we did a great job of predicting changes, we could not have foreseen what's happened to others and the moves they have had to make in order to restore their business - creating an impact on us in the short-term." (ASDA news release (http://your.asda.com/press-centre/asda-unveils-its-first-quarter-financial-results-and-strategy-update) [Last accessed October 2015])

Q2: The president of ASDA believes the company did a good job predicting changes to the market, but argues that they could not have predicted the external effects of deflation and the moves their competitors made to combat the changes in the market. (ASDA news release (http://your.asda.com/press-centre/asda-unveils-its-first-quarter-financial-results-and-strategy-update) [Last accessed October 2015])

Provide a reference (page 229)

Q3: ASDA (2015) news release [online], available http://your.asda.com/press-centre/asda-unveils-its-first-quarter-financial-results-and-strategy-update [Last accessed October 2015]

Cold calling (page 230)

Q4: Possible solution:

Schiffman (1987) says cold calling is the best and most cost-effective way for a business to increase sales. Akhabau (2015) disagrees, stating that there has been a big increase in complaints from customers about cold calling techniques in recent years. An article in The Guardian (Bachelor, 2015) backs this up with the news that "a cold-calling company that has been pestering householders with automated calls on an "industrial scale" will be hit with a record fine next week."

References

- Akhabau, I., 2015. Big increase in cold call complaints but few fines. [Online] Available at: http://www.bbc.co.uk/news/uk-politics-34618167 [last accessed 25 October 2015]
- Bachelor, L., 2015. Cold-calling 'factory' gets record fine after 180,000 complaints last year. [Online] Available at: http://www.theguardian.com/money/2015/sep/26/cold-calling-record-fine-complaints-data-protection [last accessed 25 October 2015]
- Schiffman, S., 2013. Cold Calling Techniques (That Really Work!). [Online] Available at: https://bit.ly/2OycZr8 [last accessed 25 October 2015]

End of Topic 1 test (page 233)

Q5: c) It is used to demonstrate that you have read from a small number of sources.

Q6: a) quote directly, b) paraphrase, c) cite and d) summarise

Q7: The error in the references are highlighted below:

1. Aldrich, D. The Crucial Role of Civil Society in Disaster Recovery and Japans Preparedness for Emergencies. Japan akuell, 1-12. ***(2008).***
   The year should be included after the author name, i.e. Aldrich, D (2008). The Crucial Role of Civil Society in Disaster Recovery and Japans Preparedness for Emergencies. Japan akuell, 1-12.
2. ***P M*** Bermejo (2006). Preparation and Response in Case of Natural Disasters: Cuban Programs and Experience. Journal of Public Health Policy, V.27, 13-21.
   The author's initials should be included after the author surname, i.e. Bermejo, P M (2006). Preparation and Response in Case of Natural Disasters: Cuban Programs and Experience. Journal of Public Health Policy, V.27, 13-21.
3. Garrett, L. (2000). Betrayal of the Trust: The Collapse of Global Public Health. New York: Hyperion. ***ppp***
   The page number(s) should be included instead of ppp, e.g. Garrett, L. (2000). Betrayal of the Trust: The Collapse of Global Public Health. New York: Hyperion. 1-12.

Topic 2: Analytical research

Merlin (page 237)

Q1: Possible decisions may include:

- whether or not to hire native Chinese staff to manage the new ventures or to relocate UK staff;
- how to market the new ventures;
- what attractions they should open in China that will appeal to the local market.

Force field analysis (page 238)

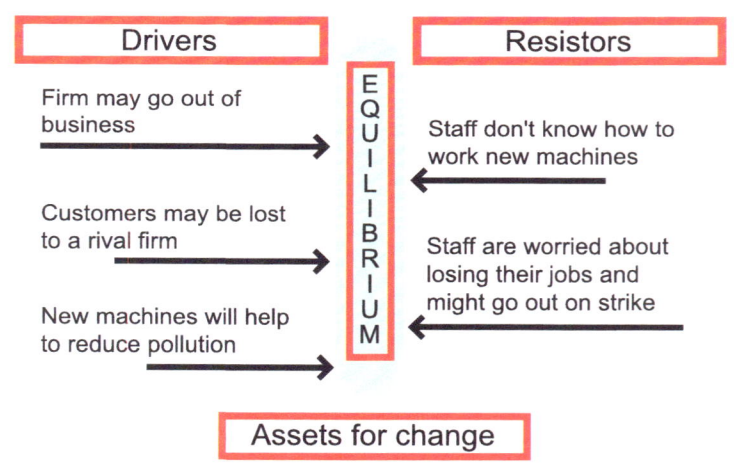

Q2:

Drivers (→ EQUILIBRIUM):
- Firm may go out of business
- Customers may be lost to a rival firm
- New machines will help to reduce pollution

Resistors (← EQUILIBRIUM):
- Staff don't know how to work new machines
- Staff are worried about losing their jobs and might go out on strike

Assets for change
- Firm has a history of good employee relations
- Firm does not need to borrow to finance new machines

Dairy Crest - case study (page 238)

Q3:

Drivers

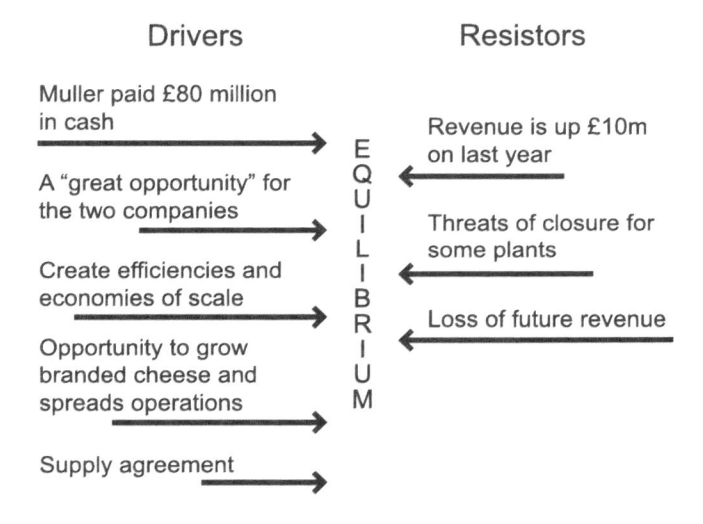

- Muller paid £80 million in cash →
- A "great opportunity" for the two companies →
- Create efficiencies and economies of scale →
- Opportunity to grow branded cheese and spreads operations →
- Supply agreement →

EQUILIBRIUM

Resistors

- ← Revenue is up £10m on last year
- ← Threats of closure for some plants
- ← Loss of future revenue

Assets for change
Pension obligations
Strengthen the UK milk market

SWOT analysis - Dairy Crest (page 241)

Q4: The SWOT analysis depends on your school so there is no suggested answer to this question. Check your answer with your teacher.

Critical path analysis (CPA) (page 242)

Q5: 12 weeks.

The critical path is A - B - C - F - G which equates to 12 weeks (4 + 2 + 3 + 1 + 2) and is shown in red in the network below.

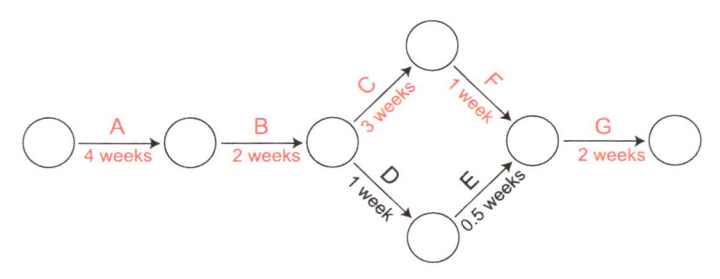

Identifying the critical path for a strategy (page 243)

Q6: The building cannot be completed until the builder has been selected. The building must be erected before plumbing and electricity are installed, decoration takes place, and shelving and computers are installed. Computers cannot be installed before shelving is in place.

Q7: Choosing the building firm because it is the first task. Ordering computers can be done at any time.

Q8: Ordering the computers along with any other tasks apart from installing them. Installing the plumbing and electricity.

Gantt chart advantages (page 245)

Q9: Creating a Gantt chart helps managers and employees to *focus* on the steps necessary to *implement* the strategy successfully. The charts help managers to see which tasks can be done *simultaneously* and which *depend* on other tasks being done first.

Updating the chart by shading in *activities* as they are completed helps to spot any *delay* before it becomes serious. They can be displayed on the wall so that everyone involved can see the *progress* made and what still needs to be done to achieve *targets*.

Gantt chart (page 246)

Q10: There is no definitive Gantt chart for this as time frames, holidays, types of activity, etc. will be different for every school.

ANSWERS: UNIT 3 TOPIC 2

End of Topic 2 test (page 247)

Q11: *Drivers*: Excessive tax demands in the UK; the USA has similar business practices and culture with the UK; British tax introduced in 2010 that targets UK-based banks' global balance sheets; systems of banking regulation in the North America appeals to HSBC; the country would easily be able to handle a financial firm of its size.

***Resistors*:** UK Chancellor said he would cut back the levy and introduce an 8% corporation tax surcharge on UK profits instead; costs involved in moving headquarters and staff; need to decide if the upheaval is worth the savings.

***Assets for change*:** Global business with local knowledge - the location of the HQ does not change this image; UK Government looking at changing the tax system but impact on HSBC may not be enough.

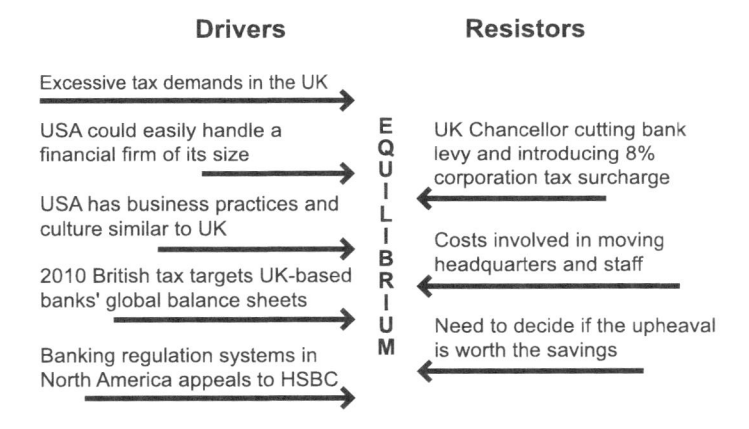

Drivers · Resistors

Drivers		Resistors
Excessive tax demands in the UK →	E	
USA could easily handle a financial firm of its size →	Q U I	← UK Chancellor cutting bank levy and introducing 8% corporation tax surcharge
USA has business practices and culture similar to UK →	L I B	← Costs involved in moving headquarters and staff
2010 British tax targets UK-based banks' global balance sheets →	R I U	
Banking regulation systems in North America appeals to HSBC →	M	← Need to decide if the upheaval is worth the savings

Assets for change

Global business with local knowledge - HQ location does not change image
UK Government's tax changes may not be enough for HSBC

Q12:

Strengths	Weaknesses
• HSBC handles $2.6 trillion worth of assets • Large business with customers all over the world	• Not finalised its decision about relocating to the USA or Hong Kong
Opportunities	**Threats**
• A move to the USA would reduce its tax burden • Growing Chinese market may increase investment opportunities	• UK tax demands larger than that of other countries • Chinese takeover possible

Topic 3: Evaluating financial information

Profitability ratios (page 251)

Q1: Gross profit Year 1= (250 / 450) x 100% = **55%**
Gross profit Year 2= (300 / 500) x 100% = **60%**
Net profit Year 1 = (100 / 450) x 100% = **22%**
Net profit Year 2 = (110 / 500) x 100% = **22%**

Liquidity ratios (page 252)

Q2: Current ratio Year 1 = 1,500,000:800,000 = **1.88:1**
Current ratio Year 2 = 1,700,000:750,000 = **2.27:1**
Acid test ratio Year 1 = (1,500,000 - 600,000):800,000 = **1.13 :1**
Acid test ratio Year 2 = (1,700,000 - 800,000):750,000 = **1.2:1**

Efficiency ratios (page 252)

Q3: ROCE Year 1 = (250,000 / 1,000,000) x 100% = **25%**
ROCE Year 2 = (300,000 / 1,100,000) x 100% = **27%**.

Ratio analysis - a worked example (page 253)

Q4:

	Year 2	Year 1
Net profit as a percentage of sales	(700 / 7,000) x 100% **10%**	(970 / 6,300) x 100% **15%**
Current ratio	10,000 / 14,300 **0.7:1**	12,000 / 10,900 **1.1:1**
Return on capital employed	(700 / 5,500) x 100% **12.7%**	(970 / 6,600) x 100% **16.1%**
Share price (in £)	1.75	2.03

Q5: The net profit as a percentage of sales for both years is low. This suggests a small operating margin, meaning a high volume of sales must be sold to make a relatively small amount of profit, or that the mark-up on goods sold is small. It might also indicate that expenses or purchasing costs are too high.

A decrease in net profit percentage from year one to year two is also concerning. This shows that the financial position of the business is declining.

A current ratio of 1.1:1 is concerning. If the business was required to pay its creditors it would struggle. Although assets are greater than liabilities, much of their assets will be tied up in stock.

A current ratio of 0.7:1 is very concerning. A business with liquidity problems is running the risk of not being able to pay employees, HMRC or suppliers. This could lead to the business going into receivership. This business requires an injection of capital if it is to survive.

A decrease in the ROCE is concerning, although a ROCE of 12.7% still compares favourably to other investment options. In the longer term, this may further reduce the share price.

A reduction in the share price is concerning as this business may need new investment in the future as it has a poor current ratio. As the share price falls, so does the net worth.

End of Topic 3 test (page 257)

Q6: b) compare a business's performance over two time periods.

Q7: a) profitability ratio.

Q8: b) False

Q9: b) False

Q10: a) True

Q11: a) True

Q12: b) False

Q13:

	Year 2	Year 1
Net profit as a percentage of sales	2,252 / 24,000 = **9.4%**	550 / 10,500 = **5.2%**
Current ratio	18,000 / 8,000 = **2.25**	12,000 / 10,900 = **1.1:1**
Return on capital employed	2,250 / 12,500 = **18%**	550 / 6,000 = **9.2%**
Share price (in £)	5.60	3.20

The net profit as a percentage of sales has doubled from year 1 to year 2. This suggests an increase in the number of sales or an increase in selling price. It is also likely that costs of production have decreased. This is all positive.

A current ratio of 1.1:1 is very concerning. If the business was required to pay its creditors it would struggle. Although assets are greater than liabilities, much of their assets will be tied up in stock. An increase to 2.25 is very good news as anything over 2:1 is positive. This means the business has been able to reduce its creditors whilst building up its assets.

A doubling of the ROCE is very good news for current shareholders, who will see their share price increase. It may also encourage them to purchase more shares if they are released in the future.

An increase in the share price is encouraging as this business may wish to expand operations in the future, funded by a release of new shares. As the share price increases, so does the net worth.